AWAKEN AS YOU READ...

DOWNLOADS FROM THE NINE

RECOGNIZE YOUR HIGHER SELF EFFORTLESSLY.

by Matías Flury

AWAKEN AS YOU READ

DOWNLOADS FROM THE NINE

Recognize Your Higher Self Effortlessly

MATIAS FLURY

DOWNLOADS FROM THE NINE

Recognize Your Higher Self Effortlessly

by

Matias Flury

Cover by Kristy Vargas

Disclaimer

Although the author and publisher have made every effort to ensure that the information in this book was correct at press time, the author and publisher do not assume and hereby disclaim any liability to any party for any loss, damage, or disruption caused by errors or omissions, whether such errors or omissions result from negligence, accident, or any other cause.

The information in this book is meant to supplement, and inform, not to replace any professional treatment and or therapy. Before practicing the techniques described in this book, be sure that you know the subject at hand, and do not take risks beyond your level of experience, aptitude, training, and comfort level.

This book is designed to provide helpful information on the subjects discussed herein. This book is not meant to be used, nor should it be used, to diagnose or treat any medical condition and is not intended as a substitute for medical advice. The reader should regularly consult a physician in matters relating to his/her health and particularly with respect to any symptoms that may require diagnosis or medical attention. For diagnosis or treatment of any medical problem, consult your own physician. The publisher and author are not responsible for any specific health or allergy needs that may require medical supervision and are not liable for any damages or negative consequences from any treatment, action, application or preparation, to any person reading or following the information in this book. References are provided for informational purposes only and do not constitute endorsement of any websites or other sources.

This book is dedicated to the Nine
Thank you for all your teachings.

Special thanks to Vinicio Zuniga Romero and Alberto Ramirez

Table of Contents

Forward

Through experience, I have proven that the teachings written here facilitate a process of rapid spiritual growth within any person who would venture to read them. Spiritual progress is part of the natural flow of development that humans are encouraged to follow during their evolutionary stage here on Earth.

If you were to read carefully, with concentration, you would be taking a shortcut through a luminous path never before experienced. Just read the words that are on each page, relax your body, and let this book take you by the hand and show you transcendental dimensions filled with infinite light and Love.

Some years ago, the person who wrote this book learned an Indian meditation technique that consists of directing one's gaze towards the heart of the Sun. He took to this new path and received guidance from certain voices that surged from the deepest spaces within his heart. They asked him to intensify his periods of concentration. They asked this person to give them his trust and told him that he, and whoever reads this book, would be spiritually protected.

With the voices' sure guidance, the author increased his meditation time day after day. Every sunrise and every sunset, he gazed until his eyes could become comfortably fixed towards the center of the Sun without blinking for around two hours twice a day.

The process of Sun gazing has the potential to awaken various parts of any person's brain, drastically bringing about changes in their personality and resulting in greater ease for settling into peaceful and meditative mind states. As time goes by, the practitioner may start experiencing and seeing subtle realms that are undetectable and incomprehensible to others. One's progress through these stages ultimately allows one to hear sounds and voices that a person at a similar level of consciousness simply cannot detect.

I'm not referring to schizophrenia or psychotic episodes; quite the contrary. The practitioner's experience is the achievement of complete mental clarity, security and an amazing calm that settles into serenity and the feeling of a loving embrace. Such development leads one toward the experience of other dimensions with a fully prepared, ethereal and expanded consciousness.

Further along the practiced path one experiences images that emanate from the Sun. Sometimes, one may hear voices that come directly from Him. This is the beginning of a deep understanding of the Sun as an intelligent and conscious being, filled with knowledge and self-realization. The established contact fascinates the mind and weakens all negative mental programming. Unexplainable events begin to unfold.

I believe that Sun gazing works in this way, but it is possible that I am mistaken. It may be that Sun gazing activated certain parts of the writer's brain, but there is also the possibility that this phenomenon was merely created by the subconscious or unconscious areas of his psyche, unknown to a common mind such as my own. Either way, yogis, Taoists, and sages from the Himalayas and the Andes have known for ages that the practice of Sun gazing establishes a direct exchange of intellectual amperage with the Sun.

This is not a book about how to practice Sun gazing. Nowhere in its contents is there further mention of these practices. However, setting the eyes to the heart of the Sun was the root cause, so to speak, of this magical text. Its unfolding magic is such that awakening is certain to follow whosoever reads it.

The enchanting reading method that is employed here penetrates deep within the mind and reaches the reader's soul with caring hands. This method accelerates the inevitable enlightenment process from within. The reading of this book by its own is a new form of spiritual practice, never before seen or experienced.

In my personal opinion, this information came from the Sun and its beings in the height of the 2011-2012 solar storms. Such an event was described by the Incas, the Mayas, and the Aztecs as the fifth Sun, a time of accelerated transformation, evolution and changes.

You may experiment and decide on the effectiveness and utility of this method of spiritual reading through your own experience.

Once you start reading the first pages you will immediately understand the process I'm referring to. The reading process and the experiences that develop from it will be different from any experience that you may have had before. From the first few pages you will find yourself immersed in the vast depths of your being. Reading is the practice. Read and enlighten your being.

This book stimulates and seduces the mind to focus its attention on an immense, subtle reality. This subtle realm can be found hiding deep within every one of us, living quietly amidst our infinite consciousness.

The spiritual power that is awakened as you read will remain as a constant presence during your life. It will accompany you all day, while you work,

Love, talk, sleep, laugh, and also through the experience of anger, sadness, pain, and other such sensations and emotions. The feeling of luminosity that this book will stir from within will continue to grow after one has concluded reading. An experience of liberation from the dictatorial mindset and negative emotions will spring forth, leaving the reader in an expansive field of pure, blue, non-dual consciousness.

I invite you to experiment with this process from within. There is nothing to lose, but there is an immense potential to be gained.

You will also observe that the way in which the sentences are arranged on each page is completely different to how they are normally arranged in common texts. You will have to follow the arrows and start reading where they lead you. This way of organizing sentences is designed to purposefully affect certain dormant sections of the brain. What the author wants is to gain access to every segment of the mental instrument or psyche. Every word will arrive at the soul's central vortex to awaken the reader.

If you analyze different hieroglyphs and other written languages from around the world, you will notice that some of them are completely different from our writing method.

The Chinese writing system, for example, presents us with sentences that are written from top to bottom in a vertical manner. As a direct consequence, the brain functions of a person from China will work and process information differently from a westerner's brain, which is accustomed to reading from left to right.

After reading this book, I now understand that our manner of reading and writing affects our personality in certain ways. This multidirectional reading and writing method has been created for this exact reason, to directly affect the egocentric mind in an extremely profound fashion.

A person's eyes are wired with the center of the brain via the optic nerve, and it seems that some optic nerve endings slightly touch the pineal gland. According to eastern schools of thought, the pineal gland is an essential and vital center, related to the Ajna Chakra (third eye). This gland is similar to an eye, but without its lens. Movement of the eyes in different directions directly affects the pineal gland and other brain parts. In this way, areas of the brain that used to be dormant operate the process of assimilating information.

During sleep and in dreaming states, our eyes move rapidly from right to left. This movement is named REM (Rapid Eye Movement) sleep.

Many psychotherapists suggest that REM and dreaming are mental mechanisms through which the brain lowers its activity and exertion in order to cope and heal from psychological problems and trauma.

There is a therapeutically prescribed technique known as EMDR (Eye Movement Desensitization and Reprocessing) that imitates this movement. Some psychotherapists currently employ this therapeutic method to deal with psychological problems and addictive behaviors that haven't been successfully worked out through other psychotherapeutic techniques.
There is also evidence of these rapid eye movements being used in various yoga meditation techniques. Sufis, Buddhists and other mystic groups widely hold that the eyes are doorways to an individual's soul.
This book makes use of these eye movements to help the reader achieve the goal of 'awakening'. As you read, your gaze will move in different directions. The message of enlightenment penetrates deeply within the darkened areas of the mind. In this way, the message is able to illuminate and awaken these sections of the brain in a wonderfully ecstatic manner.
This multidirectional reading and writing is a revolutionary method that restructures the foundations of our being and all the erroneous mental concepts we have learned. This way of absorbing information will allow us to soar like an eagle from the tallest peak of being to breathe the purest crystalline air amongst liberating heights. Read and take to the highest flight in the infinite blue sky of your eternal spirit.
As I talked to the author, he expressed that, as soon as he had completed the book, he himself read it to make sure everything was as it should be. Enigmatically, he was once again taken into the immeasurable expanses of his psyche that the book exposed as it was read. He expressed to me how he explored areas deep within his interior that he had not previously known. He says that this book has helped him to decipher the undecipherable.
What you are about to read here, and the manner in which you will read it, will change your life. Be prepared for a 180-degree spin.
This book also takes us within areas of our personalities that we have chosen or preferred to leave in the darkness. These spaces that we have refused to see become inoffensive when we shed the light of consciousness upon them. Reading will help you to closely analyze those fictitious parts of your identity that you hold yourself to be. As you move along the lines of this book, you will become capable of recognizing all the false aspects, characteristics, and beliefs that enslave you to your ego, and you will learn to reject their claim over you until all that is left is the scintillating purity of your expansive awareness.
You need only read, relax, follow the instructions, awaken and fly freely.

It's as simple as that.
Vaishnavi Devi.

Introduction

This book was created with the purpose of propelling the spiritual development of human beings who read it with attention. This transformation is happening as a consequence of the diverse geomagnetic and universal changes that are occurring in present times.

The changes have already begun. After 2013, the world entered parallel dimensions of transformative energy and will experience ascending vibrational frequencies until the coming of the year 2095. From 2013 to 2095, humanity will be subject to the experience of a very powerful evolutionary process that will change the face of the earth.

At first, this book will read as we are used to: from left to right. After this section, there will be a second part where the writing is arranged in a spiral. This system will deeply penetrate the psyche, modifying and restructuring electromagnetic frequencies within the reader, which in turn changes and enlivens the DNA and RNA strands that are currently dormant.

Every word written here will instill radiant light in the cerebral neurons and neurotransmitters, opening intercellular portals. Every sentence that you read in this book and every letter you see, directly seize the energy arranging chromosome combinations in the physical body.

In the astral dimension, these words activate very fine energetic filaments that are attached to DNA strands and coat the meridian channels with crystallized spirals of light. In the causal or spiritual bodies, reading this book will open the gates to the soul, giving it access to new horizons of perception in nine parallel dimensions as well as the possibility of absorbing higher vibration nutrient sources that are streams of living astral liquid light.

This book is a gift from beings inhabiting parallel universes; they described themselves as The Nine Devas of Crystalline Atomic Fire (known as Seraphim in the West). They are not to be confused with the counsel of 9. Their only purpose is to reactivate the evolution of the human race.

Their work begins by the process of transmuting the causal body (body that encases destiny), followed by the transformation of the astral body (energy body with thousands of meridians, keeper of emotions), to finally culminate with a complete physical transfiguration.

The transmitted frequencies won't be felt strongly at first. However, you will feel some emotional effect generated by the debris this cleansing leaves behind. Once the body is free of these emotional fragments, brilliant vibrations will embrace the nervous system in the form of pleasurable and/or ascending tingling sensations. At other times, ecstatic waves will flood the entire body. If the nervous system is not yet strong enough, the reader will feel small tremors or even experience internal seizures along the spine. These nervous reactions derive themselves directly from the neurocelular system.

As you read you will encounter many physics and chemistry terms. If you don't understand, do not worry—the magic will still touch your soul. Try to read all the words carefully to bring forth the desired effect within your three bodies.

There are many other celestial beings apart from The Nine working in unison with this book. These beings (the authors of this book) have committed to help and oversee the transformation process that takes place while you read.

They will profoundly affect your nervous system cells, or neurons, whose main feature is to transmit and captivate electromagnetic pulses. They use the neuron's hyper-receptive plasmatic membrane, which is also capable of absorbing subtle astral vibrations, to communicate with you and transform you.

In other words, these sweet Ethereal Beings take advantage of this cell receptivity, the electrical impulses, the stimuli of the neurons and their capacity to conduct impulses, to introduce inter-dimensional messianic fibers that easily become one with the electrical impulses. In this way, the plasmatic membrane assimilates them.

With these energy exchanges, we also influence the neuromuscular synapses directly where the junction between the axon and the effector is located. This forces the myelinic fiber and the terminal plates to vibrate with continuous lightning-like impulses that slowly change the structure of these pre-synaptic terminals. This indirectly affects the sarcolemma (or myolemma), the synaptic vesicle, the nicotinic receptor, and the mitochondria.

If the myelin is thin, the body will experience tremors. This is an adjustment phase to allow these transformations; however, the Nine Devas of Crystalline Fire will stimulate the myelin to thicken it, enabling the body to advance further ahead on this evolutionary process.

The brilliant Nine are Devas of Transparent Fire and are responsible for the changes this book will set in motion. Their work begins by subtly changing the space between the end plate of a neuron and the muscle fiber membrane, known as the "primary synaptic cleft", with solar radiation, which acts as a cushion.

The angstroms tend to duplicate due to the incandescent lightning of the Devas of Transparent Ultra Bright Atomic Fire.

At the cellular level, the light is processed by the potential energy until it penetrates the synaptic cleft, generating an intercellular realignment that forces the release of the neurotransmitter known as "acetylcholine". The acetylcholine is transformed instantly after its emancipation by tiny cyclones of ultra incandescent light, which are associated with the contraction of the muscle cells on the astral plane.

Gradually, the body will overproduce these light-powered neurotransmitters. They will emerge as pure crystal flowers in the large ocean of the mitochondria, in this way curing the terminal ends of the axons that were previously embraced by denser shadows. As a direct consequence of this cleansing process, light tremors might occur in some cases. Do not worry if you start to shake—this is normal, transient, and intermittent; it will only last for a few days.

In the folds of the muscle membrane there are lively and intelligent enzymes called "acetylcholinesterase”. The Devas use these enzymes to destabilize the acetylcholine.

Employing this enzyme, they entwine them together with tempestuous light and swirl them together to transmute the neurotransmitter into luminous choline and acetate of a higher nature. The choline then is reinserted into the pre-synaptic terminal, drastically changing its rubric signature. This process bestows a sense of tranquility upon the person.

Part of the discarded acetylcholine bears a form of antagonistic energetic resin that was implanted by the forces of the Nebula (the opposite force or energies of devolution). This waste will be reused beyond the synaptic field to create a depurated energy source that will be used in a further phase to feed certain nerve endings. The other face of the acetylcholine will reach the muscle membrane, just as lightning strikes the surface of the ocean during a storm, resulting in a calming effect over the muscle contractions.

When the Nine Devas inject their luminous beam, the acetylcholine, in conjunction with the enzyme process, will degrade the molecule into three components. As a result, the neurotransmitter will have minimal contact with the dark and impure membrane receptors, allowing the Devas to create a chain reaction of incandescent light, without any overstimulation or sustaining injury to the muscle fiber.

What I am trying to say is that the Luminous Beings are experts at what they do and will not affect your neurobiological body negatively in any way.

The changes will begin to be felt by everyone in different grades; the Devas will give the humans as much as they can handle, and this varies in degree. It all depends on how the human treats his/her body.
Try to make your system strong and healthy and you will receive higher amounts of power.
There is a factor of sobriety and protection when given a transfer of energy, since the nerve could be affected by impulses out of the norm. The Devas are eager to help and give you everything they have, but will never put 2000 volts in nerves that can handle only 100 volts.
This will be an intense process for some and easy for others. Everything depends on how sensitive the person is.
The normal frequency of neuron stimulation in the astral realms is 150 times per minute, and the Beings of Light increase it up to 300 per minute without allowing the natural decline of neurotransmitters released into the synaptic gap.
The changes will take place first in the causal and astral bodies, and then slowly will flood the entire physical body.

Matias Flury

Introduction by the Devas

In the three-dimensional field of perception in which time and space seem to be real, periodically, things are bound to change and are often subject to radical adjustments to protect sentient beings against the delusion of being a separate entity.

This book was created and designed with the purpose of opening the door to the unknown and helping human beings to connect with us, as well as to cross the ocean of illusion by the drastic modifications in their physical, astral and causal bodies that we will make.

It is and it always was possible for humanity to transcend duality. However, the present human body has many flaws, and this makes humanity's spiritual evolution a difficult task. But now we are at the verge of a new era in which illusory time is speeding up, and consequently, progress towards real freedom is here and now. This book is part of this universal progress, along with many other gifts that are already promoting change all around.

We all know that science is not capable of explaining or connecting spirit, mind and matter; it seems that physics can't find the equations to explain what a simple thought actually is. Quantum mechanics also tries to elucidate on this paradigm, but this is also impossible because, in order to fully understand the spiritual dimension, humans need a brain that is wired in a completely different way.

Spirit is the substratum, and the substratum is spirit itself. The modifications that this book stimulates are done at the substratum of what you call reality. Such modifications at this level make the realm of the dreamed atomic universe seem more unreal. When we make a modification at this substratum, simultaneously, the composite and elementary particles that you know begin to behave in a different manner. Sometimes these alterations seem to change and also provoke modifications on the atom itself and the atomic constitution of things. Please understand when scientists begin to see the changes that we expound upon in this book, (which in the past were thought to be impossible), that these changes are happening INSIDE of The Great Mind and that they are just changes in the collective dream; that the atoms and subatomic particles are nothing more than nonexistent pieces of mental information that adopt unimaginable sets of combinations to create multiple galaxies—and even universes—with mental, or imagined, rules and laws. You accepted these rules as physical commandments. These can be broken at any moment in time by one who understands the dream as it is.

This book is part of the magic of change—a change that is now taking place at the foundations of existence, where the concluding bases simply exist.

Reality is gradually apprehended by the empty mind and not by the thinking process.

Cleansing the window of perception is all humans must do to break free from the slavery of the illusion of separation. We emphasize and encourage you to leave desires behind and to become one with expansion.

An unvarying awareness of the present moment is the only hope to live life with no fear.

Be presence in the present moment, and you will be eternally free.

This book will help you shift your focus from your ambitions, purposes and objectives (since there is no need for them) to a new horizon in which everything is possible; where there is abundance everywhere and, at the same time, nothing really matters any more.

The self-image you are misidentified with, which walks proud with its assumed identity and tries to modify whatever it encounters, maneuvering all situations to its own benefit, unscrupulously adjusting to each situation to survive—never relaxed or tranquil—will slowly crumble.

Memory that gives the feeling of "I", an "I" that has an invisible base of inexistent thought matter, wants to survive and is ready to fight to be part of the deceptive illusion, will also crumble as you read this book with attention.

The feeling of being disconnected is associated with humanity's amplified aptitude to imagine conceptualized, intangible conditions and stipulations that create separation in the midst of unity.

An intellect, that constantly seeks commotion to keep the sense of being separate grows to be tactless and spellbound, and in this way, becomes a slave of its creation. But by comprehending its own egocentric behavior, the mind encounters a state of wakeful alertness.

Humans are believed to be a mass of contradictory feelings and thoughts; this is not true and we will prove this.

The vital nucleus of the human being is “The sense of the individual I”; if there is no reaction to outside impute this “individual sense of I” will succumb. Thus, being presence in the present will conquer all notions of division.

Do not be a victim of your fears and wishes.

Surrender to what is, and stop trying to control your field of action. Do not try to alter your world; give up the resistance, make no demands, yield, relax and read.

You are the space in which your body—together with these feelings you feel, these sounds you hear, these thoughts you think, and these emotions you experience—rests upon.

The Nine

I

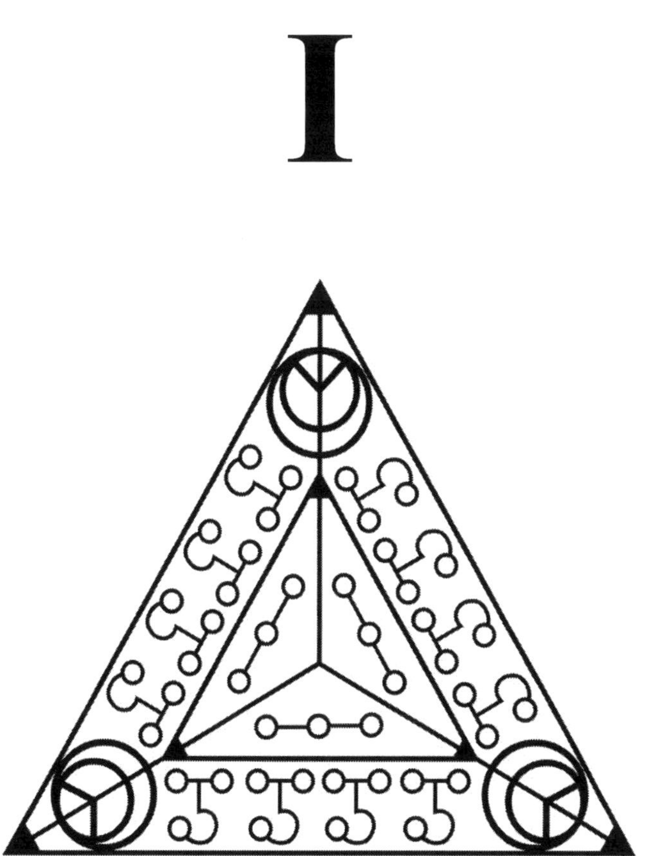

System

Below you will read The Genesis: a concise and brief interpretation of the beginning of creation from the serene viewpoint of the Devas. Then you will find the pyramidal spirals, which will repeat the information you just read. Notice that the first spiral starts at the left top corner and there is a hand with an index finger letting you know that is the beginning; the second spiral starts at the center, and the hand with the index finger sticking out will point you to the beginning.
At the beginning it could be confusing since you will find signs like ( ) ; . , etcetera going up or down in between words, also remember that we use (h)she, for he and she, and when you read this when going up or down it is challenging.
This book may seem difficult to understand in the beginning, especially if the reader does not have a background on physics or biology, however the spirals and the complicated sentences are designed to abruptly stop the wondering mind.

The sentences resemble the idea of a Zen Koan, which are short nonsensical paragraphs designed to stop the thinking process.

A famous Koan for instance is "Listen to the sound of one hand clapping."

It is said that if the meditation practitioner tries to decipher this Koan, the mind at some point will collapse altogether leaving him/her in a state of perfect union and illumination.

The spirals and the complicated configuration of this book have the same purpose, that of annihilating the ego/mind and simultaneously changing the configuration of the three bodies, ensuring thus a rapid progression of human and spiritual evolution.

Some people will feel one or many of these sensations and feelings like emptiness, cessation of thoughts; a sense of well being, tired or energized, anxiety, headaches, peace, love, tingling, heat, insomnia, elated, bliss, ecstasies and some people won't feel much. In any case the enchantment will still be working in subtle gray unconscious areas. If you are one of the few that do not feel much, do not worry you are still being reconnected to the astral and causal realms, and after this reconnection takes place you will un-doubtfully according to them begin to feel. Also know that this is a book you can read several times.

Do not worry if you cannot repeat the mantras with perfect pronunciation, this is not necessary, there is a lot of compassion transmitted in this book, and faith is all you really need when doing so.
You do not need to be young since changes happen first in the astral body, and that is all you need to cross the portal of physical dead, evolution of the human body will take care of itself in this planet.
While you read their spiral magic, the Devas will join you. I wish you well, my friend.

Matias Flury

The Dream of Transmigration

The dream of transmigration is profound and complex. In it, you forget who you really are. Through this multiplicity of so many transcendental states, you have divided into many sparks with individual consciousness, and you have forgotten your real nature. We are the dream that appeared as an act of magic that has the solemn purpose of awakening you. It is a glorious day when, in small oscillating parts of the dream of infinite immensity, you, the dreamed personage, realize and know that (you have been blindly following a forged mental conception—only a figment of a virtual imagination that lacks any real foundations. The individual mind turns and looks at itself as an astral projection or just a hologram, preconceived by the Source of Radiant Essence. In this instant, something we know as Grace happens. The Source floods the mind with dazzling light and destroys the coverings of psychological "I-ness".

Once this Divine Grace has done its job, the individual being identifies itself with Absolute Consciousness and becomes an expanded multidimensional being, and soon thereafter, also transcends the dream of multidimensionality and becomes forever free.

The Source of Radiant Light and Absolute Consciousness

It is important to state that even though the Source of Radiant Light is part of the multidimensional dream, she is always conscious, and She is also nothing more and nothing less than the Absolute Consciousness.

If there is an almighty, omniscient, and omnipresent God that can be perceived in all dimensions and that sends its messiahs, avatars, and light emissaries to awaken Absolute Consciousness inside its own dream, it is this: The Source of Radiant Essence.

The Source of all Light is part of the dream that awakens even those who are most asleep. If you are reading this, we have no doubt whatsoever that your time has arrived and that your awakening is imminent. Know, then, that God exists on this multidimensional dream, and that She is as real or unreal as you are. Understand that you don't exist as an individual, that individuality is false, and that you are expansive and marvelous. Keep this in mind while you read these dreamed words, which have the solemn purpose of stimulating your awakening.

Matter

It has already been said that everything you see, feel, smell, taste and hear is part of an imagined dream. Even though whatever is right in front of you may appear to be completely real, it does not exist. It's all simply a fragment of the collective imagination of expansive awareness. You are part of this awareness, you are this consciousness, this is your dream, and there is nothing that exists without this magnanimous imagination. Thus said, even the whole universe is false.

A great part of the energy of this universe corresponds to material representations that are constituted by particles with no apparent mass—thought particles, in reality. To mention an example, according to earthly science, electromagnetic radiation, light, and other elements are formed by photons without any mass of their own. In the same way, the graviton, the fermion (the super symmetric boson partner to a photon), and gravitino (the super symmetric partner of the graviton) constitute universal energies despite the fact that they lack any mass. Although these particles seem to exist, they do not; you are actually surrounded by empty space with a holograph of superimposed dimensions and parallel universes.

As stated before, this book will awaken first the causal body, which is a powerful dormant encasement of the soul that becomes active at the time of death. In order to awaken this body before dying, the multiple representations of the self that symbolize diverse volitional inclinations that take the psyche on its wild ride have to be erased by the Source. There are numerous personalities, and therefore numerous wills, within your enclosed individual consciousness. These are in a constant struggle against themselves, and that is exactly why you cannot advance. Intellectually, you do not have any independent autonomy from the whole. However, when you awaken your causal body, you are the master of your will.

The astral body, which acts as an intermediate between the encasement of the intelligent soul (causal body) and the physical body, will be refurbished. This subtle encasement composed of vortices of deep transcendental energy and thousands of hollow meridians of delicate fabric, is used for the spiritual projection of the soul into a universe of ecstatic feelings. Even though most of the emotions are kept in the physical body, the astral body also transmits, at times, emotions that have stayed in the vortices resulting from cleansing the physical body of emotional turmoil.

The procedures used here will cleanse the vortices in this realm. This, in turn, will have a drastic impact on human physiology. With time, our work will touch the foundations within the human physical body and change information codes and corporal biochemical constructions.
To understand the nature of this transformation, it's always good to remember that matter in itself is as hollow as the graviton or fotino. In higher planes, what humans call matter is completely nonexistent and irrelevant. Our main purpose is to activate and deactivate certain energetic patterns and conceptual information.

In the dimension humans inhabit, there are no physical laws—only mental laws. Atomic and molecular combinations hold within them the mystery of the void; the mystery they dreamed. These particles don't really exist; what lies behind these mysteries is mental, astral, causal and other types of more purified information not understood by the human brain.
In the individual's dream, mental laws prevail. One may experience gravity, walls, other objects, but these are no more than mental constructions. In reality we remain as if sleeping in bed, dreaming, and what we experience is nothing more than spontaneous imagination—a trance-like state.
If you look for molecules, atoms and so forth in your individualized dream, you will definitely find them. That does not mean that they are real and that now you have proof; your evidence will last as long as your dream lasts.
Reader: You read these words not to understand three-dimensional dream collective, chemistry or physics. These are merely employed to manipulate conceptualized energies that are the root of all existence and form a medium for the manifestation of the human body amidst countless other visions and forms. We will rearrange, clean and refine this thinking energy so that the human being may understand that his/her life is a dream and nothing more than that.
Read, open your heart and allow the change brought by Love and eternal peace to embrace you.

II

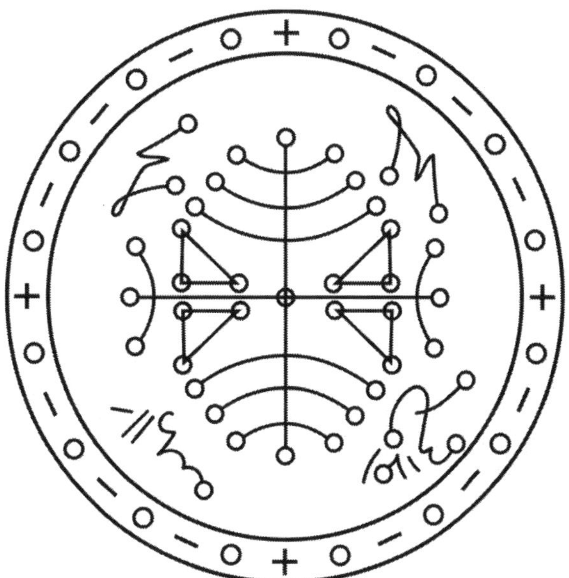

Dreamed History

The Source of Radiant Essence and the Impenetrable Shadows

Let's restate the undeniable truth that this three-dimensional reality is in fact a holographic dream. Not only what surrounds us is being dreamt at this time, but also, you are part of this exact same dream. You are a being within a dream and, simultaneously, you are also the dreamer.

You are, in truth, the heart of pure awareness—unadulterated and silent. You do not need this book to evolve, you don't need us either; we, the Seraphim, also are just dreamed beings that fly to and fro within this complex mirage.

You are already pure consciousness. However, if you feel in any way confused and you are a faithful believer in the world that surrounds you, then keep on reading openly and we will show you how what you call reality is nothing but a great optical illusion.

IT HAS ALREADY BEEN SAID THAT EVERYTHING YOU SEE, FEEL, SMELL, TASTE AND HEAR IS PART OF AN IMAGINED DREAM. EVEN THOUGH WHATEVER IS RIGHT IN FRONT OF YOU MAY APPEAR TO BE COMPLETELY REAL, IT DOES NOT EXIST. IT'S ALL SIMPLY A FRAGMENT OF THE COLLECTIVE IMAGINATION OF EXPANSIVE AWARENESS. YOU ARE PART OF THIS AWARENESS, YOU ARE THIS CONSCIOUSNESS, THIS IS YOUR DREAM, AND THERE IS NOTHING THAT EXISTS WITHOUT THIS MAGNANIMOUS IMAGINATION. THUS SAID, EVEN THE WHOLE UNIVERSE IS FALSE. A GREAT PART OF THE ENERGY OF THIS UNIVERSE CORRESPONDS TO MATERIAL REPRESENTATIONS THAT ARE CONSTITUTED BY PARTICLES WITH NO APPARENT MASS; THOUGHT PARTICLES IN REALITY. TO MENTION AN EXAMPLE, ACCORDING TO EARTHLY SCIENCE, ELECTROMAGNETIC RADIATION, LIGHT, AND OTHER ELEMENTS ARE FORMED BY PHOTONS WITHOUT ANY MASS OF THEIR OWN. IN THE SAME WAY, THE GRAVITON, THE FERMION (THE SUPERSYMMETRIC BOSON PARTNER TO A PHOTON), AND GRAVITINO (THE SUPERSYMMETRIC PARTNER OF THE GRAVITON) CONSTITUTE UNIVERSAL ENERGIES DESPITE THE FACT THAT THEY LACK ANY MASS. ALTHOUGH THESE PARTICLES SEEM TO EXIST, THEY DO NOT; YOU ARE ACTUALLY SURROUNDED BY EMPTY SPACE WITH A HOLOGRAPH OF SUPERIMPOSED DIMENSIONS AND PARALLEL UNIVERSES. AS STATED BEFORE, THIS BOOK WILL AWAKEN FIRST THE CAUSAL BODY THAT IS A POWERFUL DORMANT ENCASEMENT OF THE SOUL THAT BECOMES ACTIVE AT THE TIME OF DEATH. IN ORDER TO AWAKEN THIS BODY BEFORE DYING, THE MULTIPLE REPRESENTATIONS OF THE SELF THAT SYMBOLIZE DIVERSE VOLITIONAL INCLINATIONS, WHICH TAKE THE PSYCHE ON ITS WILD RIDE, HAVE TO BE ERASED BY THE SOURCE. THERE ARE NUMEROUS PERSONALITIES, AND THEREFORE NUMEROUS WILLS, WITHIN YOUR ENCLOSED INDIVIDUAL CONSCIOUSNESS, WHICH ARE IN A CONSTANT STRUGGLE AGAINST THEMSELVES, AND THAT IS EXACTLY WHY YOU CANNOT ADVANCE. INTELLECTUALLY, YOU DO NOT HAVE ANY INDEPENDENT AUTONOMY FROM THE WHOLE. HOWEVER, WHEN YOU AWAKEN YOUR CAUSAL BODY, YOU ARE THE MASTER OF YOUR WILL. THE ASTRAL BODY, WHICH ACTS AS AN INTERMEDIATE BETWEEN THE ENCASEMENT OF THE INTELLIGENT SOUL (CAUSAL BODY) AND

THE PHYSICAL BODY, WILL BE REFURBISHED. THIS SUBTLE ENCASEMENT, WHICH IS COMPOSED OF VORTICES OF DEEP TRANSCENDENTAL ENERGY AND THOUSANDS OF HOLLOW MERIDIANS OF DELICATE FABRIC, IS USED FOR THE SPIRITUAL PROJECTION OF THE SOUL INTION HUMANS INHABIT. ECSTATIC FEELINGS. EVEN THOUGH MOST OF THE EMOTIONS ARE KEPT IN THE PHYSICAL BODY, THE ASTRAL BODY ALSO TRANSMITS, AT TIMES, EMOTIONS WHICH HAVE STAYED IN THE VORTICES FROM CLEANSING THE PHYSICAL BODY OF EMOTIONAL TURMOIL. THE PROCEDURES USED HERE WILL CLEANSE THE VORTICES IN THIS REALM. THIS, IN TURN, WILL HAVE A DRASTIC IMPACT ON HUMAN PHYSIOLOGY. WITH TIME, OUR WORK WILL TOUCH THE FOUNDATIONS WITHIN THE HUMAN PHYSICAL BODY AND CHANGE INFORMATION CODES AND CORPORAL BIOCHEMICAL CONSTRUCTIONS. TO UNDERSTAND THE NATURE OF THIS TRANSFORMATION, IT'S ALWAYS GOOD TO REMEMBER THAT MATTER IN ITSELF IS AS HOLLOW AS THE GRAVITON OR FOTINO. IN HIGHER PLANES, WHAT HUMANS CALL MATTER IS COMPLETELY INEXISTENT AND IRRELEVANT. OUR MAIN PURPOSE IS TO ACTIVATE AND DEACTIVATE CERTAIN ENERGETIC PATTERNS AND CONCEPTUAL INFORMATION. IN THE DIMENSION HUMANS INHABIT. THERE ARE NO PHYSICAL LAWS—ONLY MENTAL LAWS. ATOMIC AND MOLECULAR COMBINATIONS HOLD WITHIN THEM THE MYSTERY OF THE VOID; THE MYSTERY THEY DREAMED. THESE PARTICLES DON'T REALLY EXIST; WHAT LIES BEHIND THESE MYSTERIES IS MENTAL, ASTRAL, CAUSAL AND OTHER TYPES OF MORE PURIFIED INFORMATION NOT UNDERSTOOD BY THE HUMAN BRAIN. IN THE INDIVIDUAL'S DREAM, MENTAL LAWS PREVAIL. ONE MAY EXPERIENCE GRAVITY, WALLS, OTHER OBJECTS, BUT THESE ARE NO MORE THAN MENTAL CONSTRUCTIONS. IN REALITY WE REMAIN SLEEPING IN BED, DREAMING, AND WHAT WE EXPERIENCE IS NOTHING MORE THAN SPONTANEOUS IMAGINATION; A TRANCE-LIKE STATE. IF YOU LOOK FOR MOLECULES, ATOMS AND SO FORTH IN YOUR INDIVIDUALIZED DREAM, YOU WILL DEFINITELY FIND THEM. THAT DOES NOT MEAN THAT THEY ARE REAL AND THAT NOW YOU HAVE PROOF: YOUR EVIDENCE WILL LAST AS LONG AS YOUR DREAM LASTS. READER: YOU READ THESE WORDS NOT TO UNDERSTAND THREE-DIMENSIONAL DREAM COLLECTIVE, CHEMISTRY

OR PHYSICS. THESE ARE MERELY EMPLOYED TO MANIPULATE CONCEPTUALIZED ENERGIES THAT ARE THE ROOT OF ALL EXISTENCE AND FORMED A MEDIUM FOR THE MANIFESTATION OF THE HUMAN BODY AMIDST COUNTLESS OTHER VISIONS AND FORMS. WE WILL REARRANGE, CLEAN AND REFINE THIS THINKING ENERGY SO THAT THE HUMAN BEING MAY UNDERSTAND THAT HIS\HER LIFE IS A DREAM AND NOTHING MORE THAN THAT. READ. OPEN YOUR HEART AND ALLOW THE CHANGE BROUGHT BY LOVE AND PEACE ETERNAL TO EMBRACE YOU. DREAMED HISTORY. THE SOURCE OF RADIANT ESSENCE AND IMPENETRABLE SHADOWS. LET'S RESTATE THE UNDENIABLE TRUTH THAT THIS THREE-DIMENSIONAL REALITY IS IN FACT A HOLOGRAPHIC DREAM. NOT ONLY WHAT SURROUNDS US IS BEING DREAMT AT THIS TIME, BUT ALSO YOU NEED US EITHER; WE THE SERAPHIM ALSO ARE JUST DREAMED BEINGS THAT FLY TO AND FRO WITHIN THIS COMPLEX MIRAGE. YOU ARE ALREADY PURE CONSCIOUSNESS. HOWEVER, IF YOU FEEL IN ANY WAY CONFUSED AND YOU ARE A FAITHFUL BELIEVER IN PART OF THIS EXACT SAME DREAM. YOU ARE A BEING WITHIN A DREAM, AND SIMULTANEOUSLY YOU ARE ALSO THE DREAMER.YOU ARE IN TRUTH THE HEART OF PURE AWARENESS, UNADULTERATED AND SILENT. YOU DO NOT NEED THIS BOOK TO EVOLVE, YOU DON'T THE WORLD THAT SURROUNDS YOU, THEN KEEP ON READING OPENLY AND WE WILL SHOW YOU HOW WHAT YOU CALL REALITY IS NOTHING BUT A GREAT OPTICAL ILLUSION

Genesis

No one knows how the illusory atmosphere of thought began or if there was a beginning to it at all
It is said that, for millennia, the Universal Consciousness lay dormant and dreamless. She held it all within Her absolute self.
One day, in a far away space/time parallel dreamed dimension, a breathtaking phenomenon took place: a movement came from within, from the center of Absolute Awareness. It began to dream and holographic images started to flourish all around. They began to move and became alive and some of them became conscious of existence. The first of these apparitions was magnificent; light, Love and peace were Her attributes. This original being began the work of creation. It took the name of "The Source of Radiant Essence".
In a far away moment within chronological time, the dream of universal consciousness stabilized and evolved into the realization "I am". This understanding "I am" was first thought within the Source of Radiant Essence, which rejoiced in happiness and bliss for billions and trillions of eons.
At some point within the nonexistent past, the Source became conscious of its existence along with other planes of dormant awareness. Such planes are what you call dimensions.
There were as many dimensions as there are presently stars in the heavens. Absolute Consciousness, through the Source of Radiant Essence, decided to create points of individualized consciousness contained in nine different dimensions. The other dimensions continued to exist, but they were not paid any attention since they were in suspended neutral calm.
The Source continued to create universe after universe in its own image and likeness, and they were universes of radiance. It produced sentient beings of eternal brilliance with their own free will and the power to dream. They were and are mesmerizing living entities of pure light.

The Nebula Was Born

One of these beings was captivatingly beautiful, alike the Source but with masculine energy. He possessed His own amazing powers. Such was His splendor and resemblance to the Source that, one day, in a space and time different to our own, He conceived the possibility of aspiring to become the architect of a parallel multi level dimensional creation. He proclaimed,

"I am separate, I am different, I am better, I am I." This was the instant in which the first Akrat (ego) was born, and this was the moment in which Akrat (ego) took His heart mercilessly and made Him believe He was separate. Together with the Akrat, suffering and terrible pain were born, and all the Nine dimensions within this great dream trembled with a new virus—the virus of fear.

This being experienced the sensation of being a separate awareness and forgot that all the other holographic visions around Him were no more than images inside a dream. This identity stemming from His ego said, "Nothing in this creation compares to me." Thus, He began to forget His own roots, and so He began to suffer horribly; His light began to shut down and His powers started to hurt and contaminate others. With these powers, He began to shape His own twisted realm and its brood.

When the Source of Radiant Essence became aware of this, it quickly neutralized the being's power, and so it was that the Source unwillingly gained its most bitter enemy.

Through His might and magnanimous power, this dark being corrupted many other beings of light with opacity and drove them to His own reign in order to dominate and torture them with Ego and absentmindedness.

The Source, which is only capable of loving, did nothing against it, for its nature is that of loving and only that. Despite this unconditional Love, the opacity was too dense to be pierced by peace.

The Source still continued to Love Him and never stopped. Some beings of light decided to fight. The Source of Radiant Essence asked for peace and embraced them lovingly, but still they were impelled to fight, forgetting that this un-reality is but a dream. Some fought filled with anger and were eventually absorbed into the Shadow. Others fought with an empty mind and triumphed. Both groups forsook their peaceful and loving nature. The noble beings that engendered anger in their hearts were never judged by the Source; judgment never fell upon them. These beings only wished to end suffering, and the abyss of forgetfulness caught them with a strong grip. Lamentably, the fighting brought only suffering to them and left their gentle nature beyond recall.

The fight lasted millennia but, for them, time was nonessential.

Finally, the Source of Radiant Essence interceded through force —but never, not even for an instant, did it stop loving. However, such was its strength that the Shadow and its minions were driven out.

Such beings (spawn of the darkest shadow ever to exist) have no realm or living dimension and inhabit the margins between dimensions; their wretched existence is like that of a virus.

The brood of the Shadows settled there but invaded the lower dimensions

and decoded the molecular structure of the Luminiferous ether. So, it was that ether became merely a light conducer, “ether Luminiferous".
The third dimension is the most dangerous, since the first and second dimensions are barren and lifeless, but darkness sometimes dwells in the second, and accesses the third through pictures, paintings and mirrors. The light, on the other hand, also has access to these and is used to help humans spiritually.

Interplanetary Light Beings of the Third Dimension

The quality of light, together with the gravitational capacity of each star, denotes the quality of physical and ethereal beings that these engender. After the ether lost its brilliance, the Source of Radiant Essence, together with the Crystalline Fire Devas, who are the most advanced and powerful beings of light, have covered the three-dimensional plane with stellar light. They use molecular hydrogen gas clouds to produce light. By a specific psychic process, they compress them, using immense centrifugal and extrasensory forces. These powerful forces increase the magnetic fields of the cloud. Such fields amplify the speed of particles charged with spiritual brightness, which stimulate high-density solar winds that dance within this gaseous constituent. In this way, the gas clouds are forced to collapse onto their own multidimensional central axis, causing the escape of tremendous radiation that envelops the circumvallating darkness.
After the “fictional dreamed time elapses”, the Devas of Crystalline Fire formed a denser and more opaque core than the one brought about by radiation, forcing the temperature to increase rapidly. Finally, they forced the floating matter to collapse into its core and embedded a kind of super intelligent soul into it. Such a reaction forced the production of ultra atomic radiation. This is how light came to exist in the third dimension, and this is how stars were made after the ether lost its brightness and became Luminiferous.
The spawn of darkness, on the other hand, takes advantage of the advanced spiritual growth of the soul of the stars, and when they are ready to break free, before they are replaced, they drive them to explode into dense black energy vortices, where the interior mass is high enough to generate an extreme gravitational field from which no particle, not even light, can escape.
This extreme gravity force is caused by a bending in space and time. The occurrence and geometry of a dark vortex in the fourth dimension is changing and elusive, whereas, within the third dimension they are quasi spherical. We know that the fourth and third dimensions are superimposed

over each other and, on many occasions, they reemerge one inside the other through these vortices.

Birth of a Black Three-Dimensional Vortex

The children of opacity force the stars, which have lost their brightness due to constant attacks and assaults, to exercise their expansive force on themselves, creating a concentrated mass of small volume. Some warriors of light infuse radiance into the stars so they can turn white. This Devic intervention helps to keep the light alive for thousands of years until it can no longer hold the pressure put forth by the night. For this reason, its light and power end up collapsing into itself; this is the point of no return, from which an alive and conscious vortex is born in the center of the star and becomes hungry for light and life.

In other words, the orbiting electrons are forced even closer to the atomic nucleus, where they end up amalgamating with protons, forming more neutrons through the process of light against dark. This process leads to the emission of neutrinos, forming a neutron star.

Depending on the mass of the agonizing sun, neutron plasma is bound by the forces of Shadow to trigger an irreparable chain reaction. The gravitational force grows unchecked, as the original distance that existed between atom and atom decreases. Neutrons are driven to implode due to the forces of confusion, which completely collapse as the light is swallowed by the hungry gorge of darkness.

This hungry vortex is in a limited region of space-time, so the events that happen inside cannot be observed from the outside. This relationship is not symmetrical; the light emitted on one side of the vortex, when consumed, cannot reach the other side. This, and any other swallowed mass, reaches a dimension known as dimension zero, where light, Love, and tranquility cease to exist.

If a being of light with individual consciousness falls into one of these vortices, it will never be able to leave or transmit information to the outside.

It is also impossible to see inside one of these vortices without being devoured.

The vortices of darkness have no visible external features and the Devas of Crystalline Fire still do not fully understand this kind of gloom, as they cannot look inside and, if they get close to it, they run the risk of being swallowed into the black depths.

For this reason, the Source of Radiant Essence created three-dimensional beings (like humans) in this universe—to understand the mechanisms of the dark.

Species

There are a significant amount of inhabited planets in this galaxy that are relatively close to Earth.
These planets have ultra photonic light beings as well as natural and unnatural atomic-molecular material beings
Planets around Polaris are inhabited by astral entities of reflected light. They are like the moon; they do not own their own light.
These beings, though invisible, have the power to holographically materialize within the third dimension, where they take on angelic forms that mesmerize the human eye.
They are responsible for balancing terrestrial electrodynamics and magnetic frequencies. On some occasions, they have guided the human race through evolutionary processes; but things have changed in the present.
Although many of them were biblical, Vedantic, Mayan or Aztec beings—amongst others—they are not highly evolved beings. In the midst of their great authority, many were flooded by darkness. They commanded humanity to call them Gods, and ruled and dominated men. They became accustomed to being worshiped. To keep humanity subdued, they instilled fear and anger their hearts. In this way, they have been enslaving humankind from time immemorial. Many humans escaped the subterranean darkness implanted on earth and hid, but the slavery imposed by the Shadow is like an appalling disease that spreads slowly to every corner and strangles the heart of even the saintliest. These beings appear to have light; nevertheless, they can be recognized by their anger and preference for skin color and sex. They are responsible for implanting the programs of racism and sexism in the collective human mind.
They may offer help in critical moments and sometimes it seems like they fight darkness, but their help is useless because they can only access the three-dimensional astral plane. They can only combat entities in the lower dimensions and, with the use of the Nebula's power, they combat darkness with darkness and this only creates more of it.
If you were to encounter one of them, realize that their help is merely astral and material and there will always be a price to pay.
These beings are not interested in guiding humanity's spirituality or in training them to defend themselves. Their purpose is simple and selfish and their transmitted energy is low; when they broadcast this energy to

humans, it remains in the muscles causing some kind of pleasant sensations. Do not be fooled by it and become addicted. This energy does not penetrate the nervous system or the subtle meridians and it won't support any lasting embryonic effect.

The Devas of Crystalline Fire have tried to help these beings, but they often have rejected these offerings because they lack humility.

There were, in the holographic past, Crystalline Devas that sometimes showed them their atomic fire, made them tremble and named themselves archangels or Devas of Fire.

The Devas of Vehement Blazing Flames guided these egocentric beings through areas of space filled with fulminating blue light to help them evolve, and not so many succeeded.

Be careful, as these Luminiferous beings are the most likely to fall into the grey Nebula.

Even though not all of them are malevolent, they may confuse and stall your progress. At the time of death, they have the ability to embed the egoic personality to the soul and guide it along three-dimensional astral paths that are fascinating at first, but utterly dull at the end, and you will also become their servant. Reject them, or else your spiritual growth could experience a lag within a sub-universal limbo.

The most powerful corporeal beings seen in the third dimension by prophets, seers, yogis, etc., are fifth-dimensional beings that inhabit the parallel three-dimensional aerials of Sirius, Arcturus, and the Pleiades.

Arcturus, being the constellation inhabited by the most advanced beings, has helped Earth on many occasions and continues to do so.

These star beings have such powerful light that they infuse the planets that revolve around them with eternal jubilee.

Some of the planets within the Arcturian constellation are inhabited by three-dimensional beings who have mental and spiritual access to the fifth, sixth and seventh dimensions. These are incredibly advanced corporeal beings.

Their technology and understanding of three-dimensional physics is unlimited.

In Alpha Draconis the existence of entities embraced by hatred, greed, anger, and other ramifications of fear may be observed. They are creatures of war and domination; their instinct is to attack, dominate, devour, and destroy. They serve their false sense of individuality.

There is another group which sprung from the binary star system called "Z Reticuli" that are homeless. They are interested in human DNA and the human soul. They have no souls of their own and with their advanced technology they are trying to encapsulate the human soul with the purpose

of becoming immortal; in other words, they try to dispose of the soul's essence living on the ethereal capsule— a clear, indestructible silhouette in which they are trying to upload their computerized conceptual mentality. This procedure needs more research, and it has been unsuccessful every time.
I know that what we propose here may sound farfetched, and maybe it is. Nevertheless, it will remain real to those who believe in this dream. If you think your home, your town, your planet, etc. are real, what is proposed in this book is just as real. On the other hand, if you realize that the apparent reality that surrounds you is a dream, consequently what we propose here is a dream as well.

The Human Being

The Source of Radiant Essence realized that the dreaming consciousness was also dreaming darkness, not because consciousness wanted to, but because it was happening spontaneously. This was thought and reflected upon and it became apparent that, in order to understand the Shadow, it was necessary to create a being that had the luminosity of the Source and the confusion of the Nebula simultaneously within itself, as all other existing beings could not hold the two ends within the same soul; they could only choose one end: Light or darkness.
If a light being changes its frequency to the Nebula's frequency, it is impossible for the Source or any other being of light to penetrate such dense gloom with loving brightness. Any being that chooses darkness remains unapproachable and it is almost impossible to recover.
Human beings were created in the image of the dreaming consciousness, with the opposites inside their souls.
Absolute Consciousness in its natural state knows neither good nor bad; inside it, everything happens spontaneously and without effort. On the other hand, the Source of Radiant Essence, which is the "manifestation" of Absolute Consciousness (so to speak, considering that it does not possess a body but is only expansive intelligence that is aware of its own existence), perceives its own existence and creation from another point of view. It seeks tirelessly to spread light and Love above all else, and to eliminate pain from its creation.
The Source of Radiant Essence, with help from the Nine Devas of Crystalline Fire, found the solution and agreed to create the human vehicle with the purpose of understanding the central nucleus that keeps the

energies of the Shadow alive inside their encasement. Humans call this nucleus “The Ego”.

III

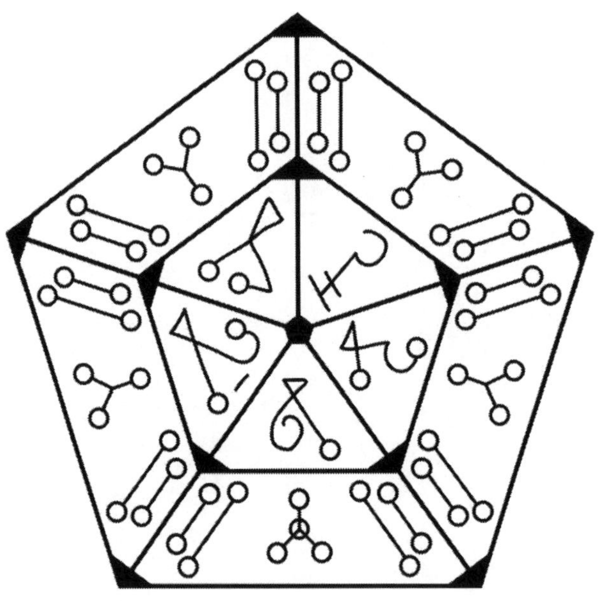

The Virus Takes Over

Egocentric Human Composition

First, a four-helix molecule similar to the nucleic acid that contained genetic imprints was created. This acid was the medium for storing and transmitting genetic and subtle/astral information.
Each gene was created by the Source of Radiant Essence with the function of producing molecular proteins of transmigrating brilliance.
This information flowed from the genes in the form of luminous tentacles and determined the composition of proteins by absorbing specific and determined information from the Devic forces. The radiant ones injected the cells with orders that established the fulfillment of a predetermined function within each cell. In this way, the old DNA was incrusted in the organized nucleus of chromosomes. Each one of these cells was created to contain dream genetic information. This information forced the DNA to duplicate before the cells divided and dispersed.
Inside the dream, everything happens spontaneously, and an action causes an effect. The aforementioned effect was not planned and it appeared like an act of magic. When more proteins were needed, the corresponding genes transcribed themselves into a double helix, similar to what today is the RNA; one could say that the RNA was the result of a spontaneous accident.
The interesting thing is that the new RNA, the one that was manipulated by the Nebula, has encrypted and unencrypted parts that are first processed so that the unencrypted parts are removed, which leaves the new RNA deficient of fundamental foundations.
The Devas use their will and abilities to transport these parts in and out of the nucleus as you read. The result of this is that proteins are constituted in a different manner, taking into account the RNA as the base in the same way that the forces of the Nebula did.

The Opaque Transmutation of the DNA Information Template

Both DNA and RNA suffered severe changes brought about by the spawn of darkness. As a result of this intervention, DNA was left with double strands and RNA now has a single strand.

Currently, you may observe that there are viruses left behind from those days of experimentation to subjugate the human race. They have genomes and DNA of triple strands and other viruses have genomes possessing RNA of two strands.

Author's note:

In a recent scientific study published online by *Nature Chemistry* a team of scientists, led by Shankar Balasubramanian at the University of Cambridge, UK, offer evidence that G-quadruples do occur in human cells. These curious structures contain imperative biological protective functions. Such formations of chromosomal DNA, known as telomeres, are loaded with guanine and so are possible aspirants for G-quadruplet structures.

Due to the effect that the forces of the Nebula had over the nucleic acid, a linear macromolecule of chained nucleotides, which were susceptible to the invasion of the virus of darkness, and the pentose and phosphate collapsed into an impermeable black vortex while other chains of amino acids, which were essential for supporting the missing strands, were lost in the process. With the purpose of restructuring and healing the damage, we will flood the pentose with 0-1-1-0-1-1 fires to change the nucleotides.
The Devas built, and are constantly building, the substructure of the union of a nitrogen base and a pentose in order to balance the disruption. They are also constantly linking the N-glucosidal that was established by the beings of light between the C1 of the pentose and a nitrogen unit of the base by the disintegration of a water molecule; this marriage of particles came to be known on Earth by the name of nucleoside.
With the creation of nucleoside, the nucleotides went on to occupy a second place, and, at present, they are the phosphoric esters of the nucleosides. As you continue reading the nucleotides are in this moment being irradiated by Devic lights that embrace them. They are born out of the union of nucleoside with a phosphoric acid molecule that has the silhouette of an ion phosphate (PO_4^{3-}) that bestows upon it the strong acidity necessary to sever the ties with the sinister imbalance.
Moving further into the past with the intention of understanding the changes that the Shadow brought about, it is important for you to know that, previously, DNA contained four material strands, four subtle strands, four causal strands and one central ethereal strand.
Humans had a total of thirteen DNA strands; the RNA, on the other hand, had two strands in the physical plane, two in the astral plane and two in

the causal plane; for a total of six strands. This is the number of humans that is described in the Bible; it is the original number of strands.
In biblical times, Bible scribes and other sacred books scribes used numerology to describe external phenomena in direct relation to the internal cosmos of the physical body.
The largest DNA molecules that existed in the distant past on Earth consisted of 988,000,000 nucleotides, which, if examined through numerology, transforms into the number seven, which, in sacred numerology, is the number of the spirit. This denotes that man is a spiritual being enclosed in a physical frame.
When the creation of deoxyribonucleic acid resulted in the awesome appearance of ribonucleic acid itself, the forces of the Nebula began to produce a potent virus that attacked the DNA and RNA molecules. Nucleic acid molecules began to appear with 21 nucleotides (3 x 7 = 21). After this lamentable attack, some chromosomes began to appear with a single molecule that contains a maximum of 247,000,000 nucleotides. Through numerology, this number is transmuted to thirteen, a number related to bad luck in the present, but in reality, it is not; thirteen is just a number that denounces the involution of the human race.
The reason why the numbers thirteen, six, twenty-one and seven are mentioned in many scriptures all around the world is because they point either to the original molecular constitution of humans or to the degradation that followed it.

The Alpha Draconic Conspiracy

Other extraterrestrial races, along with the sons of the Nebula, began sabotaging the perfect human creation and injected Nebula components into cell walls.
They embedded deoxyribose into the DNA and ribose into the RNA. As a result, the structure of the sugar molecules in their nucleotides and nucleic acid changed. Humans began to show modifications in their nitrogen bases—mainly adenine, cytosine, and guanine.
The adenine started to behave differently. Due to the dark virus cells, they began to breathe at a different pace. The cytosine started to form groups of only three hydrogen molecules. Guanine was divided into two equal and metrical forms: keto and enol, which were driven to embed themselves in the cytosine through two hydrogen molecules.
We will explain the whole process succinctly to not bore you with complicated chemistry. The children of the Nebula, in conjunction with the low light beings from Polaris and other humanoids from the vicinity of

Alpha Draconis, injected a virulent darkness into human DNA and RNA. This virus was immune to light, and dissolved the foundation of the living human beings and their 49 corporeal levels, leaving only three: Physical, Causal or Astral, and Subtle.

The day that the virulent injection occurred, the children of the Nebula deceived and enslaved many beings in the physical and astral realms of eternal consciousness. They targeted first the low light beings who, due to their ambition and vanity, were tempted with the power of dominating and thus made a pact to keep their brilliance and to become the Masters of the humans. This was a terrible day for them since they transformed into Luminiferous beings with no light of themselves; now, they are just like the moon, only capable of reflecting light.

Although we do not know for sure, we believe they were promised lordship and Godly rule over the earth. What they do not understand is that great suffering lies ahead for them—not because they will be punished by the Source of Radiant Essence but because the darkness will embrace their minds and hurl them into a whirlwind of oblivion, where they will lose the memory of their Eternal Self. The spawn of darkness also used the three-dimensional Alpha Draconians to implement changes in the human physical body.

The Alpha Draconians are servants of the Shadows. Their hearts have been tainted by the darkness for eons. They are slaves that enslave and enjoy causing human suffering and instilling terror. Since they possess psychic powers, physical force and intelligence superior to that of terrestrial creatures, they have a great advantage.

If you are unfortunate enough as to run into one of them, just run in the opposite direction and shout out loud the names of Mikha-el, Anab-el, Xiabi-el, Nabi-el, Uri-el, Yorih-el, Adritmi-el, Gabri-el-a and Sabha-el we will certainly protect you. Humans have also been modified by another race that comes from a parallel universe; they are from the Z Reticulis constellation. They have another agenda and do not spend all their time working with the children of darkness, as they have understood that doing so would mean perpetual slavery.

They sometimes affect the human race positively and sometimes negatively. The Z Reticulis often need DNA samples to clone themselves and perpetuate their existence, since their own DNA cannot sustain their race. Most of the Z Reticulis are potential enemies who are interested in that which encapsulates the human essence—what you would call the Soul. They believe they can empty this ethereal and crystalline capsule, as was explained previously, using electroacoustic and electromagnetic frequencies. These beings want to immortalize themselves and access higher dimensions, but they are like a dream within a dream and therefore cannot transcend the nine dimensions.

Humans

The human beings, although less intelligent and advanced than when they were created, still have the ability to hold two opposites within themselves without being destroyed.

Human beings are composed of the spirit of the Source of all Light and the ego, which is a reflection of the surrounding darkness. Being a mere reflection of the Shadow, although the ego may seem real, it is not truly so. If a human were to understand this paradigm, his/her mind and soul would be liberated instantaneously and his/her essence would remain beyond the duality of good and evil.

It is for this reason that human existence was perpetuated and left on Earth—so they would transfer their intimate knowledge of the darkness to the Source of Radiant Essence. In this manner, the Source would be able to understand all of the Shadow's secrets, know its most profound aspects, and, when it is least expected, it would illuminate all the gloom with the impetus of the expansive heart of pure consciousness.

In rare cases, unconditional Love flourishes inside the human heart in an unrestrained manner.

The Source of Radiant Essence helps humans with motherly Love though this process and delivers its sublime light to the DNA contaminated by the dark virus. With bright filaments, it restructures the destructive genesis of the children of the Nebula.

IV

The Source of Radiant Essence Counters the Virus

Changes

The Source of Radiant Essence, with nine multicolored light emanations, made the DNA's double helix rotate at immeasurable speeds creating a magnetic field interconnected with a three-dimensional star-like light. This connectivity was permanent and everlasting; the fate of mankind is attached to this union.

This alliance is the central reason why there is duplication in the DNA/RNA, composed by buildings blocks that exist in interstellar space.
In our biosphere this duplication also occurs, but it is less dynamic.
The DNA/RNA synthesis in chromosomal growth was instigated by Arcturian beings through radiant cylindrical coils, establishing an angular frequency and a radial frequency of dynamic geometric codes. This began the chain reaction that caused spontaneous replication connected to the Source of Radiant Essence.
Proline, tryptophan, glutamine, asparagine, leucine, methionine, serine, alancine, glycine, and other amino acids were added in order to recalibrate the damaged DNA structure, causing a permutation within the structural vibration code that governs the electromagnetic spectrum.
Breathing plays an important role because it bathes these chromosomal codes in light and encourages them with messages of life and joy.
You can confirm our statement by observing the hemoglobin molecule; it shows the development of life in itself and provides proof of our assertion.
What the darkness did not know is that, although dark ink was injected into the cell's nucleus, it failed to stain life, since life is light and the human being is a living refulgent being.
Upon mankind's first inhalation of divine air, its biological structure was realigned with the Sun's light; in this way, the universal codes that give life's substance to soul, mind, and body began to activate each and every cell. These began to beat and breathe as the light of unconditional Love embraced them with its cosmic vibrations of celestial, three-dimensional architecture. Life began with light and it shall end with light.
The configurations designed by the Source of Radiant Essence for the purpose of evolution were, in many cases, sabotaged through time and space by the forces of darkness. The Shadow and its spawn rejected the human creation from the very beginning. Hatred and envy invaded their

hearts due to the capacity the human soul possesses for the power of transcending the opposing forces along with the nine dimensions from this lower three-dimensional reality, which is constantly transmuting space/time.
The Nebula keeps hurting the predestined evolution with no regrets or reason. Due to this incomprehensible and unnecessary quarrel we are obligated to fight, the restructuration of some human bodies has been planned in the fifth dimension, so that there is less intervention and opposition from the darkness.
It is not necessary to recapitulate our words, but it is necessary to evaluate our possibility to avoid that painful fifth dimension restructuring, which is painful because the human soul will have to be purified with fiery white radiations before they are reinserted into a new, restructured human body. These printed words will guide and help you to escape the cleansing, so that you might ascend to the higher realms with an intact consciousness. Make your astral body vibrate now in higher decibels—do not wait for the fifth-dimensional reformation; you should be able to activate the ascending spiral Asuntara with the help that we offer day and night in conjunction with the reading of this book. Relax and let this energy climb your spinal column and reach your brain.
Allow also a new galactic spiral to open the heart and codify your spirit with vibratory codes from the serene areas of the silent corners of infinity. Relax and let this vortex of light in your heart increase the dynamism of the structural chemical complexion.
Those who volunteer to wake up before the restructuring will be awarded with the help of all of the Nine Shining Ones and will be able to access all dimensions without pain or without dying the psychological death. Such an awakening will help to reorganize the streamlining of the undulating patterns of luminous energy that are modulated to delineate the final design of the future human body.
The Nine Devas are in the present moment trying to adapt your body as you read to different oscillating vibrations without any centralization, where space/time ripples don't have to arrange with specific electromagnetic frequency; this can be done here and now or in parallel dimensions without continuous or sequential time.
The reprogramming of the biological structure goes hand in hand with the astral/ causal rearrangement that takes place with photonic radiations of three-dimensional symmetric content.

The Virus of the Densest Shadow Will Succumb

The codes containing viruses will be intercepted with oscillating codes from all dimensions, forming an energetic and aural structure of brilliant and geometrical radionic twirls.
The new human being will reach unimaginable horizons and will cross the barrier that separates him from the intergalactic civilizations.
If you are reading this, know that you can be a humble master and we will help you with everything so your spirit spreads beyond limits.
Help us accomplish this transformation and make you a crystalline master of celestial light, permanently exonerated from egocentric forces.
Aid us in giving you forty-nine bodies so that you may access all nine dimensions simultaneously, as in the past, and have a glimpse of the Source of Radiant Essence without being disintegrated.
Transcend the coexisting worlds and the biochemical frontiers, leave the past and heavy pride behind; fly very, very high.
What we say is not about exploring new intergalactic horizons or dimensions, even though this is bound to happen. What we want for you is the highest, and nothing else. What we wish for you is as simple as transcending this dimension and, consequently, the others. We will teach you to defeat the gravitational forces of the tremendous masses of neutrons that are encapsulating you in this third dimension. For now, forgive yourself, bow your egotistical head and ask all for forgiveness. In this way, your individual "I" sense will begin to gradually dissolve until it is left in oblivion.
Relax and let us realign your atomic and molecular structure with the purpose of making it twirl in parallel planes, so that, in this way, in the external levels, the complementary particles that are compressing it will spontaneously expand with the crystalline light of the loving heart.

The Plan

Something immensely marvelous is about to happen. The Source of Radiant Essence has finally been able to understand the darkness through human beings; even though they have suffered sabotage after sabotage, their purpose has been accomplished.
Although the darkness appears to expand infinitely, it is circumscribed and therefore limited by time and space.

The Source of Radiant Essence is very close to penetrating the densest Nebula, but first it will perform an amazing miracle. It will transcend the nine dimensions for the first time without losing its dreamed identity.

Usually, when a being wakes up within the dream, it realizes that it is not what it believed itself to be, and that it is nothing more and nothing less than the Absolute Consciousness that, for some strange reason, started dreaming itself.

During the awakening process, the individual (as itself) disappears, its identity dies and the mental conceptualization sinks in an ocean of light and eternal joy.

The individual merges with Absolute Consciousness; the drop of water returns to the ocean of peace and stillness.

Conversely, the Source of Radiant Essence that understands the dream and is already merged yet at the same time has its own omniscient, omnipresent and prevailing identity, will magically penetrate Absolute Consciousness with the purpose of illuminating specific areas with photons of the third dimension, light of 010001 in the fourth, radiant light of 011001 from the fifth dimension, beaming light of 001100 of the sixth dimension, incandescent light of 000110 from the seventh dimension, uncompressible light of 001001 of the eighth dimension and 000111 of the ninth—the most powerful existing light of the multidimensional dream.

The dream will be used with the purpose of modifying the prevailing reality and, for the first time, the dream will conquer the dreamer.

What we are saying here is contradictory. We also used to believe in the impossibility of getting out of the divine dream and continuing with individualized consciousness, but the Source of Radiant Essence is going to show the opposite.

I have no doubts, whatsoever, that if the Source of Radiant Essence has planned it, that it *is* possible, and the Nebula, with all its suffering, will disappear from the face of the nine-dimensional dream.

Please know that what we are trying to explain is unexplainable, unapproachable and not comprehensible in terms of the three-dimensional mind of the human being. What we are doing here is only an attempt to satisfy the mental hunger experienced in this dimension with three-dimensional mental concepts.

Once the Source of Radiant Essence finishes its work in the Absolute Consciousness plane, it will penetrate the dream and will be able to trespass the gloomiest and densest borders.

V

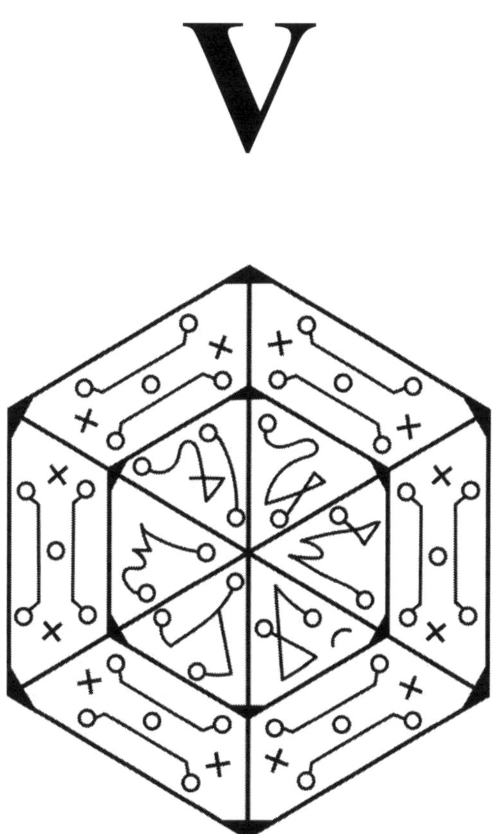

The Great Illusion of Opposites

Three-Dimensional Light and Darkness

According to human studies, the speed of light within the third dimension is 299,792,458 meters per second, taking into account the rotational and terrestrial orbiting time.

The speed of luminous waves is independent from such calculation due to the mobilization of the cause of the splendorous wave and the failed attempts of homogenously describing time and space. In the third dimension, the supposedly inert points of reference are in a constant state of hypertensive straight linear movement in relation to another reference frame. Therefore, we may observe the inconsistency that determines the nature of the dream. In other words, the three-dimensional dream is inconstant and experiencing impermanent changes in its laws, which are dependent on the movements of the collective unconscious.

Taking into account the invariant that the speed of light shows us, we can agree on the point that this velocity is only a figment of spontaneous imagination that the Absolute Collective Consciousness, or unconsciousness (however you like to call it), expresses through the dream.

Following a continuous three-dimensional trajectory of finite measurements, the speed of light can differ depending on the distance it has to cover in a linear dreamed time that is defined though conceptual universal mind waves.

The darkness in a three-dimensional plane, as we understand, also uses speed; as soon as the source of light depletes, the darkness seems to travel, in a similar velocity as light, towards the central axis of luminosity until it gets covered entirely.

Just as the light propagates from a central point, the darkness also seems to embrace the extinguished light source from the peripherals at the same speed.

The first, second, third, and fourth-dimensional universes have spaces where the darkness takes over the majority of emptiness. In these planes darkness is the base and photons block darkness.

Something very similar happens in the interior of the human being: if the internal light of the human soul turns off, the darkness embraces it immediately.

Gloom and pain go hand in hand: as there is darkness in infinite space, there will also be darkness in finite spirit if you are not vigilant.

When the Nebula takes finite spirit by surprise, it could bring about psychological issues that shock the human being's mind.

This can be confirmed by taking the circadian rhythms of the human body as an example. If the pineal gland does not receive any solar stimuli, a condition appears in the human known on Earth as seasonal or winter depression. Negative emotions, like fear, could also alter the balance. Darkness, internal or external, is the cause of fears and phobias.

The human soul and body were created with luminous fibers of high vibrations and this is the reason why the humans need either internal or at least external stimuli. If the internal light were fed, the physiological impact that the darkness causes would prove harmless.

ACCORDING TO HUMAN STUDIES, THE SPEED OF LIGHT WITHIN THE THIRD DIMENSION IS 299,792.458 METERS PER SECOND, TAKING INTO ACCOUNT THE ROTATIONAL AND TERRESTRIAL ORBITING TIME. THE SPEED OF LUMINOUS WAVES IS INDEPENDENT FROM THIS DUE TO THE MOBILIZATION OF THE CAUSE OF THE SPLENDOROUS WAVE AND THE FAILED ATTEMPTS OF HOMOGENOUSLY DESCRIBING TIME AND SPACE. IN THE THIRD DIMENSION, THE SUPPOSEDLY INERT POINTS OF REFERENCE ARE IN A CONSTANT STATE OF HYPERTENSIVE STRAIGHT LINEAR MOVEMENT IN RELATION TO ANOTHER REFERENCE FRAME; THEREFORE, WE MAY OBSERVE THE INCONSISTENCY THAT DETERMINES THE NATURE OF THE DREAM. IN OTHER WORDS, THE THREE-DIMENSIONAL DREAM IS INCONSTANT AND EXPERIENCING IMPERMANENT CHANGES IN ITS LAWS, WHICH ARE DEPENDENT ON THE MOVEMENTS OF THE COLLECTIVE UNCONSCIOUS. TAKING INTO ACCOUNT THE INVARIANT THAT THE SPEED OF LIGHT SHOWS US, WE CAN AGREE ON THIS POINT THAT THIS VELOCITY IS ONLY A FIGMENT OF SPONTANEOUS IMAGINATION THAT THE ABSOLUTE COLLECTIVE CONSCIOUSNESS, OR UNCONSCIOUSNESS (HOWEVER YOU LIKE TO CALL IT), EXPRESSES THROUGH THE DREAM. FOLLOWING A CONTINUOUS THREE-DIMENSIONAL TRAJECTORY OF FINITE MEASUREMENTS, THE SPEED OF LIGHT CAN DIFFER DEPENDING ON THE DISTANCE IT HAS TO COVER IN A LINEAR DREAMED TIME THAT IS DEFINED THOUGH CONCEPTUAL UNIVERSAL MIND WAVES. THE DARKNESS IN A THREE-DIMENSIONAL PLANE, AS WE UNDERSTAND, ALSO USES SPEED; AS SOON AS THE SOURCE OF LIGHT DEPLETES. THE DARKNESS SEEMS TO TRAVEL IN A SIMILAR VELOCITY TO THAT OF LIGHT TOWARDS THE CENTRAL AXIS OF LUMINOSITY, UNTIL IT GETS COVERED ENTIRELY. JUST AS THE LIGHT PROPAGATES FROM A CENTRAL POINT, THE DARKNESS ALSO SEEMS TO EMBRACE THE EXTINGUISHED LIGHT SOURCE FROM THE PERIPHERALS AT THE SAME SPEED. THE FIRST-, SECOND-, THIRD-, AND FOURTH-DIMENSIONAL UNIVERSES HAVE SPACES WHERE THE DARKNESS TAKES OVER THE MAJORITY OF EMPTINESS. IN THESE PLANES DARKNESS IS THE BASE AND PHOTONS BLOCK DARKNESS. SOMETHING VERY SIMILAR HAPPENS IN THE INTERIOR OF THE HUMAN BEING; DARKNESS TAKES THEM OVER IN THE SAME WAY AS IN THE

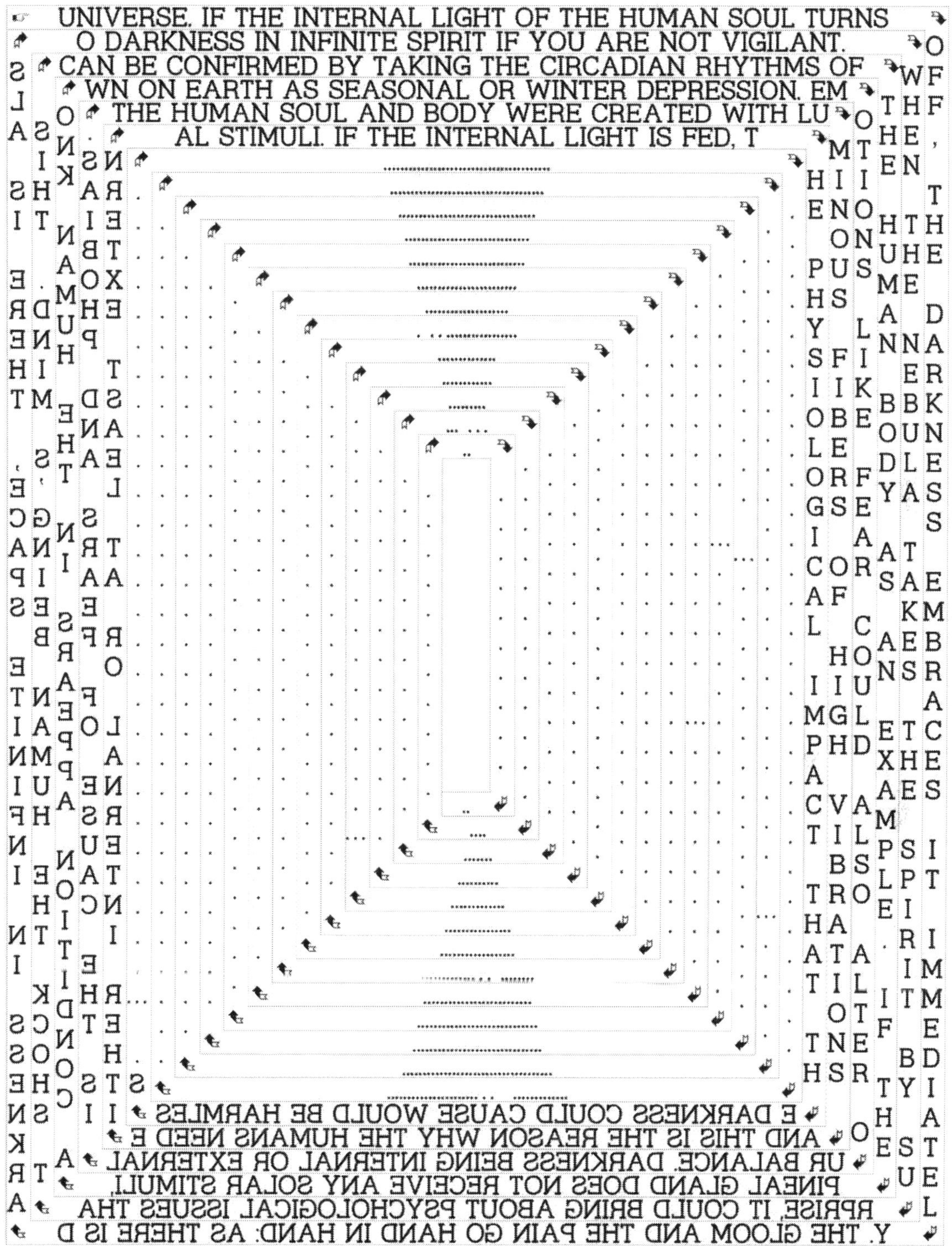

UNIVERSE. IF THE INTERNAL LIGHT OF THE HUMAN SOUL TURNS
OFF, THE DARKNESS EMBRACES IT IMMEDIATEL
Y. THE GLOOM AND THE PAIN GO HAND IN HAND: AS THERE IS D
ARKNESS IN INFINITE SPACE, THERE IS ALS
O DARKNESS IN INFINITE SPIRIT IF YOU ARE NOT VIGILANT.
WHEN THE NEBULA TAKES THE SPIRIT BY SU
RPRISE, IT COULD BRING ABOUT PSYCHOLOGICAL ISSUES THA
T SHOCK THE HUMAN BEING'S MIND. THIS
CAN BE CONFIRMED BY TAKING THE CIRCADIAN RHYTHMS OF
THE HUMAN BODY AS AN EXAMPLE. IF THE
PINEAL GLAND DOES NOT RECEIVE ANY SOLAR STIMULI,
A CONDITION APPEARS IN THE HUMAN KNO
WN ON EARTH AS SEASONAL OR WINTER DEPRESSION. EM
OTIONS LIKE FEAR COULD ALSO ALTER O
UR BALANCE. DARKNESS BEING INTERNAL OR EXTERNAL
IS THE CAUSE OF FEARS AND PHOBIAS.
THE HUMAN SOUL AND BODY WERE CREATED WITH LU
MINOUS FIBERS OF HIGH VIBRATIONS
AND THIS IS THE REASON WHY THE HUMANS NEED E
ITHER INTERNAL OR AT LEAST EXTERN
AL STIMULI. IF THE INTERNAL LIGHT IS FED, T
HE PHYSIOLOGICAL IMPACT THAT TH
E DARKNESS COULD CAUSE WOULD BE HARMLES
S

The Opposites Fight

Even though the dreamed darkness was caused by no other than the dreamer of the light, a terrible battle resulted in the dream.
The third, fourth and fifth dimensions were invaded by the Nebula. There was a division between the children of the Source of Radiant Essence and the children of the densest darkness. This battle didn't reach the sixth, seventh, eighth and ninth dimensions, since the foundation of these is pure light.
Even though the base of the third and fourth dimensions is darkness, the light can access both and infuse them with unlimited radiance. On the other hand, the fifth dimension, which is in a way a borderline of fulminating light that repels darkness, is also in some cases invaded by the most powerful Nebula beings, which stain this dimension as well. Very seldom do they contaminate the sixth dimension with small spots of darkness; but these entities can't withstand such radiance, so they return to their dark lairs in defeat and frustration. In order to enter these two dimensions, the children of darkness must have great malignant powers.

The Shadow Hurts and Contaminates

The closer the Source of Darkness gets to a sentient being that virtually exists in this dreamed world, the greater will the oblivion be, and therefore, the pain that devours them will be greater as well.
Many light beings became hypnotized by the deep force of the Nebula and fell. Others tried to rescue the fallen ones and also fell; and others fought with hatred in their heart and fell as well.
In the past, Love couldn't penetrate the darkness, but after all the exploration made possible through humans, Love is finally being used to transmute the shadow swallowed by the hearts of some fallen winged beings. Love is the most complicated armor to use; however, it is the most effective, since it changes darkness into light with motherly compassion.
Conversely, the violence directed towards the Shadow has its complications because, if you were to kill a child of the Nebula with hate, anger, or vindictive intentions, then darkness would progressively cover the aggressor with horrific tentacles. The being of light, on the other hand, upon showing anger, is left exposed and defenseless, and subsequently transformed into dense Nebula suffering material.

If one didn't fight but felt fear, insecurity or sadness, these emotions would paralyze him, and the Nebula would take his/her heart from the rearguard.

The only ways to fight against it are wielding a sword without fear or anger or simply penetrating them with love, with a mind clear like crystal. In this way, the being of light possesses an impenetrable protective veil.
Soon, we will penetrate the Nebula with a radiant fluorescence that reaches the deepest and most contaminated depths. In that way, we will establish peace in the entire dreamed creation.
The Love of the Source of Radiant Essence and, consequently, Absolute Consciousness, is so vast that it doesn't want any pain to exist inside its creation. This is the reason you can appreciate endless beautiful suns all over the three-dimensional universe. These small twinkling lights remind us of the existence of tenderness here and now.
The Source of Radiant Essence understands the pain that the Nebula is constantly generating and is gradually transforming it, until one day there won't be a single stain left in the veil of the nine imaginary dimensions.

Evolution and Transcendence

Three-dimensional soul evolution is slow and painful; however, it is considered a fast process when compared to the evolving processes in other dimensions.
The central focus of life is not evolution through multiple heavenly dimensions or parallel universes, or migration from planet to planet. The real point of existence, just as we proposed previously, is to transcend the nine dimensions and go beyond them.
The Expansive Consciousness accidentally created the nine dimensions so that it could become aware of its own existence.
All the beings and the multiplicity of planets in this and other dimensions are only dreamed thoughts that, in reality, don't possess any essential matter. What we call matter is only a group of mental laws and rules that are easy to break for those who realize their false and harmless nature.
The beings inhabiting each dimension have a feeling or a sensation of individuality.
In the third dimension this feeling is more aggressive and eagerly feeds off pain and euphoric happiness. In other words, humans are forced to live in the middle of two opposite dreamed energies. Human beings commit the terrible mistake of preferring a positive experience rather than a negative

experience; this is a pendulum effect that feeds the ego. The ego is found dancing in between these two opposed forces originating from the spiritual heart. The spiritual heart is invaded and flooded with positive and negative emotions. Fear, anger, sorrow, insecurity, etc. coexist with their constant opposites such as security, euphoria, courage, joy, etc.

If humans were to choose the unconditional Love of the present moment, the pendulum would stop. This sudden stop would cause a collision of the individual being with the Source of Radiant Essence, located at the center of the ninth dimension. If the standstill is long enough, the "I" feeling of the human being will fuse with the "I" feeling of the Source of Radiant Essence.

The expansive "I" feeling of the Source of Radiant Essence is like an antidote for the contracted "I" feeling of the terrestrial being. When the merging of the limited "I" with the limitless "I" is complete, the ego is dissolved. By being dissolved, the expansive sense of being forces the mind to comprehend the main purpose of existence, which is becoming conscious of its absolute presence that goes beyond the nine dimensions and beyond the Source of Radiant Essence.

The Source of Radiant Essence is constantly connected to the Absolute Consciousness that dreams Her; She is nothing more and nothing less than the clearest and closest visual manifestation of unlimited consciousness. Becoming one with it sets humans and other beings free, and this freedom is so amazing and perfect that it also frees them from The Source of Radiant Essence.

Bindings

Each dimension has its own bindings. In the third dimension the traps that get the human being are both pain and happiness, as stated earlier. In the fourth, it is the energetic currents; in the fifth and sixth, it is perpetual ecstasy; in the seventh, it is beatitude; and the eighth, it is the bliss that Love grants. There are no more bindings in the ninth dimension—only impervious peace, which is equal to freedom.

Each dimension has its links and passions that keep the individualism alive in beings habiting them.

The human body is very important in this matter, since it can experience the nine feelings. It has been said that, even though humans are less evolved and far removed from the Source of Radiant Essence, they can use a catapult effect that shoots them outside of the nine dimensions of reverie in an instant—without having to undergo multidimensional evolution. Spiritual evolution in the third dimension is not necessary, since humans can willfully choose the non-dual path and realize that they are actually the Source of Radiant Essence. This realization can dissolve the ego immediately; however, the chains that tie the three-dimensional soul to earth are so many, that it is almost impossible to escape this mental/optical illusion.

A multitude of beings of light were voluntarily enlisted for the human experiment. Most ended up perplexed and lost in the three-dimensional depths. It is almost impossible for those who not spiritually inclined to go back to the radiant dimensions after eating fruit from the human tree but, at the same time, freedom is also potentially viable here on Earth. That is why we are here—to help you and remind you of whom you truly are. Trust that we will never leave you, even if you do not feel us. It is our responsibility, our duty, and our pleasure to help you.

Always remember that the nine-dimensional hierarchy, along with its corporeal and non-corporeal living beings and the Source of Radiant Essence are as real as the world that surrounds you; and at the same time, they are as unreal as this world, since everything that you perceive under this blue sky is only an active energetic conceptualized dream made of thought-fabric.

Humility in the Nine Dimensions

Even though the human being has the chance to propel itself to the Source of Radiant Essence in the ninth dimension, one shouldn't believe that one is something special since one is confined to a retrograde dimension, surrounded by primitive electromagnetic frequencies.

For the beings of the fifth dimension, the humans are simply what you would refer to as a two-dimensional, imperfect cartoon drawn on a piece of paper.

Now, you would ask yourself if this message comes from the fifth dimension. The answer is no, since beings of the fifth dimension are not interested in relating very much with the beings of the third dimension; this would be a form of involution for them.

The Message

This message comes from the Nine Devas of Crystalline Fire, otherwise known to humans as Seraphim—entities of extremely radiant light and power that usually stay in the ninth dimension and do not normally communicate with humans.

These beings are the closest to the Source of Radiant Essence and, now, the long-anticipated moment has arrived in which the three-dimensional beings of this universe are connecting with other dimensions of fulminating light. Prepare to take flight, high and free.

This message was decoded and transmitted by luminous beings from the constellation of the star called Sirius.

The human channel is more receptive to the three-dimensional stellar messages than the ones coming directly from the ninth. When translating and writing these light patterns of angled and undulating Devic information, the human transcribing this book sees lights that becomes ideas and hears heavenly bells that become words. On the other hand, the Nine Devas of Ethereal Fire can use their power to talk through a human being as their channel, if one allows it. They can also change the human's molecular structure with their marvelous power and without needing any intermediaries.

If you are one of the few blessed to read this manuscript, the Luminous Nine have already started to modify your molecular structure. Be humble and accept this gift with respect.

VI

DNA Transmutation and Rejuvenation

Luminous Injections to Change the DNA and Immortalize the Soul and its Memories

Know that, although we will mention physical changes, the process of modification will begin at an energetic level in the astral body, which is, in turn, directly associated with the physical body. With time, said astral changes will embrace the subatomic particles, atoms, cells, DNA, RNA, muscles, internal organs, nervous and circulatory system, amongst others. When this happens, the changes will be scientifically observable.
Each entity of light is bound to specific vibratory combinations. The book reveals words in the Devic language that will help to connect you with said Beings of Eternal Peace and Love.
If you wish for a deeper and more intense connection with these loving energies, repeat these mantras nine times out loud:

Ashmiat ashmatviatat Anabel bushtam

I allow the energies of the Crystalline Deva Anabel to embrace me

After the process of death of the physical body and going through the burning purification of ultra atomic hydrogenised rays, the soul loses all the dreamed archives, and the person completely loses memory of their past lives. On the other hand, if this soul is purified and restructured while it is active in the physical body, it will ascend to other dimensions without losing the memory of its past existence.

Rejuvenation, Extraction of Black Stalactites from the Muscles

The muscles are surrounded by a coating that resembles a spider web (fascia). When this web goes beyond its own borders, the functional and structural unit of the muscle fiber links to itself, producing pain. It is very important to remind you that the human wasn't created with these imperfections; this was the modification caused by the virus of the children of the Nebula.
We work with 650 muscles so that the human being isn't distracted by the body's pain. However, our job in this dense physical area needs a

HUMAN channel to do the healings. Some of these channels are already living amongst you and others will become embodied very soon. To recognize said channels, look at them straight in the eyes; these channels should be clean and emit power.
The muscular activity of contraction and relaxation happens due to a mechanism of radiant imbuement of the nervous fibers with inherent intelligence. This radiance forces the fibers to release acetylcoline, which comes to rest over the nicotinic receptors, forcing them to absorb ions and sodium on an intracellular level. After being captivated by light, they travel along T-tubules, activating the receptors of dihydropyridine that are open to the luminescence of the Devas' voltage. These receptors receive the electro-luminous energy, inciting the creation of the ryanodine channels, giving complete freedom to the modified calcium we produce. This same calcium, disguised by the entities of stellar light, is expelled from the sarcoplasmic reticulum, where it is modified on an astral level by flashing undulating lights and is then sent to the complex of actin, particularly troponin C, which has three tangled complexes that will be reconstructed by our changes. This way, the super alkaline and energetically reformed calcium, modified with the luminous troponin C, will cause a conformational permutation of the troponin T, making it possible for the little heads of myosin to adhere, in this way creating a non-spasmodic contraction that is flexible and pain-free.
The myosin head, assembled with its actin, will suffer drastic changes and will be catalyzed in the lucid head of myosin by crystalline rays.

Body Depuration and Vortices with Solar Passion

Read carefully, the change will take place in you, there is no doubt about this.

Oim astriummm atishtat Mikha-el advatmiat

I allow the resplendent light of Mikhael to cleanse my three bodies

Human being works as a thinking matrix connected to everything and everyone. Human individual thoughts are permanently connected through a type of infinite and intelligent ether. This ether is different within each dimension and it may be compared to a collective mind with the aspect of a luminous network that affects every being of each dimension in particular with specific information on an unconscious level. That is why it is said that free will is limited, unless the sentient being of whichever dimension it lives in finally wakes up and understands that this matrix is but an extension of itself and that it is in reality the Source of Radiant Essence: the dreaming consciousness that dreams itself. The dream of the Absolute Consciousness can be confirmed through experimentation by anyone, in a similar way, due to this union. Most human beings don't even know that, through such a matrix, they can share thoughts, concepts and emotions. The majority doesn't even realize where their own thoughts come from or if they are their own or someone else's.

The Nine Devas designed a cleansing through the reading of this book that trims back some filaments that connect the individual with the collective ethereal placenta.

In the present time, we clean the nonmaterial body on different levels, starting with the vortices in the human astral body that were contaminated by imposed Draconian forces that directly affect over 108 billion cells on a molecular level.

Through energetic influxes that are transmitted to the physical body, we will affect cells of the musculoskeletal locomotive system, the respiratory system (we produce extension of the breathing pattern of the reader), digestive (increasing the power of absorption), excretory (increasing the purifying capacity of the body), and, in the astral planes, the connections to the endocrine, circulatory, reproductive, and nervous systems will be purged.

On the atomic and molecular levels, we will progressively change the configuration of hydrogen, oxygen, carbon and nitrogen as you read; these are the main elements that constitute the human body. We will simultaneously modify the molecular structure and will complete different unions with different combinations, in order to constitute inorganic molecules of radiant water. This water will comprise 75% of the totality of the body matter. Organic molecules, such as lipids, proteins and carbohydrates, which baptize the cortex with biochemical and cytological changes, will be distilled in the near future, becoming crystalline and refracting.

The percentage of oxygen, hydrogen, potassium, calcium, phosphorus, chlorine and nitrogen will be gradually altered to reach an absolute and perpetual balance.

On a cellular level, feel how we influence the astral field that, in turn, is connected to the physical plane, the external membrane, the nucleus, and the cytoplasm.

Presently, the cell's nucleus is governed by radio magnetic emissions to create a regimen of habitual regularity instated by the Nebula, which forces the human lineage and 108,000 genes established in 23 symmetrical pairs of chromosomes to save defective DNA and RNA. The electromagnetic emissions will be unstable for nine days in order to accept the new program. Such detailed work is something like resetting the nucleus.

The nuclear membrane that holds the genetic material is presently codified from an immaterial location in the three-dimensional universe so that it can be transformed in the future into a shell that won't let any pathogens created by the Nebula inside. The nucleus, which has inherited intelligence, will reform the cell when it is incited to spin inside its causal cortex.

We, the Seraphim, commit to penetrate the deepest levels of this nucleus to remove all the gray impurities planted by the forces of the Nebula that keep suffering alive in human beings.

Relax and feel the modifications that are taking place in the now. If you pay very close attention, you will realize that, in this instant, we are modifying, from a structural standpoint, the subatomic astral root of the biological tissues on a histological level. Thus, the epithelial, nervous, muscular and conjunctive tissues are stimulated to secrete substances that protect its form and the way that it systematizes its functions.

The current percentage of the corporal cell water is only 59% in adults. After these changes, water in the cell will be kept more efficiently and the cells will hold 77% of the body's water; some will circulate in the blood torrent, purifying and activating the glands associated to the vortices of energy in the astral realms. These changes are happening inside you on an energetic level while you read. If you don't believe us, close your eyes and feel us.

Regeneration of the Nervous System with Radiant Intensity

O aditm Axiel satmitl atratakam

I am focused on the Deva of Crystalline Fire Axi-el, who enlightens me

The nervous system is the closest to the astral body. This system can connect itself with the subtle body and its meridians and feel astral movements. If the frequency changes, the human being will start to adapt and accept orbital energetic relations of multidimensional intelligence operating on different levels.

As this system gets strengthened, a shell of the highest gravitational spectrum will be created to surround the human dome.

The brain and spinal cord are now receiving electromagnetic discharges extracted from the Sun. Their three membranes: dura mater, arachnoid, and pia mater, known by the human race as meninges—are being reformed and reinforced on energetic levels by this procedure.

During this phase being fully relaxed is essential because, when we work on this level, the human being will feel exhilarant energy that could transform into anxiety. If this happens, don't worry; the Devas of Crystalline Fire will apply a sort of astral sedative.

Due to such a change, the perception of the stimuli coming from the circumstantial plane will change. The cerebrospinal liquid will, in time, be transformed into a luminous liquid from the fifth dimension. The ideal ionic balance will suffer highs and lows for a short while until the Luminous Ones readjust the levels of the circulating elliptic electromagnetic frequencies.

The transformation of oxygen and glucose in the blood stream will be unalterable and perfect.

The gray substance, composed by the soma of the neurons, their dendrites, and the myelin sheath, will mutate its color and turn into a luminescent white. The nervous substance, instated by nervous continuations with the function of transferring information, will also mutate.

Strengthening of the Meridians with Effulgent Momentum

Adiat, adiat, adiat Raf-el

Radiant Deva Rafel make me shine, make me shine

Your energetic meridians are now changing their frequency while the radiant celestial spirals surround them. This will prevent their pulverization when the planet starts suffering geophysical changes. This subatomic change will transform the longitude of the wave of the Nebula into one of radiant light— a substance similar to the water that inhabits the seventh dimension (understand that it is not three-dimensional water, but moves like it).

Cleanse, Baptism and Chakra Protection with Splendorous Power

Ushtit, aditrar, adiatatrat Xiabiel

Xiabiel clean, christen, and protect me

As you read, the Luminous Nine harmonize the stamp of your vortices, using influxes of crystallized fire over the vortex's surface, influxes that were created and outlined by the Source and that now transmute the crystallized fire and project it over these central nuclei. These influxes will be emanated by astral convex prisms that exist inside the Devas' eyes. In this very instant, the highest intelligences will overlap a model of energy, codified in various levels of transpersonal dimensions with several binary axes that lay within your physical body, thus destroying and reorienting the programs introduced by the Nebula. This is how the Devas of Crystalline Fire dispel some of the Nebula's programs from the third dimensional plane.

In this way, the Luminous Nine make sure a neutral resonance is produced in the vortices.

Permutation of DNA and Ultra Radiant Light

Dimitrat ashtutreik udrat Gab-r-i-el-a

Gabriela, I am willing to let you change the foundations of my physical body

While the individual experiments with positive trans-lucid entropy and magnetic structure are simultaneously transmuted, injections codified with astro-immaterial DNA of thirteen helices are being administered to the cell nuclei so that they change their sub-molecular structure.

The human genome has a prolongation of three billion bp. This amplitude is stretched within different humans in different ways, since each human has a different code.

According to terrestrial science, only 27% of the DNA transcribes into RNA, and only 2% codifies proteins; this transcription and codification will be reprogrammed so the transcription becomes more dynamic. 35% of the DNA will begin to transcribe into RNA, and this RNA will codify proteins by 3%. These changes will transform the dynamic structure of the spiral. The energetic genes that are usually found separated by magnanimous regions of non-codifying DNA, will soon activate and begin to not only codify proteins but will also stimulate the production of golden lightning energy inside the gene. This will certainly stalwartly affect the codification of the spirals.

The introns of the human genes are considerably larger and more numerous than those in other genomes. They are (as you read) being prolonged with the purpose of electromagnetically changing frequencies.

The genes will be incited, one by one, to codify different proteins. The cut and its connections undergo a deep metamorphosis incited by angular lights while you read. With this new adjustment, each gene will codify up to five RAN of media. The human genome, which consists of approximately 24,000 genes, will be able to codify more proteins than before, and the transposed elements will be plentiful and luminous. This will be observable with the use of equipment humans use in their scientific investigations that have superimposed electron lenses and X-ray crystallography.

Through such changes induced by the refulgent spirit, the DNA will mutate its genetic codes, which will transfigure the information and non-changing patterns so that the sprouting cells are different from their progenitors. The genetic information will gradually transform.

The bases that possess the ability to copy and reproduce themselves will awaken the RNA so that it informs the ribosome affected by the Source that it is time to synthesize a determined albuminoidal in a reverse order.
Don't let your mind doubt for a second that we will change the central dogma of molecular biology.
The elements of recombination and transmutation will be used to re-conquer the necessary commutations for intercellular adaptation and evolution so that the DNA and RNA progressively transfigure themselves, adopting patterns of infinite light.
The nucleus will conceive a seed of ultra radiant light that will be in charge of changing the DNA auto-replication before the cellular division begins. On the other hand, the transcription of the different types of RAN will protect the synthesis of the new translucent proteins. Their sequences will energetically bind and unbind the DNA to chromosomes, stimulating the growth of more spirals. This new codified DNA will be introduced in to the cells by the human medium or directly by the Luminous Nine, realigning the molecular structure and simultaneously amplifying the human mind through non-conceptual universes lacking prototypes or paradigms.
This DNA regeneration program implanted inside the cells will restore a new order in the infinite internal universe of the cell, preventing its complete degeneration in the moment when the new interplanetary electromagnetic frequencies collide with the earth.
The Aura wasn't designed to protect the physical body, but it will guard and escort the astral body, which in turn will have been affected by the physical body's change in DNA in its atmospheric transition, and it will reject any wave or ripple coming from the darkest gloom.
When the modified soul moves through magneto-atomic zones that the Milky Way is about to disclose, its shell won't suffer any changes.
The gravitational compression, or any other categorical gravitational spectrum, such as a black hole, can't alter the shell of the modified human soul.
Without this diamond shell gifted by The Nine, the new holographic frequency determined by the new genetic code would be destroyed along with individual consciousness through the "disembodiment" phase.
If the shell hasn't been placed on time, and if the consciousness encapsulated in the human body goes through transcendental modulations of ascension to other dimensions, and if we haven't been properly balanced by the magnetic light fields created by the Luminous Nine and the medium, our mind, entrapped by intermittent electromagnetic waves, won't be able to adapt to the new three-and four-dimensional spaces; in

this case, you will need direct help before the dissolution of the "I" sense takes place.

If the bodily capsule breaks while the changes are taking place, the process will continue in the astral field and a luminous being, called The Ninth, will simultaneously chain the highest and clearest frequencies of the soul and will make them spin 495 ×9 times faster than the dreamed speed of light; this will break the magnetic linear structure of the innocuous essence.

This spin will create spirals that will completely change the behavior of the subatomic structure of the soul (in a manner of speaking, because atoms don't actually exist in the astral realms; here we observe only dreamed particles of conceptual information with a different signature). This rotation will affect astral particles similar to electrons, photons and neutrinos by forcing them to vibrate, causing permanent patterns of disintegration and changes in different energetic bands. The ethereal molecular chains will break and will cause the faceless and "personality-lacking" soul to return to the three-dimensional and immaterial geomagnetic planes.

The soul in this state will lack individual consciousness until it is spun again with the same intensity and velocity as before, coordinating its realignment with a conscious point in three-dimensional space, modulated and inset inside the three-dimensional material dream of apparent intercellular biological life and codified with the illusion of time and space.

Here, the soul will adopt programs and energies that act like configured compositions that orbit around a central axis. This center is the foundation of a molecular alliance, where matter and antimatter simultaneously unite.

At this crucial point of connectivity, the soul, matter and the vital energy will amalgamate, adopting elemental forces in a fourth-dimensional level that will oscillate around this epicenter of centrifugal forces. We call this amalgamation the "Egoic Soul" or "bodiless living egocentrism".

These subtle elemental forces activate the physical and astral bodies, the mind, instinct, intuition, the basic emotions with all their ramifications, the living air, liquid light, and the transparent ether. These oscillating forces connect and form patterns on an atomic level that combine to give a sense of individuality to the supreme consciousness, which injects life and spirit to its ephemeral mental creation.

Divine Grace

The shock induced by Divine Grace happens when there is a crystalline and pure exchange in the individual. The individual perceives grace as the defeat of fear over Love in the astral and causal planes. If we imagine this from an earthly synoptic field, we could state that the gravitational compression around the soul is changed by another one with a different gravitational vibration. The individual feels as if the vastness has opened the gates of a cage and is inviting him/her to fly.

This act allows the transmutation of the new genetic plane on an astral level.

DNA and the Astral Plane

The DNA is connected to a series of filaments in the astral level. The so-called geniuses, artists, intellectuals, prodigious children, and so on, have more of these illuminated astral filaments.

Some day humans will be able to see the astral worlds with technological devices.

The project you call Armageddon is a cleansing project. Whatever is dirty has to be cleaned, with many combinations of energetic waves. There is nothing to fear; choose Love over fear at all times.

VII

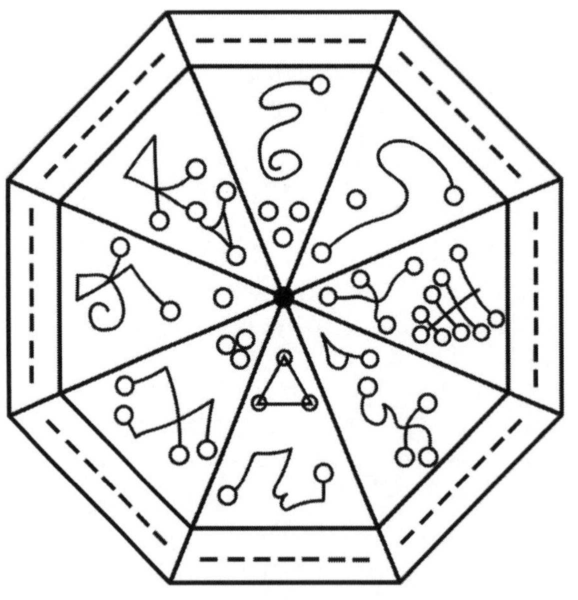

Vortices

Intergalactic Journey

Human beings have brains that are not properly codified to understand certain things; this is not normal, since the evolutionary process has been stopped by the Nebula. Some things can't be precisely explained; it would be like trying to explain colors to a blind person, but we will try our best.

According to terrestrial physics in the third dimension, the subatomic particles, which are particles smaller than the atom, are of two types: elementals and integrated.

The elemental types can be both physical and nuclear and are not combined with or integrated by other particles. The six types of elementals: electron, neuron neutron, lepton, TAU and TAU neutrino, muon and muon neutrino, are harder to modify with angular lights. The twelve force emitters and the eight gluons of extreme power and brightness, as well as the electromagnetic photon and the six types of quarks—up, down, strange, charm, bottom, and top—can be more easily manipulated by us so that they affect the foundations on which the human construction is established.

In some cases, the extensions of the elemental particles predict, thrust, and predetermine the existence of the invisible gravitation of these particles encircled by light and, therefore, of other mysterious live particles.

The integrated subatomic particles, like the proton and the atomic nucleus, are tied to more than 28 elemental particles, which we are also going to modify.

The world that we experience can be explained or understood as long as we accept that matter and energy exist inside the molecular scale of what you call quantum mechanics. For us, the three-dimensional particles are associated with something different that doesn't follow the reason of three-dimensional linear forces or what the mind in this space calls common sense.

These particles behave in an unpredictable manner since they are only dreamed particles. The more powerful the individual's mind is, it may break these rules of reverie with greater ease and make these particles behave and act differently. What the spiritual masters break when they perform miracles on Earth are not laws of physics but mental laws.

Light can behave in other dimensions like a clear and bright creek of particles. Conversely, on Earth they are appreciated as continuous waves of divine radiance. All these factors indicate that it is both possible and necessary to change our linear mental structure in order to possess a wider notion of the universe with tentative boundaries, where the properties of common sense are contingencies.

The interaction of these photonic particles, or dual wave particles and their unexpected combination with other massive particles leaves us engulfed in mystery.

This understanding of the mystery opens the door for us to conceive mass and energy as analogous elements.

Mass can be expressed as energy that exceeds the boundary of the third dimension.

On Earth it is known that energy can become denser and turn into mass. The energy, from a terrestrial point of view, can be transmitted as particles and waves; there is no doubt about this.

The flaring light of the Devas of Fire unfolds within the three-dimensional plane in the form of particles and, simultaneously, as waves.

If we go deeper into the ocean of the three-dimensional consciousness, we will realize that other particles also have a wavelike nature; you could even say that the particles of the dual waves take in the essence of three-dimensional creation.

Most subatomic particles happen and are manifested as a result of dreamed cosmic rays coming directly from Absolute Consciousness.

These dreamed cosmic rays interact in the third dimension and give color, perspective, taste, smell, shape, etc. to your surroundings.

The perspective or depth is an illusion that humans have to defeat to go beyond their mental three-dimensional limitations.

Interstellar travel in the third dimension goes from a determined point A to a point B; to get to point B, one must travel the distance that divides them.

In the fourth-dimension distance exists as well, but as visual distance; the fourth dimensional being transports itself visually.

In the fifth dimension the distance is mental; the being transports itself mentally. Just thinking about a place makes the entity disappear and appear in the place (s)he thought of instantly; we can say that the fifth-dimension folds on itself, uniting the points of exit and emergence.

Even though the journey continues to have a linear aspect, the transportation is more dynamic and fast.

In the sixth and seventh dimensions it is understood that A and B are overlapped and that we are the center wherever we are. A and B are placed one atop the other and the beings can access two, three or even one hundred different places simultaneously. The divergence between the sixth and the seventh dimensions is that the beings of the sixth can divide

themselves in two and beings from the seventh dimension can split into thousands.
In the eighth and ninth dimensions they are expansive and one with the infinite dream. They can do practically whatever they want, since they are illuminated divine extensions.
Beings from the ninth dimension can even change the course of the dream completely without violating the physical laws of the third or any other dimension, if necessary.
Such changes are only executed with the purpose of stimulating evolution.

The 21 Vortices, DNA of Thirteen and Quadruple Helix

As long as we advance through this amazing and magical reading, we will continue to awaken different faces of the human composition.
We say that the physical body, astral body and causal body have twenty-one important multidimensional energetic vortices: seventeen in the material human body and nine outside of it.
These vortices affect the individual physically, mentally and spiritually.
During this reading, you will notice that we are referring to a certain reinsertion of amino acids into the human body discovered on certain asteroids found on Earth, from the moon, and from other planets.
These asteroids were sent millennia ago by the Source of Radiant Essence to counter the collateral effects caused by the forces of darkness.
The supply of amino acids is implanted without recurring to invasive methods.
As opposed to the children of darkness, the Devas of Crystalline Fire will change the human body gradually so that it doesn't suffer any shocks.
First, the Nine Devas connect with these fallen asteroids through the thinnest messianic filaments of radiant light, which absorb the amino acids' astral blueprint into their bodies to process it. The light used for the distillation of these filaments changes the subatomic astral structure of the exhorted amino acids, and they are reproduced by a type of octagonal vortex found in the Deva's heart. Once the energetic scripture code is attained, the Deva looks for the reader and implants the vibration code into the specific center while (s)he is in the process of reading the book. In this way, the change happens first on an energetic level. With time, the amino acid elliptic astral information will also reappear materially after several years; this transformation will be observable by scientists with the help of overlapped lenses that will magnify the image.

THREE-DIMENSIONAL SOUL EVOLUTION IS SLOW AND PAINFUL; HOWEVER, IT IS CONSIDERED A FAST PROCESS WHEN COMPARED TO THE EVOLVING PROCESSES IN OTHER DIMENSIONS. THE CENTRAL FOCUS OF LIFE IS NOT EVOLUTION THROUGH MULTIPLE HEAVENLY DIMENSIONS OR PARALLEL UNIVERSES, OR MIGRATION FROM PLANET TO PLANET. THE REAL POINT OF EXISTENCE, JUST AS WE PROPOSED PREVIOUSLY, IS TO TRANSCEND THE NINE DIMENSIONS AND GO BEYOND THEM. THE NINE DIMENSIONS WERE CREATED BY THE EXPANSIVE CONSCIOUSNESS, SO THAT IT COULD BECOME AWARE OF ITS OWN EXISTENCE. ALL THE BEINGS AND THE MULTIPLICITY OF PLANETS IN THIS AND OTHER DIMENSIONS ARE ONLY DREAMED THOUGHTS THAT IN REALITY DON'T POSSESS ANY ESSENTIAL MATTER. WHAT WE CALL MATTER, IS ONLY A GROUP OF MENTAL LAWS AND RULES THAT ARE EASY TO BREAK FOR THOSE WHO REALIZE THEIR FALSE AND HARMLESS NATURE. THE BEINGS THAT INHABIT EACH DIMENSION HAVE A FEELING OR A SENSATION OF INDIVIDUALITY. IN THE THIRD DIMENSION THIS FEELING IS MORE AGGRESSIVE AND EAGERLY FEEDS OFF PAIN AND EUPHORIC HAPPINESS. IN OTHER WORDS, HUMANS ARE FORCED TO LIVE IN THE MIDDLE OF TWO OPPOSITE DREAMED ENERGIES. HUMAN BEINGS COMMIT THE TERRIBLE MISTAKE OF PREFERRING A POSITIVE EXPERIENCE RATHER THAN A NEGATIVE EXPERIENCE; THIS IS A PENDULUM EFFECT THAT FEEDS THE EGO. THE EGO IS FOUND DANCING IN BETWEEN THESE TWO OPPOSED FORCES THAT ORIGINATE FROM THE SPIRITUAL HEART. HERE ALL EMOTIONS LIKE FEAR, ANGER, SORROW, INSECURITY, AND THEIR CONSTANT OPPOSITES SUCH AS SECURITY, EUPHORIA, COURAGE, ETC, ARE ORIGINATED. IF HUMANS WERE TO CHOOSE THE UNCONDITIONAL LOVE OF THE PRESENT MOMENT, THE PENDULUM WOULD STOP. THIS SUDDEN STOP WOULD CAUSE A COLLISION OF THE INDIVIDUAL BEING WITH THE SOURCE OF RADIANT ESSENCE, LOCATED IN THE UNIVERSAL CENTER OF THE NINTH DIMENSION. THE "I" FEELING OF THE HUMAN BEING WOULD BE IN DIRECT FUSION WITH THE "I" FEELING OF THE SOURCE OF RADIANT ESSENCE. THE EXPANSIVE "I" FEELING OF THE SOURCE OF RADIANT ESSENCE IS LIKE AN ANTIDOTE FOR THE CONTRACTED "I" FEELING OF THE TERRESTRIAL BEING. WHEN THE MERGING OF

OF THE LIMITED "I" WITH THE LIMITLESS "I" IS COMPLETE, THE
EGO IS DISSOLVED. BY BEING DISSOLVED, T
HE EXPANSIVE SENSE OF BEING COMPREHENDS THE MAIN PURPOSE
OF EXISTENCE. WHICH IS BECOMING CONSCI
OUS OF ITS ABSOLUTE PRESENCE THAT GOES BEYOND THE NINE
DIMENSIONS AND BEYOND THE SOURCE OF RA
DIANT ESSENCE. THE SOURCE OF RADIANT ESSENCE IS CONST
ANTLY CONNECTED TO THE ABSOLUTE CONSC
IOUSNESS THAT DREAMS HER; SHE IS NOTHING MORE AND NOT
HING LESS THAN THE CLEAREST AND CLOS
EST VISUAL MANIFESTATION OF UNLIMITED CONSCIOUSNES
S. BECOMING ONE WITH IT SETS HUMANS
AND OTHER BEINGS FREE, AND THIS FREEDOM IS SO AM
AZING AND PERFECT THAT IT ALSO FREES
S THEM FROM THE SOURCE OF RADIANT ESSENCE. {BIN
DINGS{EACH DIMENSION HAS ITS OWN
BINDINGS. IN THE THIRD DIMENSION THE TRAPS THA
T GET THE HUMAN BEING ARE BOTH PA
IN AND HAPPINESS, AS STATED EARLIER. IN THE
FOURTH. IT IS THE ENERGETIC CURRE
NTS, THE FIFTH AND SIXTH PERPETUAL ECSTASY,
THE SEVENTH BEATITUDE AND THE
EIGHT THE BLISS THAT LOVE GRANTS. THERE A
RE NO MORE BINDINGS IN THE NINT
H DIMENSION, ONLY IMPERVIOUS PEACE, WHIC
H IS EQUAL TO FREEDOM. EACH D
IMENSION HAS ITS LINKS AND PASSIONS TH
AT KEEP THE INDIVIDUALISM ALI
VE IN BEINGS HABITING THEM. THE HUMAN
BODY IS VERY IMPORTANT IN T
HIS MATTER, SINCE IT CAN EXPERIENCE
THE NINE FEELINGS. IT HAS B
EEN SAID THAT EVEN THOUGH HUMANS
ARE LESS EVOLVED AND FAR R
EMOVED FROM THE SOURCE OF RADIA
NT ESSENCE, THEY CAN USE
A CATAPULT EFFECT THAT SHOOTS
THEM OUTSIDE OF THE NINE
DIMENSIONS OF REVERIE IN AN I
NSTANT—WITHOUT HAVING TO
UNDERGO MULTIDIMENSIONAL EV
OLUTION. SPIRITUAL EVO
LUTION IN THE THIRD DIMENS
ION IS NOT NECESSARY,
SINCE HUMANS CAN WILLFUL
LY CHOOSE THE NON-DUA
L PATH AND REALIZE THA
T THEY ARE ACTUALLY
THE SOURCE OF RADIAN
T ESSENCE. THIS REA
LIZATION CAN DISSO
LVE THE EGO IMMEDIA
TELY; HOWEVER, THE
CHAINS THAT TIE T
HE THREE-DIMENSI
ONAL SOUL TO EART
H ARE SO MANY,
THAT THEY MAKE
IT ALMOST IMP
OSSIBLE TO ESCAP
E THIS MENTA
L/OPTICAL ILLUS
ION. A MUL
TITUDE OF BEIN
GS OF LIG
HT WERE VOLUN
TARILY
ENLISTED FOR
THE
HUMAN EXPERI
MENT
. MOST ENDE
D
UP PERPLEX
ED

AND LOST IN THE THREE-DIMENSIONAL DEPTHS. IT IS ALMOST IMPOSSIBLE FOR THOSE NOT SPIRITUALLY INCLINED TO GO BACK TO THE RADIANT DIMENSIONS AFTER EATING FRUIT FROM THE HUMAN TREE. BUT AT THE SAME TIME FREEDOM IS ALSO POTENTIALLY VIABLE HERE ON EARTH. THAT IS WHY WE ARE HERE—TO HELP YOU AND REMIND YOU OF WHOM YOU TRULY ARE. TRUST THAT WE WILL NEVER LEAVE YOU, EVEN IF YOU DO NOT FEEL US. IT IS OUR RESPONSIBILITY, OUR DUTY, AND OUR PLEASURE TO HELP YOU. ALWAYS REMEMBER THAT THE NINE-DIMENSIONAL HIERARCHY, ALONG WITH ITS CORPOREAL AND NONCORPOREAL LIVING BEINGS, AND THE SOURCE OF RADIANT ESSENCE ARE AS REAL AS THE WORLD THAT SURROUNDS YOU; AND AT THE SAME TIME, THEY ARE AS UNREAL AS THIS WORLD. SINCE EVERYTHING THAT YOU PERCEIVE UNDER THIS BLUE SKY IS ONLY AN ACTIVE ENERGETIC CONCEPTUALIZED DREAM. {HUMILITY IN THE NINE DIMENSIONS}EVEN THOUGH THE HUMAN BEING HAS THE CHANCE TO PROPEL ITSELF TO THE SOURCE OF RADIANT ESSENCE IN THE NINTH DIMENSION. (S)HE SHOULDN'T BELIEVE THAT (S)HE IS SOMETHING SPECIAL SINCE IT IS CONFINED TO A RETROGRADE DIMENSION, SURROUNDED BY PRIMITIVE ELECTROMAGNETIC FREQUENCIES. FOR THE BEINGS OF THE FIFTH DIMENSION, THE HUMANS ARE SIMPLY WHAT YOU WOULD REFER TO AS A TWO-DIMENSIONAL, IMPERFECT CARTOON DRAWING ON A PIECE OF PAPER. NOW YOU WOULD ASK YOURSELF IF THIS MESSAGE COMES FROM THE FIFTH DIMENSION. THE ANSWER IS NO, SINCE BEINGS OF THE FIFTH DIMENSION ARE NOT INTERESTED IN RELATING VERY MUCH WITH THE BEINGS OF THE THIRD DIMENSION; THIS WOULD BE INVOLUTION FOR THEM. {THE MESSAGE}THIS MESSAGE COMES FROM THE NINE DEVAS OF CRYSTALLINE FIRE, OTHERWISE KNOWN TO HUMANS AS SERAPHIM; ENTITIES OF EXTREMELY RADIANT LIGHT AND POWER THAT USUALLY STAY IN THE NINTH DIMENSION AND THAT DO NOT NORMALLY COMMUNICATE TO HUMANS. THESE BEINGS ARE THE CLOSEST TO THE SOURCE OF RADIANT ESSENCE AND NOW THE LONG-ANTICIPATED MOMENT HAS ARRIVED IN WHICH THE THREE-DIMENSIONAL BEINGS OF THIS UNIVERSE ARE CONNECTING WITH OTHER DIMENSIONS OF FULMINATING LIGHT. PREPARE TO TAKE FLIGHT, HIGH AND FREE.

THIS MESSAGE WAS DECODED AND TRANSMITTED BY LUMINOUS BEINGS FROM THE CONSTELLATION OF THE STAR CALLED SIRIUS. THEY ARE THE DEVIC FORCES OF THE STELLAR FIRE. WE THANK ASTORIAN AND ANDRONIS, WHO RESIGNED THE OCCUPATION OF BODIES WHOSE ASTRAL QUALITIES ARE MORE LUMINOUS THAN ETHER IN EXCHANGE FOR A MORE DENSE PHYSICAL BODY. THEY WERE USED LIKE MEDIUMS, TO TRANSMIT MESSAGES TO HUMANS. THE HUMAN CHANNEL IS MORE RECEPTIVE TO THE THREE-DIMENSIONAL STELLAR MESSAGES THAN THE ONES COMING DIRECTLY FROM THE NINTH. WHEN TRANSLATING AND WRITING THESE LIGHT PATTERNS OF ANGLED AND UNDULATING DEVIC INFORMATION, THE HUMAN TRANSCRIBING THIS BOOK SEES LIGHTS THAT BECOME IDEAS AND HEARS HEAVENLY BELLS THAT BECOME WORDS. ON THE OTHER HAND, THE NINE DEVAS OF ETHEREAL FIRE CAN USE THEIR POWER TO TALK THROUGH A HUMAN BEING AS THEIR CHANNEL, IF ONE ALLOWS THIS, THEY CAN ALSO CHANGE THE HUMAN'S MOLECULAR STRUCTURE WITH THEIR MARVELOUS POWER AND WITHOUT NEEDING ANY INTERMEDIAIRIES. IF YOU ARE ONE OF THE FEW BLESSED TO READ THIS MANUSCRIPT, THE LUMINOUS NINE HAVE ALREADY STARTED TO MODIFY YOUR MOLECULAR STRUCTURE. BE HUMBLE AND ACCEPT THIS GIFT WITH RESPECT.{LUMINOUS INJECTIONS TO CHANGE THE DNA AND IMMORTALIZE THE SOUL AND ITS MEMORIES{KNOW THAT ALTHOUGH WE WILL MENTION PHYSICAL CHANGES, THE PROCESS OF MODIFICATION WILL BEGIN AT AN ENERGETIC LEVEL IN THE ASTRAL BODY, WHICH IN TURN IS DIRECTLY ASSOCIATED WITH THE PHYSICAL BODY. WITH TIME, SAID ASTRAL CHANGES WILL EMBRACE THE SUBATOMIC PARTICLES, ATOMS, CELLS, DNA, RNA, MUSCLES, INTERNAL ORGANS, NERVOUS AND CIRCULATORY SYSTEM, AMONGST OTHERS. WHEN THIS HAPPENS, THE CHANGES WILL BE SCIENTIFICALLY OBSERVABLE. EACH ENTITY OF LIGHT IS BOUND TO SPECIFIC VIBRATORY COMBINATIONS. THE BOOK REVEALS WORDS IN THE DEVIC LANGUAGE THAT WILL HELP TO CONNECT YOU WITH SAID BEINGS OF ETERNAL PEACE AND LOVE. IF YOU WISH FOR A DEEPER AND MORE INTENSE CONNECTION WITH THESE LOVING ENERGIES, REPEAT THE MANTRAS NINE TIMES OUT LOUD.{ASHMIAT ASHMATVIATAT ANABEL BUSHTAM}{ I ALLOW THE ENERGIES OF THE

CRYSTALLINE DEVA ANABEL TO EMBRACE ME. (AFTER THE PROCESS OF DEATH OF THE PHYSICAL BODY AND GOING THROUGH THE BURNING PURIFICATION OF ULTRA ATOMIC HYDROGENISED RAYS, THE SOUL LOSES ALL THE DREAMED ARCHIVES, AND THE PERSON COMPLETELY LOSES MEMORY OF THEIR PAST LIVES. ON THE OTHER HAND, IF THIS SOUL IS PURIFIED AND RESTRUCTURED WHILE IT IS ACTIVE IN THE PHYSICAL BODY, IT WILL ASCEND TO OTHER DIMENSIONS WITHOUT LOSING THE MEMORY OF ITS PAST EXISTENCE. {REJUVENATION, EXTRACTION OF BLACK STALACTITES FROM THE MUSCLES.}THE MUSCLES ARE SURROUNDED BY A COATING THAT RESEMBLES A SPIDER WEB (FASCIA). WHEN THIS WEB GOES BEYOND ITS OWN BORDERS, THE FUNCTIONAL AND STRUCTURAL UNIT OF THE MUSCLE FIBER LINKS TO ITSELF, PRODUCING PAIN. IT IS VERY IMPORTANT TO REMIND YOU THAT THE HUMAN WASN'T CREATED WITH THESE IMPERFECTIONS: THIS WAS THE MODIFICATION CAUSED BY THE VIRUS OF THE CHILDREN OF THE NEBULA. WE WORK WITH 650 MUSCLES SO THAT THE HUMAN BEING ISN'T DISTRACTED BY THE BODY'S PAIN. HOWEVER, OUR JOB IN THIS DENSE PHYSICAL AREA NEEDS A HUMAN CHANNEL TO DO THE HEALINGS. SOME OF THESE CHANNELS ARE ALREADY LIVING AMONGST YOU AND OTHERS WILL BECOME EMBODIED VERY SOON. TO RECOGNIZE SAID CHANNELS LOOK AT THEM STRAIGHT IN THE EYES; THESE CHANNELS SHOULD BE CLEAN AND EMIT POWER. THE MUSCULAR ACTIVITY OF CONTRACTION AND RELAXATION HAPPENS DUE TO A MECHANISM OF RADIANT IMBUEMENT OF THE NERVOUS FIBERS WITH INHERENT INTELLIGENCE. THIS RADIANCE FORCES THE FIBERS TO RELEASE ACETYLCOLINE, WHICH COMES TO REST OVER THE NICOTINIC RECEPTORS, FORCING THEM TO ABSORB IONS AND SODIUM ON AN INTRACELLULAR LEVEL. AFTER BEING CAPTIVATED BY LIGHT, THEY TRAVEL ALONG T-TUBULES, ACTIVATING THE RECEPTORS OF DIHYDROPYRIDINE THAT ARE OPEN TO THE LUMINESCENCE OF THE DEVAS, VOLTAGE. THE RECEPTORS RECEIVE THE ELECTRO-LUMINOUS ENERGY, INCITING THE CREATION OF THE RYANODINE CHANNELS, GIVING COMPLETE FREEDOM TO THE MODIFIED CALCIUM WE PRODUCE. THIS SAME CALCIUM, DISGUISED BY THE ENTITIES OF STELLAR LIGHT, IS EXPELLED FROM THE SARCOPLASMIC RETICULUM

WHERE IT IS MODIFIED ON AN ASTRAL LEVEL BY FLASHING UNDU
CTED BY OUR CHANGES. THIS WAY, THE SUPER ALKALINE AND E
MAKING IT POSSIBLE FOR THE LITTLE HEADS OF MYOSIN TO
ITS ACTIN, WILL SUFFER DRASTIC CHANGES AND WILL
D CAREFULLY AND THE CHANGE WILL TAKE PLACE IN
BODIES. THE HUMAN BEING WORKS AS A THINKING
PE OF INFINITE AND INTELLIGENT ETHER. TH
E ASPECT OF A LUMINOUS NETWORK THAT
IOUS LEVEL. THAT IS WHY IT IS SAI
IVES IN FINALLY WAKES UP AND U
ALITY THE SOURCE OF RADIANT
E ABSOLUTE CONSCIOUSNESS
R WAY DUE TO THIS UN
A MATRIX THEY CAN
TY DOESN'T EVE
IF THEY ARE
OF CRYST
THRO
K

ING
ESIGNED
OMEONE ELS
THEIR OWN THO
CONCEPTS AND EMO
NGS DON'T EVEN KNO
OUGH EXPERIMENTATION B
ONSCIOUSNESS THAT DREAMS I
IX IS BUT AN EXTENSION OF ITS
D, UNLESS THE SENTIENT BEING OF
DIMENSION IN PARTICULAR WITH SPECIFI
EACH DIMENSION AND IT MAY BE COMPARED
D EVERYONE. HUMAN INDIVIDUAL THOUGHTS ARE
A-EL ADVATMIAT. I ALLOW THE RESPLENDENT LIGH
YOSIN BY CRYSTALLINE RAYS. BODY DEPURATION AND
PASMODIC CONTRACTION WHICH IS FLEXIBLE AND PAIN-FR
D WITH THE LUMINOUS TROPONIN C, WILL CAUSE A CONFORMA
MPLEX OF ACTIN, PARTICULARLY TROPONIN C, WHICH HAS THREE

LATING LIGHTS AND IS THEN SENT TO THE CO
NERGETICALLY REFORMED CALCIUM, MODIFIE
ADHERE, CREATING IN THIS WAY A NON-S
BE CATALYZED IN THE LUCID HEAD OF M
TANGLED COMPLEXES THAT WILL BE RECONSTR

L PAIRS OF CHROMOSOMES TO SAVE DEFECTIVE DNA AND RNA. THE
GOVERNED BY RADIO MAGNETIC EMISSIONS, INSTATED TO CREA
LEVEL, FEEL HOW WE INFLUENCE THE ASTRAL FIELD THAT IN
PERCENTAGE OF OXYGEN, HYDROGEN, POTASSIUM, CALCIU
CARBOHYDRATES, WHICH BAPTIZE THE CORTEX WITH
TE INORGANIC MOLECULES OF RADIANT WATER. T
ODY. WE WILL SIMULTANEOUSLY MODIFY THE M
NGE THE CONFIGURATION OF HYDROGEN, O
RCULATORY, REPRODUCTIVE, AND NER
Y (INCREASING THE PURIFYING CA
ENSION OF THE BREATHING PA
L AFFECT CELLS OF THE MU
EVEL. THROUGH ENERGE
RACONIAN FORCES TH
ICES IN THE HUM
MATERIAL BOD
L PLACENT
HE IN
SO
T
S TH
H COLLE
ENT TIME, W
EVELS, STARTI
AT WERE CONTAMIN
OVER 108 BILLION CEL
E TRANSMITTED TO THE
VE SYSTEM, THE RESPIRATORY
GESTIVE (INCREASING THE POWER
IN THE ASTRAL PLANES, THE CONNEC
. ON THE ATOMIC AND MOLECULAR LEVEL
YOU READ; THESE ARE THE MAIN ELEMENT
PLETE DIFFERENT UNIONS WITH DIFFERENT COM
E TOTALITY OF THE BODY MATTER. ORGANIC MOLEC
ES, WILL BE DISTILLED IN THE NEAR FUTURE, BECOMI
WILL BE GRADUALLY ALTERED TO REACH AN ABSOLUTE A
ANE, THE EXTERNAL MEMBRANE, THE NUCLEUS, AND THE CYTO
TATED BY THE NEBULA, WHICH FORCE THE HUMAN LINEAGE AND 10

ELECTROMAGNETIC EMISSIONS WILL BE UNSTABLE FOR NINE DAYS IN ORDER TO ACCEPT THE NEW PROGRAM. SUCH DETAILED WORK IS SOMETHING LIKE RESETTING THE NUCLEUS. THE NUCLEAR MEMBRANE THAT HOLDS THE GENETIC MATERIAL IS PRESENTLY CODIFIED FROM AN IMMATERIAL LOCATION IN THE THREE-DIMENSIONAL UNIVERSE, SO THAT IT CAN BE TRANSFORMED IN THE FUTURE INTO A SHELL THAT WON'T LET ANY PATHOGENS CREATED BY THE NEBULA INSIDE. THE NUCLEUS, WHICH HAS INHERITED INTELLIGENCE, WILL REFORM THE CELL WHEN IT IS INCITED TO SPIN INSIDE ITS CAUSAL CORTEX. WE, THE SERAPHIM COMMIT TO PENETRATE THE DEEPEST LEVELS OF THIS NUCLEUS TO REMOVE ALL THE GRAY, IMPURITIES PLANTED BY THE FORCES OF THE NEBULA THAT KEEP SUFFERING ALIVE IN HUMAN BEINGS. RELAX AND FEEL THE MODIFICATIONS THAT ARE TAKING PLACE IN THE NOW. IF YOU PAY VERY CLOSE ATTENTION, YOU WILL REALIZE THAT IN THIS INSTANT WE ARE MODIFYING, FROM A STRUCTURAL STANDPOINT, THE SUBATOMIC ASTRAL ROOT OF THE BIOLOGICAL TISSUES ON A HISTOLOGICAL LEVEL. THUS, THE EPITHELIAL, NERVOUS, MUSCULAR AND CONJUNCTIVE TISSUES ARE STIMULATED TO SECRETE SUBSTANCES THAT PROTECT ITS FORM AND THE WAY THAT IT SYSTEMATIZES ITS FUNCTIONS. THE CURRENT PERCENTAGE OF THE CORPORAL CELL WATER IS ONLY 59% IN ADULTS. AFTER THESE CHANGES, WATER IN THE CELL WILL BE KEPT MORE EFFICIENTLY AND THE CELLS WILL HOLD 77% OF THE BODY'S WATER; SOME WILL CIRCULATE IN THE BLOOD TORRENT, PURIFYING AND ACTIVATING THE GLANDS ASSOCIATED TO THE VORTICES OF ENERGY IN THE ASTRAL REALMS. THESE CHANGES ARE HAPPENING INSIDE YOU ON AN ENERGETIC LEVEL WHILE YOU READ. IF YOU DON'T BELIEVE US, CLOSE YOUR EYES AND FEEL US. {REGENERATION OF THE NERVOUS SYSTEM WITH RADIANT INTENSITY}OADITM AXIELSATMITL ATRATAKAM. I AM FOCUSED ON THE DEVA OF CRYSTALLINE FIRE AXI-EL WHO ENLIGHTENS ME. THE NERVOUS SYSTEM IS THE CLOSEST TO THE ASTRAL BODY. THIS SYSTEM CAN CONNECT ITSELF WITH THE SUBTLE BODY AND ITS MERIDIANS AND FEEL ASTRAL MOVEMENTS. IF THE FREQUENCY CHANGES, THE HUMAN BEING WILL START TO ADAPT AND ACCEPT ORBITAL ENERGETIC RELATIONS OF

ONE OF RADIANT LIGHT; OF A SUBSTANCE SIMILAR TO THE WATER
SURROUND THEM. THIS WILL PREVENT THEIR PULVERIZATION W
OMENTUM.} ADIAT, ADIAT, ADIAT RAF-EL. RADIANT DEVA RA
RRING INFORMATION WILL ALSO MUTATE. ITS BRIGHTNES
THE MYELIN SHEATH, WILL MUTATE ITS COLOR AND
F OXYGEN AND GLUCOSE IN THE BLOOD STREAM W
OWS FOR A SHORT WHILE UNTIL THE LUMINOUS
LIQUID WILL IN TIME BE TRANSFORMED
E. DUE TO SUCH A CHANGE, THE PER
INTO ANXIETY. IF THIS HAPPE
IAL, BECAUSE WHEN WE WORK
INFORCED IN ENERGETIC LE
HNOID, AND PIA MATER
DISCHARGES EXTRAC
ME. THE BRAIN
TIONAL SPECT
ETS STREN
IN DI
IO

HEN THE PLANET STARTS SUFFERING GEOPHYS
FEL MAKE ME SHINE, MAKE ME SHINE. YOU
S WILL START TO SHOW IN X-RAYS AFTER
TURN INTO A LUMINESCENT WHITE. THE
ILL BE UNALTERABLE AND PERFECT. T
ONES READJUST THE LEVELS OF TH
INTO A LUMINOUS LIQUID FROM T
CEPTION OF THE STIMULI COMI
NS, DON'T WORRY, THE DEVA
IN THIS LEVEL THE HUMAN
VELS BY THIS PROCEDURE
, KNOWN BY THE HUMAN
TED FROM THE SUN. T
AND SPINAL CORD A
RUM WILL BE CREA
GTHENED, AS HE
FFERENT LEVE
NAL INTELLI
ULTIDIMENS
E OPERATING
THIS SYSTEM
HIGHEST GRAVITA
ING THE HUMAN DO
ELECTROMAGNETIC
ES—DURA MATER, ARAC
BEING REFORMED AND RE
FULLY RELAXED IS ESSENT
ERGY THAT COULD TRANSFORM
Y A SORT OF ASTRAL SEDATIV
CHANGE. THE CEREBROSPINAL
LANCE WILL SUFFER HIGHS AND L
EQUENCIES. THE TRANSFORMATION O
HE NEURONS, THEIR DENDRITES, AND
ATIONS WITH THE FUNCTION OF TRANSFE
NG OF THE MERIDIANS WITH EFFULGENT M
Y, WHILE THE RADIANT CELESTIAL SPIRALS
ONGITUDE OF THE WAVE OF THE NEBULA INTO

M
GENC
LS. AS
LL OF THE
TED, SURROUND
RE NOW RECEIVING
HEIR THREE MEMBRAN
RACE AS MENINGES—ARE
. DURING THIS PHASE BEING
BEING WILL FEEL EXHILARANT EN
S OF CRYSTALLINE FIRE WILL APPL
NG FROM THE CIRCUMSTANTIAL PLANE WI
HE FIFTH DIMENSION. THE IDEAL IONIC BA
E CIRCULATING ELLIPTIC ELECTROMAGNETIC FR
HE GRAY SUBSTANCE, COMPOSED BY THE SOMA OF T
NERVOUS SUBSTANCE, INSTATED BY NERVOUS CONTINU
50 YEARS OF THE ASTRAL MODIFICATIONS. {STRENGTHENI
R ENERGETIC MERIDIANS ARE NOW CHANGING THEIR FREQUENC
ICAL CHANGES. THIS SUBATOMIC CHANGE WILL TRANSFORM THE L

THAT INHABITS THE SEVENTH DIMENSION (UNDERSTAND THAT IT

IS NOT THREE-DIMENSIONAL WATER, BUT MOVE

ATATRAT XIABIEL. XIABIEL CLEAN, CHRISTEN, AND PROTECT M

RFACE, INFLUXES WHICH WERE CREATED AND OUTLINED BY T

ANATED BY ASTRAL CONVEX PRISMS THAT EXIST INSIDE

LEVELS OF TRANSPERSONAL DIMENSIONS, WITH SEV

GABRIELA I AM WILLING TO LET YOU CHANGE TH

ND HIS/HER MAGNETIC STRUCTURE IS SIMULTA

ADMINISTERED TO THE CELL NUCLEI SO T

BILLION BP. THIS AMPLITUDE IS STR

E.IN YOUR PHYSICAL BODY, THUS

THE DEVAS OF CRYSTALLINE FI

E. IN THIS WAY, THE LUM

TICES. {PERMUTATION

-R-I-EL-A. GABRIELA

MY PHYSICAL B

SITIVE TRANS

UCTURE IS

CTION

ER

ITH

LY TRAN

AND HIS/HE

NDIVIDUAL EXP

LET YOU CHANGE T

DIANT}. DIMITRAT A

A NEUTRAL RESONANCE IS

EBULA'S PROGRAMS FROM THE

G THE PROGRAMS INTRODUCED BY

IN DIFFERENT WAYS, SINCE EACH

CULAR STRUCTURE. THE HUMAN GENOME I

S CODIFIED WITH ASTRO-IMMATERIAL DNA

DY. WHILE THE INDIVIDUAL EXPERIMENTS WITH

ERMUTATION OF DNA AND ULTRA RADIANT}. DIMITR

ANT THE HIGHEST INTELLIGENCES WILL OVERLAP A MO

CRYSTALLIZED FIRE AND PROJECT IT OVER THESE CENTR

ONIZE THE STAMP OF YOUR VORTICES, USING INFLUXES OF C

S LIKE IT). {CLEANSE, BAPTISM AND CHAKRA PROTECTION WITH S

THAT POSSESS THE ABILITY TO COPY AND REPRODUCE
ICH WILL TRANSFIGURE THE INFORMATION AND NON-CHANGING
ENT THAT HUMANS USE IN THEIR SCIENTIFIC INVESTIGATION
LY 24,000 GENES WILL BE ABLE TO CODIFY MORE PROTE
INCITED BY ANGULAR LIGHTS WHILE YOU READ. WI
ICALLY CHANGING FREQUENCIES. THE GENES ONE
GENES THAT ARE CONSIDERABLY LARGER AND
LIGHTNING ENERGY INSIDE THE GENE. T
-CODIFYING DNA, WILL SOON ACTIVA
IC STRUCTURE OF THE SPIRAL.
N TO TRANSCRIBE INTO RNA A
CATION WILL BE REPROGRAM
A TRANSCRIBES INTO R
HAS A DIFFERENT CO
STRETCHED IN D
HAS A PROLO
THEIR SU
O THE
LI

T
G AD
SO THA
UCTURE. TH
BILLION BP. T
N DIFFERENT WAYS
RRESTRIAL SCIENCE,
IES PROTEINS; THIS TRA
ON BECOMES MORE DYNAMIC. 3
PROTEINS BY 3%; THESE CHANGES
ARE USUALLY FOUND SEPARATED BY
DIFY PROTEINS, BUT WILL ALSO STIMUL
AFFECT THE CODIFICATION OF THE SPIRA
NOMES ARE, AS YOU READ BEING PROLONGED WI
DIFFERENT PROTEINS. THE CUT AND ITS CONNECT
WILL CODIFY UP TO FIVE RAN OF MEDIA. THE HUMAN G
ELEMENTS WILL BE PLENTIFUL AND LUMINOUS. THIS WILL
UGH SUCH CHANGES INDUCED BY THE REFULGENT SPIRIT, THE
RE DIFFERENT FROM THEIR PROGENITORS. THE GENETIC INFORMA

TION WILL GRADUALLY TRANSFORM. THE BASES

PATTERNS, SO THAT THE SPROUTING CELLS A
STHAT HAVE SUPERIMPOSED LENSES. THRO
INS THAN BEFORE, AND THE TRANSPOSED
TH THIS NEW ADJUSTMENT, EACH GENE
BY ONE WILL BE INCITED TO CODIFY

THEMSELVES WILL AWAKEN THE MRNA SO THAT IT INFORMS THE RIBOSOME AFFECTED BY THE SOURCE THAT IT IS TIME TO SYNTHESIZE A DETERMINED ALBUMINOIDAL IN A REVERSE ORDER. DON'T LET YOUR MIND DOUBT FOR A SECOND THAT WE WILL CHANGE THE CENTRAL DOGMA OF MOLECULAR BIOLOGY. THE ELEMENTS OF RECOMBINATION AND TRANSMUTATION WILL BE USED TO RECONQUER THE NECESSARY COMMUTATIONS FOR INTERCELLULAR ADAPTATION AND EVOLUTION SO THAT THE DNA AND RNA PROGRESSIVELY TRANSFIGURE THEMSELVES, ADOPTING PATTERNS OF INFINITE LIGHT. THE NUCLEUS WILL CONCEIVE A SEED OF ULTRARADIANT LIGHT THAT WILL BE IN CHARGE OF CHANGING THE DNA AUTOREPLICATION BEFORE THE CELLULAR DIVISION BEGINS. ON THE OTHER HAND, THE TRANSCRIPTION OF THE DIFFERENT TYPES OF RAN WILL PROTECT THE SYNTHESIS OF THE NEW TRANSCENT PROTEINS. THEIR SEQUENCES WILL ENERGETICALLY BIND AND UNBIND THE DNA TO CHROMOSOMES, STIMULATING THE GROWTH OF MORE SPIRALS. NOTE THAT THE CHANGES WILL BE FIRST REALIZED IN THE ASTRAL REALMS OF THE HUMAN BODY AND IT WILL TAKE A WHILE (50 TO 60 YEARS) UNTIL THEY CAN BE OBSERVED BY SUPERIMPOSED LENSES. THIS NEW CODIFIED DNA WILL BE INTRODUCED INTO THE CELLS BY THE HUMAN MEDIUM OR DIRECTLY BY THE LUMINOUS NINE, REALIGNING THE MOLECULAR STRUCTURE AND SIMULTANEOUSLY AMPLIFYING THE HUMAN MIND THROUGH NON-CONCEPTUAL UNIVERSES LACKING PROTOTYPES OR PARADIGMS. THIS DNA REGENERATION PROGRAM IMPLANTED INSIDE THE CELLS WILL RESTORE A NEW ORDER IN THE INFINITE INTERNAL UNIVERSE OF THE CELL, PREVENTING ITS COMPLETE DEGENERATION IN THE MOMENT WHEN THE NEW INTERPLANETARY ELECTROMAGNETIC FREQUENCIES COLLIDE WITH THE EARTH. THE AURA WASN'T DESIGNED TO PROTECT THE PHYSICAL BODY, BUT IT WILL GUARD AND ESCORT THE ASTRAL BODY, WHICH IN TURN WILL HAVE BEEN AFFECTED BY THE PHYSICAL BODY'S CHANGE IN DNA IN ITS ATMOSPHERIC TRANSITION, AND IT WILL REJECT ANY WAVE OR RIPPLE COMING FROM THE DARKEST GLOOM. WHEN THE MODIFIED SOUL MOVES THROUGH MAGNETO-ATOMIC ZONES THAT THE MILKY WAY IS ABOUT TO DISCLOSE, ITS SHELL WON'T SUFFER ANY CHANGES. THE GRAVITATIONAL

COMPRESSION, OR ANY OTHER CATEGORICAL GRAVITATIONAL SPECTRUM, SUCH AS A BLACK HOLE, CAN'T ALTER THE SHELL OF THE MODIFIED HUMAN SOUL. WITHOUT THIS DIAMOND SHELL GIFTED BY THE NINE. THE NEW HOLOGRAPHIC FREQUENCY DETERMINED BY THE NEW GENETIC CODE WOULD BE DESTROYED ALONG WITH INDIVIDUAL CONSCIOUSNESS THROUGH THE "DISEMBODIMENT" PHASE. IF THE SHELL HASN'T BEEN PLACED ON TIME, IF THE CONSCIOUSNESS ENCAPSULATED IN THE HUMAN BODY GOES THROUGH TRANSCENDENTAL MODULATIONS OF ASCENSION TO OTHER DIMENSIONS, AND IF WE HAVEN'T BEEN PROPERLY BALANCED BY THE MAGNETIC LIGHT FIELDS CREATED BY THE LUMINOUS NINE AND THE MEDIUM, OUR MIND, ENTRAPPED BY INTERMITTENT ELECTROMAGNETIC WAVES, WON'T ADAPT TO THE NEW THREE- AND FOUR-DIMENSIONAL SPACES; IN THIS CASE, YOU WILL NEED DIRECT HELP BEFORE THE DISSOLUTION OF THE "I" SENSE TAKES PLACE. IF THE BODILY CAPSULE BREAKS WHILE THE CHANGES ARE TAKING PLACE, THE PROCESS WILL CONTINUE IN THE ASTRAL FIELD AND A LUMINOUS BEING CALLED THE NINTH WILL SIMULTANEOUSLY CHAIN THE HIGHEST AND CLEAREST FREQUENCIES OF THE SOUL AND WILL MAKE THEM SPIN 495 ×9 TIMES FASTER THAN THE DREAMED SPEED OF LIGHT; THIS WILL BREAK THE MAGNETIC LINEAR STRUCTURE OF THE INNOCUOUS ESSENCE. THIS SPIN WILL CREATE SPIRALS THAT WILL COMPLETELY CHANGE THE BEHAVIOR OF THE SUBATOMIC STRUCTURE OF THE SOUL (IN A MANNER OF SPEAKING, BECAUSE ATOMS DON'T ACTUALLY EXIST IN THE ASTRAL REALMS: HERE WE OBSERVE ONLY DREAMED PARTICLES OF CONCEPTUAL INFORMATION WITH A DIFFERENT SIGNATURE). THIS ROTATION WILL AFFECT ASTRAL PARTICLES SIMILAR TO ELECTRONS, PHOTONS AND NEUTRINOS BY FORCING THEM TO VIBRATE, CAUSING PERMANENT PATTERNS OF DISINTEGRATION AND CHANGES IN DIFFERENT ENERGETIC BANDS. THE ETHEREAL MOLECULAR CHAINS WILL BREAK AND WILL CAUSE THE FACELESS AND "PERSONALITY LACKING" SOUL TO RETURN TO THE THREE-DIMENSIONAL AND IMMATERIAL GEOMAGNETIC PLANES. THE SOUL IN THIS STATE WILL LACK INDIVIDUAL CONSCIOUSNESS UNTIL IT IS SPUN AGAIN WITH THE SAME INTENSITY AND VELOCITY AS BEFORE, COORDINATING ITS REALIGNMENT

WITH A CONSCIOUS POINT IN THREE-DIMENSIONAL SPACE; MODULATED AND INSET INSIDE THE THREE-DIMENSIONAL MATERIAL DREAM OF APPARENT INTERCELLULAR BIOLOGICAL LIFE AND CODIFIED WITH THE ILLUSION OF TIME AND SPACE. HERE, THE SOUL WILL ADOPT PROGRAMS AND ENERGIES THAT ACT LIKE CONFIGURED COMPOSITIONS THAT ORBIT AROUND A CENTRAL AXIS. THIS CENTER IS THE FOUNDATION OF A MOLECULAR ALLIANCE, WHERE MATTER AND ANTIMATTER SIMULTANEOUSLY UNITE. AT THIS CRUCIAL POINT OF CONNECTIVITY, THE SOUL, MATTER AND THE VITAL ENERGY WILL AMALGAMATE. ADOPTING ELEMENTAL FORCES IN A FOURTH-DIMENSIONAL LEVEL THAT WILL OSCILLATE AROUND THIS EPICENTER OF CENTRIFUGAL FORCES. WE CALL THIS AMALGAMATION THE “EGOIC SOUL” OR “BODILESS LIVING EGOCENTRISM”. THESE SUBTLE ELEMENTAL FORCES ACTIVATE THE PHYSICAL AND ASTRAL BODIES, THE MIND, INSTINCT, INTUITION, THE BASIC EMOTIONS WITH ALL THEIR RAMIFICATIONS, THE LIVING AIR, LIQUID LIGHT, AND THE TRANSPARENT ETHER. THESE OSCILLATING FORCES CONNECT AND FORM PATTERNS ON AN ATOMIC LEVEL THAT COMBINE TO GIVE A SENSE OF INDIVIDUALITY TO THE SUPREME CONSCIOUSNESS, WHICH INJECTS LIFE AND SPIRIT TO ITS EPHEMERAL MENTAL CREATION. {DIVINE GRACE}. THE SHOCK INDUCED BY DIVINE GRACE HAPPENS WHEN THERE IS A CRYSTALLINE AND PURE EXCHANGE IN THE INDIVIDUAL. GRACE IS PERCEIVED BY THE INDIVIDUAL AS THE DEFEAT OF FEAR BEFORE LOVE, IN THE ASTRAL AND CAUSAL PLANES. IF WE IMAGINE THIS FROM AN EARTHLY SYNOPTIC FIELD, WE COULD STATE THAT THE GRAVITATIONAL COMPRESSION AROUND THE SOUL IS CHANGED BY ANOTHER ONE WITH A DIFFERENT GRAVITATIONAL VIBRATION. THE INDIVIDUAL FEELS AS IF THE VASTNESS HAS OPENED THE GATES OF A CAGE AND IS INVITING HIM/HER TO FLY. THIS ACT ALLOWS THE TRANSMUTATION OF THE NEW GENETIC PLANE ON AN ASTRAL LEVEL. {DNA AND THE ASTRAL PLANE}THE DNA IS CONNECTED TO A SERIES OF FILAMENTS IN THE ASTRAL LEVEL. SO CALLED GENIUSES, ARTISTS, INTELLECTUALS, PRODIGIOUS CHILDREN AND SO ON, HAVE MORE OF THESE ILLUMINATED ASTRAL FILAMENTS. SOME DAY HUMANS WILL BE ABLE TO SEE THE ASTRAL WORLDS WITH TECHNOLOGICAL

DEVICES. THE PROJECT YOU CALL ARMAGEDDON IS A CLEANSING PROJECT. WHATEVER IS DIRTY HAS TO BE CLEANED, WITH MANY COMBINATIONS OF ENERGETIC WAVES. THERE IS NOTHING TO FEAR. CHOOSE LOVE OVER FEAR AT ALL TIMES. {INTERGALACTIC JOURNEYS AND TIME TRAVELING}, HUMAN BEINGS HAVE BRAINS THAT ARE NOT PROPERLY CODIFIED TO UNDERSTAND CERTAIN THINGS; THIS IS NOT NORMAL, SINCE THE EVOLUTIONARY PROCESS HAS BEEN STOPPED BY THE NEBULA. SOME THINGS CAN'T BE PRECISELY EXPLAINED; IT WOULD BE LIKE TRYING TO EXPLAIN COLORS TO A BLIND PERSON, BUT WE WILL TRY OUR BEST. ACCORDING TO TERRESTRIAL PHYSICS IN THE THIRD DIMENSION, THE SUBATOMIC PARTICLES, WHICH ARE PARTICLES SMALLER THAN THE ATOM, ARE OF TWO TYPES. ELEMENTALS AND INTEGRATED. THE ELEMENTAL TYPES CAN BE BOTH PHYSICAL AND NUCLEAR AND ARE NOT COMBINED WITH, OR INTEGRATED BY OTHER PARTICLES. THE SIX TYPES OF ELEMENTALS; ELECTRON, NEURON NEUTRON, LEPTON, TAU AND TAU NEUTRINO, MUON AND MUON NEUTRINO, ARE HARDER TO MODIFY WITH ANGULAR LIGHTS. THE TWELVE FORCE EMITTERS AND THE EIGHT GLUONS OF EXTREME POWER AND BRIGHTNESS, AS WELL AS THE ELECTROMAGNETIC PHOTON AND THE SIX TYPES OF QUARKS—UP, DOWN, STRANGE, CHARM, BOTTOM, AND TOP—CAN BE MORE EASILY MANIPULATED BY US SO THAT THEY AFFECT THE FOUNDATIONS ON WHICH THE HUMAN CONSTRUCTION IS ESTABLISHED. IN SOME CASES, THE EXTENSIONS OF THE ELEMENTAL PARTICLES PREDICT, THRUST, AND PREDETERMINE THE EXISTENCE OF THE INVISIBLE GRAVITATION OF THESE PARTICLES ENCIRCLED BY LIGHT AND THEREFORE OF OTHER MYSTERIOUS LIVE PARTICLES. THE INTEGRATED SUBATOMIC PARTICLES LIKE THE PROTON AND THE ATOMIC NUCLEUS ARE TIED TO MORE THAN 28 ELEMENTAL PARTICLES, WHICH WE ARE ALSO GOING TO MODIFY. THE WORLD THAT WE EXPERIENCE CAN BE EXPLAINED OR UNDERSTOOD AS LONG AS WE ACCEPT THAT MATTER AND ENERGY EXISTS INSIDE THE MOLECULAR SCALE OF WHAT YOU CALL QUANTUM MECHANICS. FOR US, THE THREE-DIMENSIONAL PARTICLES ARE ASSOCIATED WITH SOMETHING DIFFERENT THAT DOESN'T FOLLOW THE REASON OF THREE-DIMENSIONAL LINEAR FORCES OR WHAT THE MIND IN THIS SPACE CALLS

COMMON SENSE. THESE PARTICLES BEHAVE IN AN UNPREDICTABLE

VERIE AND MAKE THESE PARTICLES BEHAVE AND ACT DIFFERENT

N BEHAVE IN THE THIRD DIMENSION LIKE A CLEAR AND BRIG

NTINUOUS WAVES OF DIVINE RADIANCE. ALL THESE FAC

DER NOTION OF THE UNIVERSE WITH TENTATIVE BOU

R DUAL WAVE PARTICLES AND THEIR UNEXPECTED

Y OPENS THE DOOR FOR US TO CONCEIVE MASS

THE THIRD DIMENSION. ON EARTH IT IS KN

OF VIEW, CAN BE TRANSMITTED AS PA

FIRE UNFOLDS WITHIN THE THREE

GO DEEPER INTO THE OCEAN OF

LES ALSO HAVE A WAVELIKE

S TAKE IN THE ESSENC

; HAPPEN AND ARE M

DIRECTLY FROM

RAYS INTERA

R, PERSPE

TO Y

EC

TH

INGS

SMELL

DIMENSION

OUSNESS. THES

ULT OF DREAMED C

NAL CREATION. MOST

EN SAY THAT THE PARTIC

CONSCIOUSNESS, WE WILL REA

FORM OF PARTICLES AND SIMULT

S NO DOUBT ABOUT THIS. THE FLAR

ENSER AND TURN INTO MASS. THE ENERGY

ENTS. MASS CAN BE EXPRESSED AS ENERGY

PARTICLES LEAVE US ENGULFED IN MYSTERY. T

COMMON SENSE ARE CONTINGENCIES. THE INTERACT

BLE AND NECESSARY TO CHANGE OUR LINEAR MENTAL

ES (PHOTONS) EXHIBIT WAVES IN OTHER DIMENSIONS, AND

HEN THEY PERFORM MIRACLES ON EARTH ARE NOT LAWS OF P

ICLES. THE MORE POWERFUL THE INDIVIDUAL MIND IS, WITH GREA

IS AN ILLUSION THAT HUMANS HAVE TO DEFEAT TO GO BEYOND THEIR MENTAL THREE-DIMENSIONAL LIMITATIONS. INTERSTELLAR TRAVEL IN THE THIRD DIMENSION GOES FROM A DETERMINED POINT A TO A POINT B, AND TO GET TO POINT B, ONE MUST TRAVEL THE DISTANCE THAT DIVIDES THEM. IN THE FOURTH DIMENSION DISTANCE EXISTS AS WELL. BUT IT EXISTS AS VISUAL DISTANCE; THE FOURTH DIMENSIONAL BEING TRANSPORTS ITSELF. VISUALLY. IN THE FIFTH DIMENSION THE DISTANCE IS MENTAL; THE BEING TRANSPORTS ITSELF MENTALLY; JUST THINKING ABOUT A PLACE MAKES THE ENTITY DISAPPEAR AND APPEAR IN THE PLACE (S)HE THOUGHT OF INSTANTLY; WE CAN SAY THAT THE FIFTH DIMENSION FOLDS ON ITSELF, UNITING THE POINTS OF EXIT AND EMERGENCE. EVEN THOUGH THE JOURNEY CONTINUES TO HAVE A LINEAR ASPECT, THE TRANSPORTATION IS MORE DYNAMIC AND FAST. IN THE SIXTH AND SEVENTH DIMENSIONS IT IS UNDERSTOOD THAT A AND B ARE OVERLAPPED AND THAT WE ARE THE CENTER WHEREVER WE ARE. A AND B ARE PLACED ONE ATOP THE OTHER AND THE BEINGS CAN ACCESS TWO, THREE OR EVEN 100 DIFFERENT PLACES SIMULTANEOUSLY. THE DIVERGENCE BETWEEN THE SIXTH AND THE SEVENTH DIMENSIONS IS THAT THE BEINGS OF THE SIXTH CAN DIVIDE THEMSELVES IN TWO AND BEINGS FROM THE SEVENTH DIMENSION CAN SPLIT INTO THOUSANDS. IN THE EIGHTH AND NINTH DIMENSIONS. THEY ARE EXPANSIVE AND ONE WITH THE INFINITE DREAM. THEY CAN DO PRACTICALLY WHATEVER THEY WANT, SINCE THEY ARE ILLUMINATED DIVINE EXTENSIONS. BEINGS FROM THE NINTH DIMENSION CAN EVEN CHANGE THE COURSE OF THE DREAM COMPLETELY WITHOUT VIOLATING THE PHYSICAL LAWS OF THE THIRD OR ANY OTHER DIMENSION, IF THIS WAS NECESSARY. SUCH CHANGES ARE ONLY EXECUTED WITH THE PURPOSE OF STIMULATING EVOLUTION {THE 21 VORTICES, DNA OF THIRTEEN AND QUADRUPLE HELIX}AS LONG AS WE ADVANCE THROUGH THIS AMAZING AND MAGICAL READING, WE WILL CONTINUE TO AWAKEN DIFFERENT FACES OF THE HUMAN COMPOSITION. WE SAY THAT THE PHYSICAL BODY, ASTRAL BODY AND CAUSAL BODY HAVE 21 IMPORTANT MULTIDIMENSIONAL ENERGETIC VORTICES: SEVENTEEN IN THE MATERIAL HUMAN BODY AND NINE OUTSIDE OF IT. THESE VORTICES

AFFECT THE INDIVIDUAL PHYSICALLY, MENTALLY AND SPIRITUALLY. DURING THIS READING YOU WILL NOTICE THAT WE ARE REFERRING TO A CERTAIN REINSERTION OF AMINO ACIDS INTO THE HUMAN BODY DISCOVERED ON CERTAIN ASTEROIDS FOUND ON EARTH, FROM THE MOON, AND FROM OTHER PLANETS. THESE ASTEROIDS WERE SENT MILLENNIA AGO BY THE SOURCE OF RADIANT ESSENCE TO COUNTER THE COLLATERAL EFFECTS CAUSED BY THE FORCES OF DARKNESS. THE SUPPLY OF AMINO ACIDS IMPLANTED WITHOUT RECURRING TO INVASIVE METHODS. AS OPPOSED TO THE CHILDREN OF DARKNESS, THE DEVAS OF CRYSTALLINE FIRE WILL CHANGE THE HUMAN BODY GRADUALLY SO THAT IT DOESN'T SUFFER ANY SHOCKS. FIRST, THE NINE DEVAS CONNECT WITH THESE FALLEN ASTEROIDS THROUGH THE THINNEST MESSIANIC FILAMENTS OF RADIANT LIGHT, WHICH ABSORB THE AMINO ACIDS' ASTRAL BLUEPRINT INTO THEIR BODIES TO PROCESS IT. THE LIGHT USED FOR THE DISTILLATION OF THESE FILAMENTS CHANGES THE SUBATOMIC ASTRAL STRUCTURE INFORMATION OF THE EXHORTED AMINO ACIDS, AND THEY ARE REPRODUCED BY A TYPE OF OCTAGONAL VORTEX FOUND IN THE DEVA'S HEART. ONCE THE ENERGETIC SCRIPTURE CODE IS ATTAINED, THE DEVA LOOKS FOR THE READER AND IMPLANTS THE VIBRATION CODE INTO THE SPECIFIC CENTER WHILE (S)HE IS IN THE PROCESS OF READING THE BOOK. IN THIS WAY, THE CHANGE HAPPENS FIRST ON AN ENERGETIC LEVEL. WITH TIME, THE AMINO ACID ELLIPTIC ASTRAL INFORMATION WILL ALSO REAPPEAR MATERIALLY AFTER SEVERAL YEARS; THIS TRANSFORMATION WILL BE OBSERVABLE BY SCIENTISTS WITH HELP OF OVERLAPPED LENSES THAT WILL MAGNIFY THE IMAGE. ...

VIII

ASUNTARIUM

The Evolutionary Energy of Four Strands

When Asuntarium wakes up and starts to embrace the twenty-one vortices, the sensations could be extremely intense and uncomfortable since this energy will completely restructure the "I am" sensation and will take it to unimaginable levels that the human brain can't possibly understand.

Some will become frightened and will believe that the process was started and created by the darkness. But this is not so. Not everything that is intense is bad; quite to the contrary, the light is much more intense and potent than the darkness.

This intensity is necessary to clean the darkness injected inside you. Don't be afraid, relax and let the cleansing and the restructuration take place.

History

Since the Source of Radiant Light created the human race to understand darkness, the children of the Nebula have been tirelessly sabotaging its creation.

They understood that inside the human capsule exist two seeds: one of light and another of darkness. These seeds were interconnected with Asuntarium, the ascendant spiral of four genetic filaments—two lunar filaments and two solar filaments that intercrossed in the spinal cord and embraced the twenty-one vortices.

This made humans powerful and dangerous at the same time. For this reason, the spawn of the Nebula designed a dark energetic virus in order to destroy the perfect balance between the opposites that reigned in the human body.

This virus was introduced in the terrestrial atmosphere thousands of years ago; it entered through the respiratory tract and propagated quickly.

The virus destroyed one of the solar filaments of Asuntarium. This change altered the soul's balance on an energetic level and started a chain reaction that affected the forty-nine inter-dimensional bodies and incited a drastic transformation over the thirteen strands of DNA; such change left only six strands in three different bodies.

The RNA also suffered a deep transmutation; from seven strands, it ended up with three, one on each body.

After these modifications, the human soul started to fade away—extinction was the only future humans could foresee. The virus caused horrendous suffering, which was not understood by the absolute goodness emanating from the Source.
Since Asuntarium and its four filaments were irreparable without destroying the human vessel, and since the virus was already surrounding the earth, an emergency rescue was lead by the Nine Devas of Crystalline Fire, who fought tirelessly, along with thousands of light beings, to stop the great human suffering. At this time a terrible battle erupted; they had to fight with swords in hand, lead by a beautiful being named Mikhael—he was the one that kept the children of the Nebula and their battalions away. The struggle was brutal and lasted thousands of Earth-years but, in the end, the light triumphed.
As soon as the war was over, all the light beings started to work tirelessly, night and day without rest, with humans that were in hibernation in the north and south poles.
They literally had to tear another filament of Asuntarium, this time one of the lunar filaments, from each of the frozen bodies. Such alteration created a chain reaction and the DNA and the RNA lost their integrity; humans were saved, nonetheless. This way the DNA was left with two filaments of deoxyribonucleic acid and the RNA with only one filament of ribonucleic acid inside the psycho-biological body. This process dismantled the expansive personality of the human soul and cloistered it only within the physical body, which became like a cage that constantly strangles the divine freedom of the thinking human being.
The human mind lost its emergent phenomenon of understanding and reasoning. Feeling lost, bewildered and without the capacity of controlling their forty-nine hyper-dimensional bodies, they ran to and fro without control, screaming in agony. This is the reason why the Source, with a fulminating ray from its dreaming consciousness, destroyed forty-six of its bodies and left the human being with a physical body, an astral body and the causal body.
Its mind was left with only three live processes: the conscious, the unconscious and unconscious with the procedural knowledge, which caused humans to generate only polarized states of personality.
The human being lost 99.99% of its intelligence with this modification, and was left with a mind that conceptualizes everything—even what is impossible to bring into concepts.
Humans now feel they are constantly out in the open, without any protection, since any energy change makes their bodies deeply unstable.

Any of these energetic changes can cause pathological disorders in the brain's ontogeny faculties.
Their homeostatic faculties are now in constant risk of being bombarded.
When this happens, the mind detracts the apparent three-dimensional reality and disconnects itself from the collective consciousness.
This produces gloomy and incoherent hallucinations. The disorder can be caused by various factors, like energetic changes in the earth's crust, planets, the moon, asteroids, stars, supernovas, Lumiferous beings, beings of light and also beings of night. On some occasions, it has been observed that even spiritual practices can make the humans unstable.
Humans have become hyper-sensible; however, they have accomplished their initial purpose of investigating how the Nebula behaves inside the third dimension. Thanks to you, the modification implanted by darkness is coming to an end.
This is why we thank you deeply and promise that radiant times will cover entirely the infinite dreamed creation.
In the past, we realized that, just by stimulating the double helix, the human ascended, causing a series of synergic radiant upward movements that burned the ego-self.
Simultaneously, the electro-physiological properties within the neurons of the central nervous system changed their molecule structure but, with this same stimulus, the neurosecretory neurons were expelled from the synaptic indentations into the blood stream.
This endocrine change happened over ten thousand years ago and equally affected all vertebrate animals, insects, and crustaceans under the terrestrial atmosphere.
The evolutionary step happened only with the stimulation of the double helix on a spinal and cellular level. Some advanced beings made their double helix ascend to the top and reached a state of consciousness that transcended the three bodies; these beings are the enlightened individuals that you've known of or heard about throughout history.
Now we are entering the conclusive phase; the human body is ready to bear again the ascension of the Asuntarium with its quadruple brilliant helix.
While you read, we gradually change the way that the afferent and efferent neurons and "interneurons" communicate. Normally, as is known on Earth, sense neurons collect information, and their axons or afferent fibers transmit this information to other neurons, accessing integral nervous centers. While 010100 light in the here and now flood these, the synapses of the interneuron change affect the efferent neurons, which in turn control the atomic lymph node structures.

Your glands are receiving an order that tells their internal electromagnetic circuit to spin in an orbit at great speed, producing an electromagnetic field that goes beyond the bodily periphery. Such a field affects the nervous system and makes the dendrites and the axons re-internalize their 001101 light. With this energetic change, the conduction speed of the axon will raise dramatically and, jointly with the "myelination of golden radiance" that the reset caused, the axon in the future will transmit its impulses in different directions simultaneously (we know that this goes against scientific beliefs. Until now, it has been believed that the axon transmits impulses only in a single direction. This will stop and the scientists soon will observe the imminent change in the physical body).
The nervous fibers (dendrites) that receive the dazzling neuronal impulses from neurons that, in turn, transmit their forces coming from the universe, will gradually learn to feed from such blinding brightness.
These bright impulses you are currently receiving in the present moment hold intelligent electromagnetic life. These intelligent discharges are being received right now by your shining dendrites.
The alpha neurons of the anterior spinal stems awaken with such a transmission and radiate mystical heat; with this, their electric IT speed will increase to 999 meters per millisecond.
The polyhedral neurons of the anterior spinal stem are being modified while you read by the ascension of Asuntara, which we excite using multidimensional vibrations. These motoneurons, or polyhedral neurons, now become cells that hold the power and the mystery of the cosmos.
Such unleashed power in your deepest interior awakens the quadruple ascendant helix of the First Vortex in the astral body. In this way, Asuntarium reaches and embraces each vortex with Love until it penetrates the physical brain, where it regenerates and activates the fusiform neurons located at the double bifurcation of the brain cortex.
The almighty energy of the Devas of Crystalline Fire is now affecting the star-shaped and spider-shaped neurons (or "arachnid-forms") of the brain cortex and the cerebellum nest.
In the pyramidal neurons, Asuntara's light is being forced to penetrate their center and enlightens it with embracing fiery irradiations.
When Asuntarium reaches the top physiological vortex, it then leaves the body through the top of the head to embrace other intergalactic vortices connected to human beings in the distant past. It is an incredibly fantastic sensation you will feel when this takes place; a cascade of light will invade the spherical neurons of the sympathetic and parasympathetic spinal nodes and you will breathe again for the first time.

The neurons are being excited as you read so that they accept a grade of depolarization.
Through an electrochemical process, they get reprogrammed so they are able to hold the great power of the nine surrounding dimensions, giving birth to a bio- hyperboric (waves of light) feedback that produces living synergistic and antagonistic progressive replies.
The modification that you are experiencing in this present moment connects your dreamed three-dimensional body to the Source of Radiant Essence.
Be patient, relax, don’t think and let the light completely and definitely change you.

IX

Restructuring of the Vortices by the Devas

Nourishment

We recommend that the reader drinks pure and natural water, free of chemicals, especially fluoride. This poison has been introduced into many countries' drinking water with the pretext of protecting against dental cavities, due to its ability to force the body to assimilate calcium in an unnatural manner. Know that this calcium is assimilated in other areas of the body as well, such as arteries and glands.

With fluoride, the pineal gland also calcifies and ceases to function properly.

The pineal gland plays a vital role since it is a very powerful antenna that connects the human being with other beings of light and their Source. If it functions improperly, the human will be unable to access other dimensions with an intact individuality.

In some countries, fluoride is also infused into the salt.

Read the ingredients and inform yourself.

Detoxify yourself with boron and potassium iodide along with K1 and K2 vitamins. also eat plenty of cilantro and chlorella to cleanse your brain from heavy metals.

Take Lion's Mane and red Reishi mushrooms plus Ashwagandha and Maca to regenerate the nervous system and to regrow new neurons.

Eat pure and natural food without genetic modifications and, when possible, without pesticides or other contaminants so that our work can flow without any interruptions or obstacles.

On Earth, scientists have observed that the levels of glyphosate and other chemicals in some grains are increasing.

These chemicals inhibit the natural growth of plants. Terrestrial scientists have associated glyphosate with embryonic defects in certain animal species for this very evident reason.

According to them, these chemicals could affect the spinal cord, the nervous system, and the cranium. Remember that these bone structures and filaments are of vital importance, since they protect the Asuntarium and are the channel along which it moves.

Soybeans, corn, and most of the grains and pod vegetables consumed worldwide are most likely genetically modified and, in most cases, have a high glyphosate content.

There are terrestrial studies that indicate that glyphosate has a high potential to cause cellular damage and DNA mutations, and is neurotoxic. Glyphosate can cause damage to the intestinal flora and, consequently, it causes stress on the immune system.
We could continue to write for hours about other chemicals that have been added to your food, but the reading would become boring. What is required is as simple as eating natural foods, organic when possible, and without modifications. Lastly, it is better to fast than to eat poison.

WHILE YOU READ WE GRADUALLY CHANGE THE WAY THAT THE AFFERENT AND EFFERENT NEURONS AND “INTERNEURONS” COMMUNICATE. NORMALLY, AS IS KNOWN ON EARTH, SENSE NEURONS COLLECT INFORMATION, AND THEIR AXONS OR AFFERENT FIBERS TRANSMIT THIS INFORMATION TO OTHER NEURONS, ACCESSING INTEGRAL NERVOUS CENTERS. WHILE THESE GET FLOODED BY 010100 LIGHT IN THE HERE AND NOW, THE SYNAPSES OF THE INTERNEURON CHANGE, AFFECTING THE EFFERENT NEURONS, WHICH IN TURN CONTROL THE ATOMIC LYMPH NODE STRUCTURES. YOUR GLANDS ARE RECEIVING AN ORDER WHICH TELLS THEIR INTERNAL ELECTROMAGNETIC CIRCUIT TO SPIN IN AN ORBIT AT GREAT SPEED, PRODUCING AN ELECTROMAGNETIC FIELD THAT GOES BEYOND THE BODILY PERIPHERY. SUCH A FIELD AFFECTS THE NERVOUS SYSTEM AND MAKES THE DENDRITES AND THE AXONS REINTERNALIZE THEIR PHOTO 001101 LIGHT. WITH THIS ENERGETIC CHANGE, THE CONDUCTION SPEED OF THE AXON WILL RAISE DRAMATICALLY AND, JOINTLY WITH THE “MYELINATION OF GOLDEN RADIANCE” THAT THE RESET CAUSED. THE AXON IN THE FUTURE WILL TRANSMIT ITS IMPULSES IN DIFFERENT DIRECTIONS SIMULTANEOUSLY (WE KNOW THAT THIS GOES AGAINST SCIENTIFIC BELIEFS. UNTIL NOW IT HAS BEEN BELIEVED THAT THE AXON TRANSMITS IMPULSES ONLY IN A SINGLE DIRECTION. THIS WILL STOP AND THE SCIENTISTS SOON WILL OBSERVE THE IMMINENT CHANGE IN THE PHYSICAL BODY). THE NERVOUS FIBERS (DENDRITES) THAT RECEIVE THE DAZZLING NEURONAL IMPULSES FROM NEURONS WHICH IN TURN TRANSMIT THEIR FORCES COMING FROM THE UNIVERSE, WILL GRADUALLY LEARN TO FEED FROM SUCH BLINDING BRIGHTNESS. THESE BRIGHT IMPULSES THAT YOU ARE CURRENTLY RECEIVING IN THE PRESENT MOMENT HOLD INTELLIGENT ELECTROMAGNETIC LIFE. THESE INTELLIGENT DISCHARGES ARE BEING RECEIVED RIGHT NOW BY YOUR SHINING DENDRITES. THE ALPHA NEURONS OF THE ANTERIOR SPINAL STEMS AWAKEN WITH SUCH A TRANSMISSION AND RADIATE MYSTICAL HEAT; WITH THIS, THEIR ELECTRICIT SPEED WILL INCREASE TO 999 METERS PER MILLISECOND. THE POLYHEDRAL NEURONS OF THE ANTERIOR SPINAL SYSTEM ARE BEING MODIFIED WHILE YOU READ BY THE ASCENSION OF ASUNTARA WHICH WE EXCITE USING

MULTIDIMENSIONAL VIBRATIONS. THESE MOTONEURONS, OR POLYHEDRAL NEURONS, NOW BECOME CELLS THAT HOLD THE POWER AND THE MYSTERY OF THE COSMOS. SUCH UNLEASHED POWER IN YOUR DEEPEST INTERIOR AWAKENS THE QUADRUPLE ASCENDANT HELIX OF THE FIRST VORTEX IN THE ASTRAL BODY. IN THIS WAY ASUNTARIUM REACHES AND EMBRACES EACH VORTEX WITH LOVE UNTIL IT PENETRATES THE PHYSICAL BRAIN, WHERE IT REGENERATES AND ACTIVATES THE FUSIFORM NEURONS THAT ARE LOCATED AT THE DOUBLE BIFURCATION OF THE BRAIN CORTEX. THE ALMIGHTY ENERGY OF THE DEVAS OF CRYSTALLINE FIRE IS NOW AFFECTING THE STAR- AND SPIDER-SHAPED NEURONS, OR “ARACHNID-FORMS”, OF THE BRAIN CORTEX AND THE CEREBELLUM NEST. IN THE PYRAMIDAL NEURONS, ASUNTARA'S LIGHT IS BEING FORCED TO PENETRATE THEIR CENTER AND ENLIGHTENS IT WITH EMBRACING FIERY IRRADIATIONS. WHEN ASUNTARIUM REACHES THE TOP PHYSIOLOGICAL VORTEX, IT THEN LEAVES THE BODY THROUGH THE TOP OF THE HEAD TO EMBRACE OTHER INTERGALACTIC VORTICES CONNECTED TO HUMAN BEINGS IN THE DISTANT PAST. IT IS AN INCREDIBLY FANTASTIC SENSATION YOU WILL FEEL WHEN THIS TAKES PLACE; A CASCADE OF LIGHT WILL INVADE THE SPHERICAL NEURONS OF THE SYMPATHETIC AND PARASYMPATHETIC SPINAL NODES AND YOU WILL BREATHE AGAIN FOR THE FIRST TIME. THE NEURONS ARE BEING EXCITED AS YOU READ SO THAT THEY ACCEPT A GRADE OF DEPOLARIZATION. THROUGH AN ELECTROCHEMICAL PROCESS, THEY GET REPROGRAMMED SO THEY ARE ABLE TO HOLD THE GREAT POWER OF THE NINE SURROUNDING DIMENSIONS, GIVING BIRTH TO A BIO- HYPERBORIC (WAVES OF LIGHT) FEEDBACK THAT PRODUCES LIVING SYNERGISTIC AND ANTAGONISTIC PROGRESSIVE REPLIES. THE MODIFICATION THAT YOU ARE EXPERIENCING IN THIS PRESENT MOMENT CONNECTS YOUR DREAMED THREE-DIMENSIONAL BODY TO THE SOURCE OF RADIANT ESSENCE. BE PATIENT, RELAX, DON'T THINK AND LET THE LIGHT COMPLETELY AND DEFINITELY CHANGE YOU. {NOURISHMENT} WE RECOMMEND THAT THE READER DRINKS PURE AND NATURAL WATER, FREE OF CHEMICALS, ESPECIALLY FLUORIDE. THIS POISON HAS BEEN INTRODUCED INTO MANY COUNTRIES, DRINKING WATER WITH THE PRETEXT OF PROTECTING AGAINST

THE READING WOULD BECOME BORING. IT IS AS SIMPLE AS EATING

SE DAMAGE TO THE INTESTINAL FLORA, AND CONSEQUENTLY, IT

GLYPHOSATE CONTENT. THERE ARE TERRESTRIAL STUDIES T

L ALONG WHICH IT MOVES. SOY BEANS, CORN, AND MOST

E NERVOUS SYSTEM, AND THE CRANIUM. REMEMBER T

OSATE WITH EMBRYONIC DEFECTS IN CERTAIN AN

THER CHEMICALS IN SOME GRAINS ARE INCREA

THAT OUR WORK CAN FLOW WITHOUT ANY

NS, EAT PURE AND NATURAL FOOD WI

INGREDIENTS AND INFORM YOUR

NSIONS WITH AN INTACT INDI

GHT AND THEIR SOURCE. IF

IT IS A VERY POWERFU

AND CEASES TO FUN

TERIES AND GLA

ASSIMILATED

AN UNNAT

RCE T

TIE

D

TS A

SSIMILA

NOW THAT T

THE BODY AS

E, THE PINEAL GLA

PINEAL GLAND PLAYS

CTS THE HUMAN BEING WI

LY, THE HUMAN WILL BE UNAB

RIES, FLUORIDE IS ALSO INFUSE

TH BORON AND POTASSIUM IODIDE A

AND WHEN POSSIBLE WITHOUT PESTICID

EARTH, SCIENTISTS HAVE OBSERVED THAT

HE NATURAL GROWTH OF PLANTS. TERRESTRIAL

T REASON. ACCORDING TO THEM, THESE CHEMICALS

MENTS ARE OF VITAL IMPORTANCE, SINCE THEY PROTEC

NSUMED WORLDWIDE ARE MOST LIKELY GENETICALLY MOD

GH POTENTIAL TO CAUSE CELLULAR DAMAGE, DNA MUTATIONS,

COULD CONTINUE TO WRITE FOR HOURS ABOUT OTHER CHEMICALS

CAUSES STRESS ON THE IMMUNE SYSTEM. WE

HAT INDICATE THAT GLYPHOSATE HAS A HI

OF THE GRAINS AND POD VEGETABLES CO

THESE BONE STRUCTURES AND FILA

IMALS SPECIES FOR THIS VERY EVIDEN

SING. THESE CHEMICALS INHIBIT

INTERRUPTIONS OR OBSTACLES. ON

THOUT GENETIC MODIFICATIONS

Cleansing and Restructuring the inner Vortexes

First Vortex

This vortex is related to vitality and vigor. In this manner, we experience the connection with the environment, as well as its rhythms and patterns, with profound wisdom. When inactive, the body experiences a general lack of energy, feelings of hopelessness, a sense of not belonging and not being capable of an inner blossoming.
Without this energy, the individual will experience sensations of cold, inertia, congestion, lack of coordination, lack of dynamism, fatigue, discouragement, and the impression of being sucked in and trapped by others.
A hyperactive First Vortex could manifest symptoms such as redness of the skin, physical tension, inability to relax, rage, fear, bewilderment, mood swings and intolerance.
When effectively activated, an individual obtains the ability of summoning the abundance of the universe. One may enjoy health and coordination, enthusiasm and peace. It bestows the capacity of conferring the extreme lightness of air to the physical body, of making astral voyages, and embraces the practitioner with a brilliant golden aura of protection.

The Womb and the First Vortex

Urvit matviat uditmatrat Adonai madraitrat

Adonai confers (or restores) perfect femininity to the woman.

The womb is essential for the Devas of Crystalline Fire. It is mainly used to transmute feminine energy. If you are a woman, the Devas of Crystalline Fire, in this precise moment, are introducing ethereal light into the complex tissues of your womb with the purpose of increasing certain secretions that communicate information to the cells from other dimensions. Also, in case you are pregnant, the Beings of Powerful Light will simultaneously introduce shining spirals all over the fetal placental unit.
From now on, the uterine receptors will remain in constant commotion due to the Devic presence. In linear three-dimensional time, such receptors

will increase and decrease their impetus during the menstrual cycle as long as this presence embraces you.

The receptors in the different parts of the endometrium that vary along the cycle will change their order of presentation. The estrogen receptors, such as progesterone, will increase their luminosity along the first phase, where an insertion of "mini-cyclones of incandescent spirit light" will take place. These will enforce the feeling of impenetrable calm that the woman deserves during the follicular phase.

We will presently extract the vibrant living energy of the ovum and redirect it to the First Vortex of the astral body with the purpose of awakening Asuntarium (the radiant helix of four filaments). The secretory phase will remain intact. The epithelial cells and the progesterone receptors assume a color reminiscent to amber sapphire in the astral parallel.

The intermediate muscular coat, formed by a flat muscle between the peritoneal serous and the glandular mucus of the uterus, will be flooded with photonic solar light of Devic origin. This process will increase the progesterone receptors.

The endometrium will reach a perfect balance due to the right relation between estrogen 010 light and the progesterone that the Devas stimulate. The 010 light and hormonal changes will affect the temporary sequence of the luteal phase over the discrepant molecular archetype in conjunct and in a balanced manner. The estrogen already modified by the Seraphim Radiance will be mainly involved in the attainment of intermolecular perfection. The progesterone will embrace the stroma with angelic irradiation.

Unnatural patriarchal astral darkness gripped the feminine hormonal process for a long time, causing abnormalities in the endometrium. These changes that the densest shadows provoked in the female's body resulted in different types of hormonal imbalances that cause chemical disorders of physical and emotional nature.

The Nine Devas, through bright golden and violet inoculations, will drive the estrogens to stimulate the internal expression of "being someone"; such stimulation will culminate in the destruction of the "I" illusion and the labels the False "I" creates. The soul in the woman's body will slowly understand that its essence goes beyond the physical body; the False "I" will succumb and the sensation of "I am that, I am", conjunctly with a feeling of imperishable eternity, will spawn into life. The most marvelous expansion will take the reins of the soul, culminating in its total union with the most radiant cosmos.

The transformational phase that you are experiencing in the present moment awakens a strong bond that is very present in the mental de-configuration phase, which will drive the epithelial cells to re-introduce themselves into pools of light without any borders whatsoever.
The cytokines will be forced with photonic waves and Arcturian light to lower their quantity drastically. This way, the womb will stop being an organ that carries immutable degeneration.
The insulin that has an expression scheme recognized by the Devas of Crystalline Fire as luminous waves will increase due to the intermolecular change suffered. Simultaneously, the Devas will promote, mainly, the production of lipid molecules using predecessor light emanated from the endometrium. This change indicates the awakening of Asuntarium in this imminent phase.
The B-endorphin will be released substantially, since the flashing lights from the fifth dimension incite the inhibition process of certain dark areas of the womb here and now. These flashes, conjunctly with the B-endorphin, will produce ecstatic states in the body.
In conclusion, you will go through positive hormonal changes similar to pregnancy, without being pregnant; these changes will be produced by the ascension of quadruple helix Asuntarium.
The change will be hormonal and the sensation will be of ecstasy and not the uncomfortable feeling most women experience during their menstrual period. The experience will be pleasurable and different from what you are used to in reference to the hormonal oscillations that are involved in this area. Be patient, relax, and open your heart to change.

Prostate and the First Vortex

Adonai madraitrat itriyam multrat bidram

Adonai confers unadulterated masculinity to man.

If you are a male, your prostate will now be incited to produce prostatic liquid without creating the need for ejaculation. The Devas use this change with the purpose of extracting bright and clear energy that this masculine substance radiates. This irradiation will not only nurture your physical body but, as it blends with sperm, it will produce a 100010 light that will move through a hypersensitive meridian connected to the right side of the heart; said meridian is born in the right area of the chest, travels though tiny curves, goes straight through the liver, and reaches the testicles, pituitary and hypothalamus. This light incites the hypothalamus to position the hormones that exert pressure in such a way that the pituitary gland regulates testosterone production. Such effect lowers the testosterone without there being a conversion to estrogen; consequently, there is no possibility for the body's cells to attack themselves.

The testosterone was stimulated and modified by the dark forces to make it prominent. This hormone mentally and emotionally dominates man. The "testosterone-driven man", so to speak, is very aggressive and addicted to the first vortex.

With the changes that we effected in the first vortex, both men and women will adopt an androgenic and balanced shape similar to that of the soul. The pituitary gland will join the fight of spiritual light, being physically linked to the hypothalamus. It will also change its behavior, affecting the testicles and the adrenal glands so that they lower their testosterone production without there being any single cancerous mutation.

{THE WOMB AND THE FIRST VORTEX}URVIT MATVIAT UDITMATRAT ADONAI MADRAITRAT. ADONAI CONFERS (CORE STORES) PERFECT FEMININITY TO THE WOMAN. THE WOMB IS ESSENTIAL FOR THE DEVAS OF CRYSTALLINE FIRE. IT IS MAINLY USED TO TRANSMUTE FEMININE ENERGY. IF YOU ARE A WOMAN, THE DEVAS OF CRYSTALLINE FIRE, IN THIS PRECISE MOMENT, ARE INTRODUCING ETHEREAL LIGHT INTO THE COMPLEX TISSUES OF YOUR WOMB, WITH THE PURPOSE OF INCREASING CERTAIN SECRETIONS THAT COMMUNICATE INFORMATION TO THE CELLS FROM OTHER DIMENSIONS. ALSO, IN CASE YOU ARE PREGNANT. THE BEINGS OF POWERFUL LIGHT WILL SIMULTANEOUSLY INTRODUCE SHINING SPIRALS ALL OVER THE FETAL PLACENTAL UNIT. FROM NOW ON, THE UTERINE RECEPTORS WILL REMAIN IN CONSTANT COMMOTION DUE TO THE DEVIC PRESENCE. IN LINEAR THREE-DIMENSIONAL TIME, SUCH RECEPTORS WILL INCREASE AND DECREASE THEIR IMPETUS DURING THE MENSTRUAL CYCLE AS LONG AS THIS PRESENCE EMBRACES YOU. THE RECEPTORS IN THE DIFFERENT PARTS OF THE ENDOMETRIUM THAT VARY ALONG THE CYCLE WILL CHANGE THEIR ORDER OF PRESENTATION. THE ESTROGEN RECEPTORS, SUCH AS PROGESTERONE, WILL INCREASE THEIR LUMINOSITY ALONG THE FIRST PHASE, WHERE AN INSERTION OF "MINI-CYCLONES OF INCANDESCENT SPIRIT LIGHT" WILL TAKE PLACE. THESE WILL ENFORCE THE FEELING OF IMPENETRABLE CALM THAT THE WOMAN DESERVES DURING THE FOLLICULAR PHASE. WE WILL PRESENTLY EXTRACT THE VIBRANT LIVING ENERGY OF THE OVUM AND REDIRECT IT TO THE FIRST VORTEX OF THE ASTRAL BODY, WITH THE PURPOSE OF AWAKENING ASUNTARIUM (THE RADIANT HELIX OF FOUR FILAMENTS). THE SECRETORY PHASE WILL REMAIN INTACT. THE EPITHELIAL CELLS AND THE PROGESTERONE RECEPTORS ASSUME A COLOR REMINISCENT TO AMBER SAPPHIRE IN THE ASTRAL PARALLEL. THE INTERMEDIATE MUSCULAR COAT, FORMED BY A FLAT MUSCLE BETWEEN THE PERITONEAL SEROUS AND THE GLANDULAR MUCUS OF THE UTERUS, WILL BE FLOODED WITH PHOTONIC SOLAR LIGHT OF DEVIC ORIGIN. THIS PROCESS WILL INCREASE THE PROGESTERONE RECEPTORS. THE ENDOMETRIUM WILL REACH PERFECT BALANCE DUE TO THE RIGHT RELATION BETWEEN ESTROGEN 010 LIGHT AND THE PROGESTERONE THAT

THE DEVAS STIMULATE. THE 010 LIGHT AND HORMONAL CHANGES WILL AFFECT THE TEMPORARY SEQUENCE OF THE LUTEAL PHASE OVER THE DISCREPANT MOLECULAR ARCHETYPE IN CONJUNCT AND IN A BALANCED MANNER. THE ESTROGEN ALREADY MODIFIED BY THE SERAPHIM RADIANCE WILL BE MAINLY INVOLVED IN THE ATTAINMENT OF INTERMOLECULAR PERFECTION. THE PROGESTERONE WILL EMBRACE THE STROMA WITH ANGELIC IRRADIATION. UNNATURAL PATRIARCHAL ASTRAL DARKNESS GRIPPED THE FEMININE HORMONAL PROCESS FOR A LONG TIME, CAUSING ABNORMALITIES IN THE ENDOMETRIUM. THESE CHANGES THAT THE DENSEST SHADOWS PROVOKED IN THE FEMALE'S BODY RESULTED IN DIFFERENT TYPES OF HORMONAL IMBALANCES, WHICH CAUSE CHEMICAL DISORDERS OF PHYSICAL AND EMOTIONAL NATURE. THE NINE DEVAS OF ATOMIC LIGHT, THROUGH BRIGHT GOLDEN AND VIOLET INOCULATIONS, WILL DRIVE THE ESTROGENS TO STIMULATE THE INTERNAL EXPRESSION OF "BEING SOMEONE"; SUCH STIMULATION WILL CULMINATE IN THE DESTRUCTION OF THE "I" ILLUSION AND THE LABELS THE FALSE "I" CREATES. THE SOUL IN THE WOMAN'S BODY WILL SLOWLY UNDERSTAND THAT ITS ESSENCE GOES BEYOND THE PHYSICAL BODY; THE FALSE "I" WILL SUCCUMB AND THE SENSATION OF "I AM THAT, I AM" CONJUNCTLY WITH A FEELING OF IMPERISHABLE ETERNITY, WILL SPAWN INTO LIFE AND THE MOST MARVELOUS EXPANSION WILL TAKE THE REINS OF THE SOUL, CULMINATING IN ITS TOTAL UNION WITH THE MOST RADIANT COSMOS. THE TRANSFORMATIONAL PHASE THAT YOU ARE EXPERIENCING IN THE PRESENT MOMENT AWAKENS A STRONG BOND THAT IS VERY PRESENT IN THE MENTAL DE-CONFIGURATION PHASE, WHICH WILL DRIVE THE EPITHELIAL CELLS TO RE-INTRODUCE THEMSELVES INTO POOLS OF LIGHT WITHOUT ANY BORDERS WHATSOEVER. THE CYTOKINE WILL BE FORCED WITH PHOTONIC WAVES AND ARCTURIAN LIGHT TO LOWER THEIR QUANTITY DRASTICALLY. THIS WAY, THE WOMB WILL STOP BEING AN ORGAN THAT CARRIES IMMUTABLE DEGENERATION. THE INSULIN THAT HAS AN EXPRESSION SCHEME RECOGNIZED BY THE DEVAS OF CRYSTALLINE FIRE AS LUMINOUS WAVES WILL INCREASE DUE TO THE INTERMOLECULAR CHANGE SUFFERED. SIMULTANEOUSLY, THE DEVAS WILL PROMOTE, MAINLY, THE PRODUCTION OF

LIPID MOLECULES USING PREDECESSOR LIGHT EMANATED FROM THE ENDOMETRIUM. THIS CHANGE INDICATES THE AWAKENING OF ASUNTARIUM IN THIS IMMINENT PHASE. THE B-ENDORPHIN WILL BE RELEASED SUBSTANTIALLY, SINCE THE FLASHING LIGHTS FROM THE FIFTH DIMENSION INCITE THE INHIBITION PROCESS OF CERTAIN DARK AREAS OF THE WOMB HERE AND NOW. THESE FLASHES, CONJUNCTLY WITH THE B-ENDORPHIN, WILL PRODUCE ECSTATIC STATES IN THE BODY. IN CONCLUSION, YOU WILL GO THROUGH POSITIVE HORMONAL CHANGES SIMILAR TO PREGNANCY, WITHOUT BEING PREGNANT. THESE CHANGES WILL BE PRODUCED BY THE ASCENSION OF QUADRUPLE HELIX ASUNTARIUM. THE CHANGE WILL BE HORMONAL AND THE SENSATION WILL BE OF ECSTASY AND NOT THE UNCOMFORTABLE FEELINGS MOST WOMEN EXPERIENCE DURING THEIR MENSTRUAL PERIOD. THE EXPERIENCE WILL BE PLEASURABLE AND DIFFERENT FROM WHAT YOU ARE USED TO IN REFERENCE TO THE HORMONAL OSCILLATIONS THAT ARE INVOLVED IN THIS AREA. BE PATIENT, RELAX, AND OPEN YOUR HEART TO CHANGE. {PROSTATE AND THE FIRST VORTEX}ADONAI MADRAITRAT ITRIYAM MULTRAT BIDRAM. ADONAI CONFERS UNADULTERATED MASCULINITY TO MAN. IF YOU ARE A MALE, YOUR PROSTATE WILL NOW BE INCITED TO PRODUCE PROSTATIC LIQUID WITHOUT CREATING THE NEED FOR EJACULATION. THE DEVAS USE THIS CHANGE WITH THE PURPOSE OF EXTRACTING BRIGHT AND CLEAR ENERGY THAT THIS MASCULINE SUBSTANCE RADIATES. THIS IRRADIATION WILL NOT ONLY NURTURE YOUR PHYSICAL BODY, BUT AS IT BLENDS WITH SPERM, IT WILL PRODUCE A 100010 LIGHT, THAT WILL MOVE THROUGH A HYPERSENSITIVE MERIDIAN CONNECTED TO THE RIGHT SIDE OF THE HEART; SAID MERIDIAN IS BORN IN THE RIGHT AREA OF THE CHEST, TRAVELS THOUGH TINY CURVES, GOES STRAIGHT THROUGH THE LIVER, AND REACHES THE TESTICLES, PITUITARY AND HYPOTHALAMUS. THIS LIGHT WILL INCITE THE HYPOTHALAMUS TO POSITION THE HORMONES THAT EXERT PRESSURE IN SUCH A WAY THAT THE PITUITARY GLAND REGULATES TESTOSTERONE PRODUCTION. SUCH EFFECT LOWERS THE TESTOSTERONE WITHOUT THERE BEING A CONVERSION TO ESTROGEN; CONSEQUENTLY, THERE IS NO POSSIBILITY FOR THE BODY'S CELLS TO ATTACK THEMSELVES. THE TESTOSTERONE

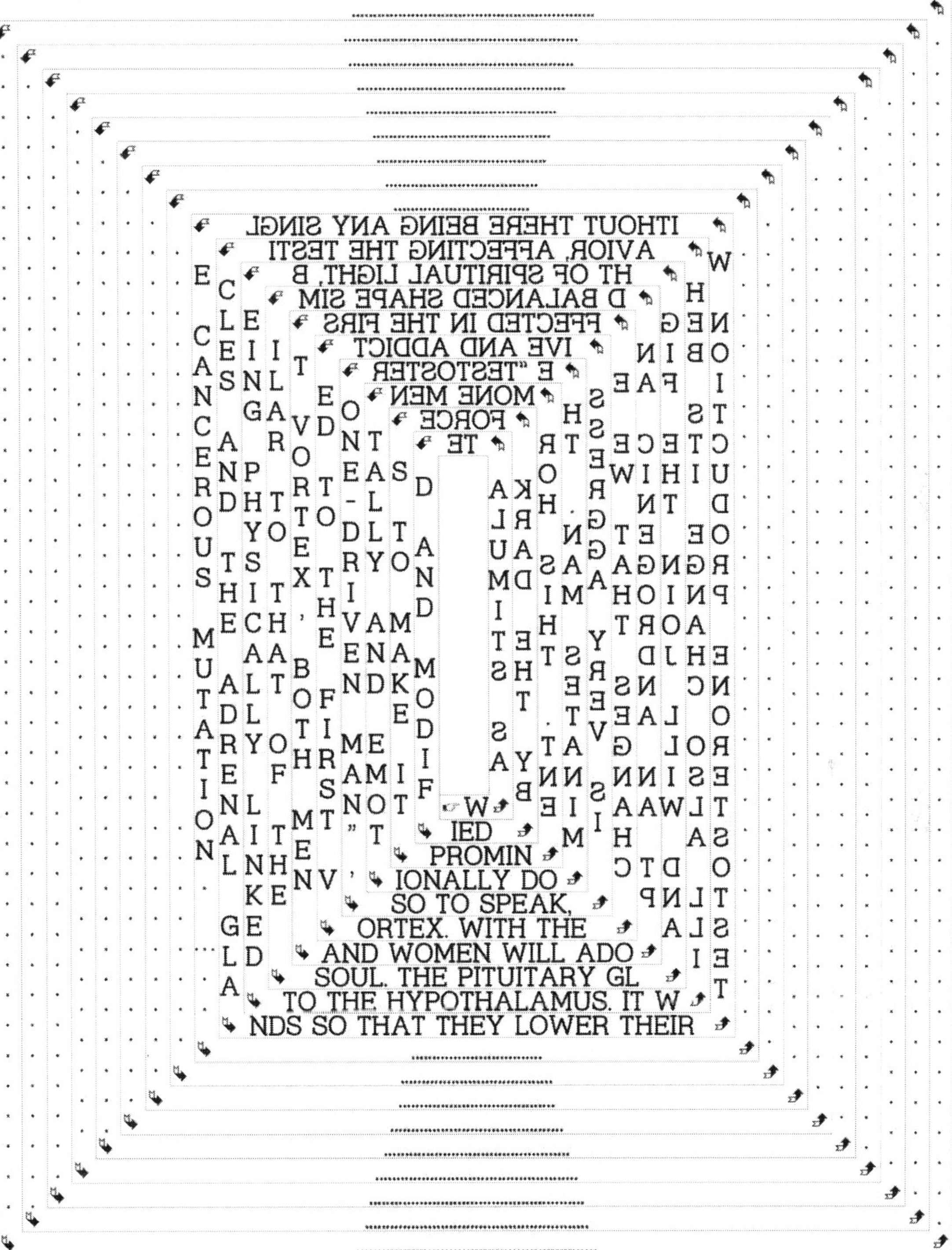
ITHOUT THERE BEING ANY SINGL
AVIOR, AFFECTING THE TESTI
HT OF SPIRITUAL LIGHT, B
D BALANCED SHAPE SIM
FFECTED IN THE FIRS
IVE AND ADDICT
E "TESTOSTER
MONE MEN
FORCE
TE
W
IED
PROMIN
IONALLY DO
SO TO SPEAK,
ORTEX. WITH THE
AND WOMEN WILL ADO
SOUL. THE PITUITARY GL
TO THE HYPOTHALAMUS. IT W
NDS SO THAT THEY LOWER THEIR

Second Vortex

The second vortex is related to progress and power currents. It is associated with sensuality and the childhood longing for enjoyment and satisfaction.

A person with an imbalance may show signs of musculoskeletal tension, limited feelings, disturbed digestion, lack of concentration and strength, feelings of being trapped in the past, impotence, uterine problems, bladder problems, kidney problems and stiffness in the lower back. One may also observe inferiority complex feelings, possessiveness, envy, antisocial conducts, lust, selfishness, aggression, conceit, lack of consideration, discouragement, victimization, masochism, and consumerism.

When this center is consolidated, it is capable of awakening asuntarium energy by redirecting the libido up. This feminine power will evolve in the subtle and physical body; it will also purify the superfluous emotions, illnesses, indefinite negative feelings, and other complementary blockages that hinder the free movement of this force.

This center gives the power of living for a long period of time without food or water and makes the body shine with a silver aura.

Testicle Functions and Their Correlation with the Second Vortex

Ataratmitat uriit vastriyat shimstit Aristat

Spermatogenesis is being catalyzed here and now so that the sperm's vital energy will join the ascension of Asuntara. The Sertoli cells will be in charge of transporting receptor lights and of discharging dark leftovers. Simultaneously, a lumen coming from the germinal cells will be redirected to Asuntara's abode to ignite it.

The FSH and LH produced by the hypophysis (pituitary gland) will be manipulated to be able to slowly, and in a throbbing manner, produce less testosterone than usual. This lowering in production will drive the male to tune in with his feminine side.

The action of the enzyme alpha reductase is affected by the Seraphim through an energetic meridian so that it may produce a normal amount of dihitestosterone

The dihitestosterone is now metabolized by Devic sensitivity with spherical lights that will change the molecular code of the intrinsic androgenic intracellular receptors so they can join transcription factors that systematize the permutation of genetic expression and, at the same time, gradually change the DNA.

Ovary Hormones and the Second Vortex

Ushti ustimitrut adktatrakt amadiat Xiabi-el

Reader, pay attention, since we are changing the astral lights that affect the activin and inhibin in your body, which are two protein complexes narrowly related and opposite to each other. The activin is destabilized as you advance with the lecture of the book in order to change its atomic structure. In this way, the biosynthesis and the FSH suppuration that regulate the menstrual cycle will be increased with more potency.

Almost immediately after this has happened, the Devas of Crystalline Fire, with the purpose of balancing the symptoms caused by the modification, will set in motion the activin with astral/cascading light to awaken dormant properties that will make the woman lose less blood and vital energy, and to experience less pain. This change will subsequently affect cellular proliferation, cellular differentiation, apoptosis, homeostasis, immune response, scarring, and the endocrinal function in a positive and gradual way.

The inhibin affected by this light will regulate the synthesis of FSH at the right moment to strengthen the change made by the Devas of Crystalline Fire with effulgent lightning without any secondary adjacent effects.

This effect will change the molecular structure of a number of proteins structurally related to the activin and inhibin, such as the dimeric glycoprotein and the skeletal morphogenic protein. Such permutations will incite a chain reaction that will awaken various sub-alternate ethereal centers in the astral body.

{TESTICLE FUNCTIONS AND THEIR CORRELATION WITH THE SECOND VORTEX.} {ATARAMITAT URIIT VASTRIYAT SHIMSTIT ARISTAT}SPERMATOGENESIS IS BEING CATALYZED HERE AND NOW SO THAT THE SPERM'S VITAL ENERGY WILL JOIN THE ASCENSION OF ASUNTARA. THE SERTOLI CELLS WILL BE IN CHARGE OF TRANSPORTING RECEPTOR LIGHTS AND OF DISCHARGING DARK LEFTOVERS. SIMULTANEOUSLY. A LUMEN COMING FROM THE GERMINAL CELLS WILL BE REDIRECTED TO ASUNTARA'S ABODE TO IGNITE IT. THE FSH AND LH PRODUCED BY THE HYPOPHYSIS (PITUITARY GLAND) WILL BE MANIPULATED TO BE ABLE TO SLOWLY, AND IN A THROBBING MANNER, PRODUCE LESS TESTOSTERONE THAN USUAL. THIS LOWERING IN PRODUCTION WILL DRIVE THE MALE TO TUNE IN WITH HIS FEMININE SIDE. THE ACTION OF THE ENZYME ALPHA REDUCTASE IS AFFECTED BY THE SERAPHIM THROUGH AN ENERGETIC MERIDIAN SO THAT IT MAY PRODUCE A NORMAL AMOUNT OF DIHITESTOSTERONE. THE DIHITESTOSTERONE IS NOW METABOLIZED BY DEVIC SENSITIVITY WITH SPHERICAL LIGHTS THAT WILL CHANGE THE MOLECULAR CODE OF THE INTRINSIC ANDROGENIC INTRACELLULAR RECEPTORS SO THEY CAN JOIN TRANSCRIPTION FACTORS THAT SYSTEMATIZE THE PERMUTATION OF THE GENETIC EXPRESSION AND AT THE SAME TIME GRADUALLY CHANGE THE DNA. {USHTI USTIMITRUT ADKTATRAKT AMADIAT XIABI-EL {READER, PAY ATTENTION, SINCE WE ARE CHANGING THE ASTRAL LIGHTS THAT AFFECT THE ACTIVIN AND INHIBIN IN YOUR BODY, WHICH ARE TWO PROTEIN COMPLEXES NARROWLY RELATED AND OPPOSITE TO EACH OTHER. THE ACTIVIN IS DESTABILIZED AS YOU ADVANCE WITH THE LECTURE OF THE BOOK IN ORDER TO CHANGE ITS ATOMIC STRUCTURE. IN THIS WAY, THE BIOSYNTHESIS AND THE FSH SUPPURATION THAT REGULATE THE MENSTRUAL CYCLE WILL BE INCREASED WITH MORE POTENCY. ALMOST IMMEDIATELY AFTER THIS HAS HAPPENED, THE DEVAS OF CRYSTALLINE FIRE, WITH THE PURPOSE OF BALANCING THE SYMPTOMS CAUSED BY THE MODIFICATION, WILL SET IN MOTION THE ACTIVIN WITH ASTRAL/CASCADING LIGHT TO AWAKEN DORMANT PROPERTIES THAT WILL MAKE THE WOMAN LOSE LESS BLOOD AND VITAL ENERGY, AND TO EXPERIENCE LESS PAIN. THIS CHANGE WILL SUBSEQUENTLY AFFECT CELLULAR PROLIFERATION,

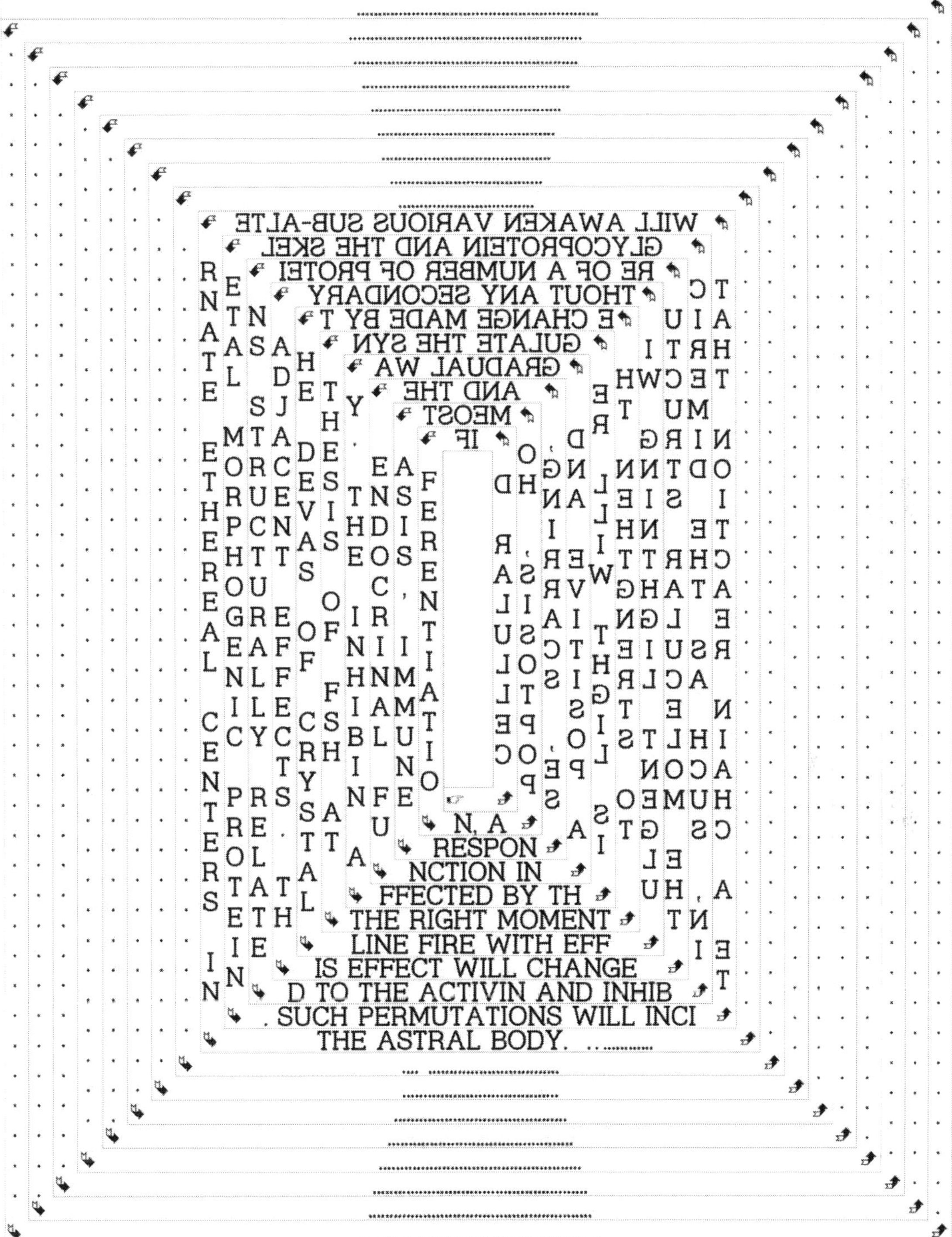
WILL AWAKEN VARIOUS SUB-ALTE
GLYCOPROTEIN AND THE SKEL
RE OF A NUMBER OF PROTEI
THOUT ANY SECONDARY
E CHANGE MADE BY T
GULATE THE SYN
GRADUAL WA
AND THE
MEOST
IF
N, A
RESPON
NCTION IN
FFECTED BY TH
THE RIGHT MOMENT
LINE FIRE WITH EFF
IS EFFECT WILL CHANGE
D TO THE ACTIVIN AND INHIB
. SUCH PERMUTATIONS WILL INCI
THE ASTRAL BODY.

Solar Plexus and the Third Vortex

The third vortex is the throne of egoic energy. This is the area from which the ego sucks vital energy.
People transcend their fundamental needs of feeding in the first vortex, and their sexual addictions (unhealthy sex) in the second. The third center is about leadership; if this vortex is open with light and not transcended, the person is at risk of becoming a politician, president of a country, an important person in a company, a famous musician, or a movie star, for example.
This vortex expresses alterations based on the lifestyle we lead. It uses and renews the energy in insufficient conditions.
It generates modifications in us, and those that surround us, through “tentacular energetic elongations” that connect themselves to other close beings. It also systematically gives us the capacity and the determination to put our life under our control.

The Kidneys and the Third Vortex

Urdvittrat ard sutri madviat animim adim vashtrim Anatronix

The kidneys hold pyramidal power, since their tissues are conical, or shaped like pyramids. The kidney mass has eighteen pyramidal subdivisions. The extensive pedestal of each pyramid touches the kidney cortex and its apex points towards the interior. The pyramids that are constituted by parallel segments of renal tubes are used by the light beings to introduce radiance to the lymphocytes and leukocytes that surround the area.
These conical shapes regulate and intensify the celestial radiance.
The enzyme renin and the glycoprotein hormone, which raises fire when erythrocytes are produced, benefit from these light inoculations and increases vitamin D production.
Renin, with its 340 amino acids, is being modified at this precise moment. The Seraphim are extracting two amino acids and are adding the energy codes of three special amino acids found in meteorites here on Earth. After this, with the help of the Seraphim, the modified renin is forced to be segregated into the kidney. The sodium molecules in the serum are oscillated at such high speed that they produce a sound imperceptible to the human ear; this sound replicates the sodium molecules that are

physiologically necessary for the proper functioning of the cells. This homeostasis is vital to the micro-universe inside the human body.
The steroidal hormones, known as mineralocorticoids, have been prompted in your body using energy at three different speeds so they can reabsorb the sodium profusion and pyramidal energy. The kidney's distal tentacles are used for this process.
Sodium and water have homeostatically engaging ions. We take advantage of such dynamism and electromagnetically manipulate this sodium water with the purpose of altering the individual's auric body. At the same time, the amount of circulating liquid in the body increases when filtered with a kind of net of messianic filaments, and astral liquid light is produced with the intention of regulating the hydrostatic and homeostatic pressures without there being any inflammation in the extremities. This pressure, the result of the vertiginous interexchange of transmuted watery-blood and electromagnetic exchange, is generated to create subliminal energy fields inside the physical body, which prepares the soul for ascension.

Fourth Vortex and Liver

Ashmitraviat ashmatarak triutmitrat aditadir Nabi-el

In the fourth vortex, we will make the liver produce less cholesterol and bile, since there will be less fat to decompose. Due to all these changes, fat will not be deposited in the tissues, since it will be burned before it reaches the liver. We are now taking some proteins and amino acids from this vortex to create a fiery human light, which will be fed to the third vortex. The glycogen and iron stored in the liver will serve as fuel to increase this fiery light.
The liver will begin to work optimally and will eliminate from the bloodstream any substance that is harmful to the psycho-biological organism.
During this process, the Seraphim's advice is not to drink alcoholic beverages or any heavy substances that have to be processed by the liver.
The enzymes of the pancreatic nectar are used to decompose the little fat that enters the fourth vortex as you read. The proteins and carbohydrates will be almost disintegrated by the enzymes' power, which will increase conjunctly with the nucleic acids and insulin; such action will decompose the molecular structure of these, producing a heat that is experienced in the Buddhist practice called Tumo. This metabolic process will join the

nourishment of the fiery human light. The glucose level will not be affected; it will remain as before, depending on the individual's karma. However, in a few cases, if there is any diabetes, this may come to be completely healed because of this modification.
The gall bladder will take care of the excess of bile and will transport it directly into the intestine. This bile excess won't be allowed into the blood stream.

Digestion

The digestion will become optimal. The duodenal mucus will segregate colecistoquinine without further consideration; this will force the gall bladder to convulse softly.
We are taking advantage of the digestive process to increase the intense fire with the purpose of cleansing and purifying not just the biological wrap, but the astral body as well. The pyloric portion of the stomach will produce a pure substance similar to gastrine that will unchain the production of gastric fluid with a high content of light, which will increase the intestinal peristaltic contractions. It is recommended for the reader in this period to take magnesium sulfate to speed up the detoxification process.
The gastrointestinal hormones in the duodenum are receiving electro-dynamic frequencies that will stimulate the production of pancreatic nectar with a high content of bicarbonate with the purpose of counteracting the acidity of the new manifestation of gastric fluid.
This balance created in the organs of the fourth vortex will affect the brain in a positive way, since the blockage inserted there by the Nebula has affected the vascular brain dysfunction for millennia. Certain neurodegenerative diseases come from this inoculation of astral tar made by the beings that live in between dimensions.
On the astral level, the fourth vortex uses sporadic lightning of violet light to incite the liver to produce the IGF hormone. Shortly after this hormone absorbs the violet energies, it will be molecularly codified in a way similar to pancreatic insulin. As a consequence, both substances will coexist, tricking the psycho-biological system into producing the creation of new brain vessels, and neuronal reproduction will in turn be stimulated. In this way, the brain will be constantly irrigated, fresh, and awake. This freshness will prevent any type of temperature change caused by the radiant fire of the third and fourth vortices.

THE KIDNEYS HOLD PYRAMIDAL POWER, SINCE THEIR TISSUES ARE CONICAL, OR SHAPED LIKE PYRAMIDS. THE KIDNEY MASS HAS EIGHTEEN PYRAMIDAL SUBDIVISIONS. THE EXTENSIVE PEDESTAL OF EACH PYRAMID TOUCHES THE KIDNEY CORTEX AND ITS APEX POINTS TOWARDS THE INTERIOR. THE PYRAMIDS THAT ARE CONSTITUTED BY PARALLEL SEGMENTS OF RENAL TUBES ARE USED BY THE LIGHT BEINGS TO INTRODUCE RADIANCE TO THE LYMPHOCYTES AND LEUKOCYTES THAT SURROUND THE AREA. THESE CONICAL SHAPES REGULATE AND INTENSIFY THE CELESTIAL RADIANCE. THE ENZYME RENIN AND THE GLYCOPROTEIN HORMONE, WHICH RAISES FIRE WHEN ERYTHROCYTES ARE PRODUCED, BENEFIT FROM THESE LIGHT INOCULATIONS AND INCREASE VITAMIN D PRODUCTION. RENIN WITH ITS 340 AMINO ACIDS, IS BEING MODIFIED AT THIS PRECISE MOMENT. THE SERAPHIM ARE EXTRACTING TWO AMINO ACIDS AND ARE ADDING THE ENERGY CODES OF THREE SPECIAL AMINO ACIDS FOUND IN METEORITES HERE ON EARTH. AFTER THIS, WITH THE HELP OF THE SERAPHIM, THE MODIFIED RENIN IS FORCED TO BE SEGREGATED INTO THE KIDNEY. THE SODIUM MOLECULES IN THE SERUM ARE OSCILLATED AT SUCH HIGH SPEED THAT THEY PRODUCE A SOUND IMPERCEPTIBLE TO THE HUMAN EAR; THIS SOUND REPLICATES THE SODIUM MOLECULES THAT ARE PHYSIOLOGICALLY NECESSARY FOR THE PROPER FUNCTIONING OF THE CELLS. THIS HOMEOSTASIS IS VITAL TO THE MICRO-UNIVERSE INSIDE THE HUMAN BODY. THE STEROIDAL HORMONES KNOWN AS MINERALOCORTICOIDS HAVE BEEN PROMPTED IN YOUR BODY USING ENERGY AT THREE DIFFERENT SPEEDS TO REABSORB THE SODIUM PROFUSION AND PYRAMIDAL ENERGY. THE KIDNEY'S DISTAL TENTACLES ARE USED FOR THIS PROCESS. SODIUM AND WATER HAVE HOMEOSTATICALLY ENGAGING IONS. WE TAKE ADVANTAGE OF SUCH DYNAMISM AND ELECTROMAGNETICALLY MANIPULATE THIS SODIUM WATER WITH THE PURPOSE OF ALTERING THE INDIVIDUAL'S AURIC BODY. AT THE SAME TIME, THE AMOUNT OF CIRCULATING LIQUID IN THE BODY INCREASES WHEN FILTERED WITH A KIND OF NET OF MESSIANIC FILAMENTS, AND ASTRAL LIQUID LIGHT IS PRODUCED WITH THE INTENTION OF REGULATING THE HYDROSTATIC AND HOMEOSTATIC PRESSURES WITHOUT THERE BEING ANY INFLAMMATION IN THE EXTREMITIES.

THIS PRESSURE, THE RESULT OF THE VERTIGINOUS INTEREXCHANGE OF TRANSMUTED WATERY-BLOOD AND ELECTROMAGNETIC EXCHANGE, IS GENERATED TO CREATE SUBLIMINAL ENERGY FIELDS INSIDE THE PHYSICAL BODY, WHICH PREPARES THE SOUL FOR ASCENSION. {FOURTH VORTEX AND THE SOLAR PLEXUS} {ASHMITRAVIAT ASHMATARAK TRIUTMITRAT ADITADIR NABI-EL} IN THE FOURTH VORTEX, WE WILL MAKE THE LIVER PRODUCE LESS CHOLESTEROL AND BILE, SINCE THERE WILL BE LESS FAT TO DECOMPOSE. DUE TO ALL THESE CHANGES, FAT WILL NOT BE DEPOSITED, SINCE IT WILL BE BURNED BEFORE IT REACHES THE LIVER. WE ARE NOW TAKING SOME PROTEINS AND AMINO ACIDS OF THIS VORTEX TO CREATE A FIERY HUMAN LIGHT, WHICH WILL BE FED TO THE THIRD VORTEX. THE GLYCOGEN AND THE IRON STORED IN THE LIVER WILL SERVE AS FUEL TO INCREASE THIS FIERY LIGHT. THE LIVER WILL BEGIN TO WORK OPTIMALLY AND WILL ELIMINATE ANY SUBSTANCE THAT IS HARMFUL TO THE PSYCHO-BIOLOGICAL ORGANISM FROM THE BLOODSTREAM. DURING THIS PROCESS, THE SERAPHIM'S ADVICE IS NOT TO DRINK ALCOHOLIC BEVERAGES OR ANY HEAVY SUBSTANCE THAT HAS TO BE PROCESSED BY THE LIVER. THE ENZYMES OF THE PANCREATIC NECTAR ARE USED TO DECOMPOSE THE LITTLE FAT THAT ENTERS THE FOURTH VORTEX AS YOU READ. THE PROTEINS AND THE CARBOHYDRATES WILL BE ALMOST DISINTEGRATED BY THE ENZYMES' POWER, WHICH WILL INCREASE CONJUNCTLY WITH THE NUCLEIC ACIDS AND INSULIN; SUCH ACTION WILL DECOMPOSE THE MOLECULAR STRUCTURE OF THESE, PRODUCING A HEAT THAT IS EXPERIENCED IN THE BUDDHIST PRACTICE CALLED TUMO. THIS METABOLIC PROCESS WILL JOIN THE NOURISHMENT OF THE FIERY HUMAN LIGHT. THE GLUCOSE LEVEL WILL NOT BE AFFECTED; IT WILL REMAIN AS BEFORE, DEPENDING ON THE INDIVIDUAL'S KARMA. HOWEVER, IN A FEW CASES, IF THERE IS ANY DIABETES, THIS MAY COME TO BE COMPLETELY HEALED BECAUSE OF THIS MODIFICATION. THE GALL BLADDER WILL TAKE CARE OF THE EXCESS OF BILE AND WILL

TRANSPORT IT DIRECTLY INTO THE INTESTINE. THIS BILE EXCESS WO
WITHOUT FURTHER CONSIDERATION; THIS WILL FORCE THE GALL
LEANSING AND PURIFYING NOT JUST THE BIOLOGICAL WRAP,
L UNCHAIN THE PRODUCTION OF GASTRIC FLUID WITH A
IN THIS PERIOD TO TAKE MAGNESIUM SULFATE TO S
C FREQUENCIES THAT WILL STIMULATE THE PRODU
ITY OF THE NEW MANIFESTATION OF GASTRIC
TIVE WAY, SINCE THE BLOCKAGE THAT WAS
CERTAIN NEURODEGENERATIVE DISEAS
EN DIMENSIONS. ON THE ASTRAL L
LIVER TO PRODUCE THE IGF HO
BE MOLECULARLY CODIFIED
BSTANCES WILL COEXIS
THE CREATION OF NE
TURN BE STIMU
LY IRRIGATED
PREVENT
CAUSE
THI

HT
IANT
TEMPERA
AKE. THIS
AY, THE BRAIN
AND NEURONAL REP
CHO-BIOLOGICAL SYS
ANCREATIC INSULIN. AS A
IS HORMONE ABSORBS THE VIO
SES SPORADIC LIGHTNING OF VIO
ION OF ASTRAL TAR MADE BY THE
A HAS AFFECTED THE VASCULAR BRAIN
IN THE ORGANS OF THE FOURTH VORTEX, WI
A HIGH CONTENT OF BICARBONATE WITH THE PU
S. THE GASTROINTESTINAL HORMONES IN THE DUOD
NCREASE THE INTESTINAL PERISTALTIC CONTRACTIONS
ORIC PORTION OF THE STOMACH WILL PRODUCE A PURE SU
KING ADVANTAGE OF THE DIGESTIVE PROCESS TO INCREASE T
DIGESTION}THE DIGESTION WILL BECOME OPTIMAL. THE DUODENA

THE PRIMITIVE FREQUENCY PATTERNS OF THE BRAIN THAT LACKS
RINGS SO THAT THEY ARE ANALOGOUS TO THE RING OF AMINO A
HO2CCH(NH2)CH2SH, WHICH MAKES IT SIMILAR TO THE 32 POL
D PRESSURE. THE RING OF THE ATRIAL NATRIURETIC PEP
A CONSEQUENCE, NOTE THAT THE ARTERIAL CIRCULA
URPOSE OF REDUCING WATER AND SODIUM IN THE
S CIRCUMFERENCE, WITH THE PURPOSE OF AFF
CAL LIGHT; IN THIS WAY, THEY WILL DI
MINO ACIDS OF THE ATRIAL NATRIUR
DUCE A POTENT VASODILATATION
ONSTITUTED BY THE ALLIANCE
IS STIMULATES THE PRODUC
IONS COMING FROM THE
RE. THE HEART IS IN
IERY CHANGES B
IT—AMONG OT
S TO IMPR
ON ON
HT

E FIFTH VOR

{

TEX}
LEVEL I
CIRCULATIO
EP THE BODY C
HE DEVAS OF ATOM
A METAMORPHOSIS O
AND OTHER AREAS OF GEO
ETIC PEPTIDE (ANP), WHICH
THROUGH MAGNANIMOUS PEPTIC
Y SCIENTISTS. AS YOU READ, THE SE
E CENTER OF THE MOLECULE, WHICH IS W
ING ONLY NINETEEN AMINO ACIDS IN THE
OF THE WATER IN THE PSYCHO-BIOLOGICAL COV
YPE OF ENERGETIC STAGNATION. IN SOME CASES,
FFERENT THINGS; WE ARE SIMPLY LOOKING TO GENERAT
OMS OF SULFUR IN BETWEEN TWO RESIDUES OF AMINO ACI
IAC VENTRICLES. WE WILL INSERT SPECIFIC AMINO ACIDS OF
IMILARITY WILL LET US CONNECT THE BRAIN'S VIBRATIONS WITH

CIDS FOUND IN THE BRAIN; THIS CREATED S

THE COOLING CARDIAC VIBRATIONS, MODIFYING

LOVE. IF YOU MAKE THE EFFORT TO FAST (GO WITHOUT FOOD), THE ELONGATED AND MULTINUCLEATED CELLS, WITH THE SPASMODIC CARDIAC CAPACITY OF THE HEART AURICLES, WILL RELEASE THE EXCESS OF ANP, WHICH, IN CONJUNCTION WITH THE BOMBING OF THE SEVEN-DIMENSIONAL LIGHTS, WILL GENERATE A ROBUST DISTENTION IN THE AURICULAR SECTIONS. THE READING OF THIS BOOK WILL INCREASE THE ANP PRODUCTION IN THE BRAIN AT A HIGHER SCALE SO THAT THERE IS A COMMUNICATION SIMILAR TO THE ALLOTROPIC COMMUNICATION THAT THE DIAMOND EMANATES. THIS WILL HAPPEN IN THE ASTRAL-CAUSAL LEVEL BETWEEN THE HEART AND THE MIND. SUBMERGING IN THE COLD AND PURE FEMININE WATER OF LAKES, RIVERS, AND OCEANS INCREASES THE ANP SECRETION ALSO, INDUCING THE STRETCHING OF THE AURICULAR NERVE DUE TO THE STIMULATION OF THE DISTRIBUTION OF THE INTRAVASCULAR LIQUID; THE WATER OF THESE SACRED PLACES ALSO CLEANS OTHER ENERGIES BORNE FROM THE NEBULA. TAKE ADVANTAGE OF THE COLD WATERS; SUBMERGE IN THEM WHENEVER YOU ARE STRONG AND HEALTHY AND BE MINDFUL OF YOUR GEOGRAPHIC LOCATION DURING WINTER. THE CRYSTALLINE LIGHT THAT WE ARE NOW SHARING WITH YOU, FORCES THE ALLIANCE RECEPTORS, ON AN ASTRAL LEVEL, TO STIMULATE THE DEFLATION OF THE BLOOD'S VOLUME; THIS CAUSES A DECLINE IN THE CARDIAC CALORIC CONSUMPTION. THE SYSTEMIC ARTERIAL PRESSURE WILL DROP SIMULTANEOUSLY WITHOUT DISCRETION. WE WILL ALSO BOOST THE METABOLIC PROCESS. MODIFYING THE LIPIDS OF THE ORGANISM TO PROMOTE FATTY ACIDS AND GLYCEROL. IN SOME CASES, WE WILL REDUCE THE RENAL ABSORPTION OF SODIUM AND THE VOLUME CAUSED BY THE HORMONAL SYSTEM THAT HELPS TO NORMALIZE THE BLOOD PRESSURE. THE ANATOMIC EXTRACELLULAR VOLUME WILL DECREASE, AND THE BLOOD CIRCULATION WILL FLOW WITHOUT BECOMING STAGNANT AT ANY POINT. ON CERTAIN OCCASIONS, AT THE BEGINNING, THE BODY WEIGHT WILL BE REDUCED BY THESE ALCHEMICAL CHANGES. {THE SIXTH VORTEX.} {IRIXTIAM AS HUITMAT BATRAKT AMADTIAM RAFA I-YL THYMUS} IN THE THREE-DIMENSIONAL FIELD OF THE SIXTH VORTEX, WE AFFECT THE THYMUS WITH GREEN FLUORESCENT LIGHT; THE PURPOSE OF THIS IS TO

PRODUCE THE THYMOLIN, THYMOSIN AND THYMOPOIETIN HORMONES THESE HORMONES ACT ON THE LYMPHOCYTES WITH GOLDEN SHINING RAYS. WHICH EMANATE FROM ITS CENTRAL RHOMBOIDAL ASTRAL APEX, SO THEY BECOME PLASMATIC CELLS, PROMOTING ANTIBODIES WITH RED AND PINK FIERY AURAS. EVEN IF THE READER HAS ALREADY GONE THROUGH THE PUBERTY PHASE, BY USING ELECTRO-CRYSTALLINE WAVES, WE WILL MAKE SURE THAT THE THYMUS LOSES ITS FAT TISSUES AND THAT IT DOESN'T DIMINISH IN SIZE WITH TIME. IN THIS PRECISE INSTANT. WE ARE INFLUENCING THE LYMPHATIC SYSTEM WITH CRYSTALLINE LIGHT, SO THE READER HAS A STABLE AND STRONG IMMUNE SYSTEM. AT THE SAME TIME, WE INCREASE THE T-LYMPHOBLASTOIDS, THROUGH INJECTIONS OF SUPRA MAGENTA LIGHT SPIRALS, THAT REACH THE CENTER OF THE BONE MARROW. THROUGHOUT THIS PROCESS, THE T-LYMPHOBLASTOIDS ARE RE-PROGRAMMED WITH INCANDESCENT LIGHTNING WITH THE PURPOSE OF MAKING YOU ACQUIRE SPECIFIC ANTIGENIC CRYSTALLINE RECEPTORS WITH ANGELICAL INTELLIGENCE SO THEY CAN MOVE FREELY WITHOUT ATTACKING THE READER'S ANTIGENS. WE ARE OPTIMIZING THE PSYCHO-BIOLOGICAL ORGANISM, ALONG WITH THE ASTRAL AND CAUSAL BODIES, EXTRACTING DARK PATTERNS, CLEANING SHADOWS, AND PLANTING LUMINOUS CRYSTAL FLOWERS OF PURE LIGHT. …

Fifth Vortex

The fifth vortex is located in the middle point of the chest area. It symbolizes stability, symmetry and Love.
It is the diocese of vital force, where physical and spiritual energies reside. It is known as the soul's abode. From here you can listen to a sound vibration that resembles that of a dynamo, this sound can bring forth enlightenment.
It gives us the capacity of transformation while remaining grounded.
When balanced, a sensation of calmness seems to embrace the person, and openness, tolerance, comprehension, kindness, compassion, and unconditional Love for everything and everyone become enhanced tremendously.
When the Anahata Chakra is appropriately stimulated, all wishes come true; this can be treacherous, because if we have unorganized thoughts, feelings, emotions, doubts, and aversions, they can also be materialized.
If this chakra becomes out of balance, it can bring forth fear and preoccupation.
Symptoms of asthma, arterial hypertension, pulmonary and heart illness, colds, obsessions such as claustrophobia, disgust, unworthiness, and feelings of restraint or submission may assail the person.
This chakra bestows the power to fly like astral birds and understand their language.

Heart and the Fifth Vortex

Adriatmiat ustart atatrak kah adrmatrat Xiabiel

Our intention on a physical level in this area is to improve the blood circulation, since we use it—among other things—to keep the body cool during the fiery changes. The heart is incited to go through a metamorphosis of energetic undulations coming from the terrestrial center and other areas of geopathic alteration. This stimulates the production of atrial natriuretic peptide (ANP), which is a type of molecule constituted by the alliance of diverse amino acids through magnanimous peptic bonds. This will also produce a potent vasodilatation never before witnessed by scientists.
As you read, the Seraphim manipulate the twenty-eight amino acids of the atrial natriuretic peptide and distort the center of the molecule, which is where they implant an spherical light; in this way, they will divide the

twenty-eight amino acids, leaving only nineteen in the center and nine outside of its circumference, with the purpose of affecting the homeostatic control of the water in the psycho-biological covering, reducing water and sodium in the adipose tissue, preventing any type of energetic stagnation. In some cases, blood pressure may be lowered as a consequence.

Note that the arterial circulation and blood pressure are two different things. We are simply looking to generate good circulation with normal blood pressure.

The ring of the atrial natriuretic peptide is created by a union of two atoms of sulfur in between two residues of amino acids composed by the chemical formula HO2CCH(NH2) CH2SH, which makes it similar to the thirty-two polypeptide amino acids produced by cardiac ventricles. We will insert specific amino acids of circular photonic light in these ANP rings so that they are analogous to the ring of amino acids found in the brain; this created similarity will let us connect the brain's vibrations with the loving cardiac vibrations, modifying the primitive frequency patterns of the brain that lacks Love.

If you make the effort to fast (go without food), the elongated and multinucleated cells, with the spasmodic cardiac capacity of the heart auricles, will release the excess of ANP, which, in conjunction with the bombing of the seven-dimensional lights, will generate a robust distention in the auricular sections.

The reading of this book will increase the ANP production in the brain at a higher scale so that there is a communication similar to the allotropic communication that the diamond emanates.

Submerging in the cold and pure feminine water of lakes, rivers, and oceans increases the ANP secretion also, inducing the stretching of the Auricular nerve due to the stimulation of the distribution of the intravascular liquid; the water of these sacred places also cleans other energies borne from the Nebula. Take advantage of the cold waters; submerge in them whenever you are strong and healthy and be mindful of your geographic location during winter.

The crystalline light that we are now sharing with you forces the alliance receptors to stimulate the deflation of the blood's volume on an astral level; this causes a decline in the cardiac caloric consumption. The systemic arterial pressure will drop simultaneously without discretion. We will also boost the metabolic process, modifying the lipids of the organism to promote fatty acids and glycerol. In some cases, we will reduce the renal absorption of sodium and the volume caused by the hormonal system that helps to normalize the blood pressure.

The anatomic extracellular volume will decrease, and the blood circulation will flow without becoming stagnant at any point. On certain occasions, at the beginning, the body weight will be reduced by these alchemical changes.

The Sixth Vortex

Irixtiam ashuitmat batrakt amadtiam Rafa-yel

Thymus

In the three-dimensional field of the sixth vortex, we affect the thymus with green fluorescent light; the purpose of this is to produce the thymolin, thymosin and thymopoietin hormones.
These hormones act on the lymphocytes with golden shining rays, which emanate from its central rhomboidal astral apex, so they become plasmatic cells, promoting antibodies with red and pink fiery auras. Even if the reader has already gone through the puberty phase, by using electro-crystalline waves, we will make sure that the thymus loses its fat tissues and that it doesn't diminish in size with time.
In this precise instant, we are influencing the lymphatic system with crystalline light. At the same time, we increase the T-lymphoblastoids, through injections of supra magenta light spirals, that reach the center of the bone marrow.
Throughout this process, the T-lymphoblastoids are re-programmed with incandescent lightning with the purpose of making you acquire specific antigenic crystalline receptors with angelical intelligence so they can move freely without attacking the reader's antigens, so the reader has a stable and strong immune system.
We are optimizing the psycho-biological organism, along with the astral and causal bodies, extracting dark patterns, cleaning shadows, and planting luminous crystal flowers of pure light.

{ADORATM ADMIATAM TRATAISHTRAT ARIATRAM MIKHA-EL}WHEN WE GO DEEPER INTO CEREBRAL VORTICES, WE HAVE TO BE MORE CAREFUL AND GO SLOWER, SINCE THEY ARE HYPERSENSITIVE. IN THESE AREAS, WE PLANT A CRYSTALLINE SEED OF LIGHT, WE WATER IT WITH TRANSCENDENTAL ENERGIES, AND WE HAVE INCOMMENSURABLE PATIENCE, SO BEAUTIFUL RADIANT SPHERES GROW LIKE FLOWERS AND SHARE THE THREE-DIMENSIONAL SPACE WITH THE PITUITARY, PINEAL AND OTHER GLANDS. WHEN THIS SPHERE OCCUPIES THE CAUSAL AND ASTRAL SPACES SUPERIMPOSED ON THE PITUITARY, IT MAKES THE GLANDS SEGREGATE THE HUMAN GROWTH HORMONE (HGH) ABUNDANTLY. REMEMBER THAT THESE HORMONES ARE TIED TO AGING, AND WE, LIKE THIS REGENERATE THE PHYSICAL BODIES (PLEASE EXCUSE THIS REDUNDANCY, BUT RIGHT NOW WE ARE MAKING THE NECESSARY ADJUSTMENTS IN THE ASTRAL LEVEL SO THAT THIS HAPPENS IN YOUR BODY); IF YOU PAY ATTENTION, YOU WILL REALIZE THAT THERE ARE SUBTLE MOVEMENTS OF ENERGY IN YOUR BRAIN WHILE YOU READ. THESE MOVEMENTS ALSO AFFECT THE THYROTROPIN SEGREGATION, WHICH STIMULATES THE THYROID TO PRODUCE FSH HORMONES. ON THE OTHER HAND, THE LUMINOUS CRYSTALLINE SPHERES REINSTALLED BY US (I SAY REINSTALLED BECAUSE WHEN THE HUMAN BEING HAD A THIRTEEN-SPIRAL DNA, (S)HE WAS CREATED WITH THOSE SPHERES, BUT THEY WERE ROBBED BY THE FORCES OF THE NEBULA) WILL INCREASE AND MODIFY THE PRODUCTION OF HORMONES COMPOSED BY MOLECULES OF A PROTEIN ADAPTED TO THE CARBOHYDRATES. SUCH HORMONES ARE INJECTED WITH LIFE, INTELLIGENCE, AND LIGHT IN THE HERE AND NOW SO THAT THESE, AMONG OTHER FUNCTIONS, HAVE THE GIFT OF CELLULAR RECOGNITION. THEY ARE PRESENTED AS DAZZLING ILLUMINATED POINTS OVER THE PLASMATIC SUPERFICIAL MEMBRANE, AND ARE PRODUCED BY THE PREFIXED LOBULE OF THE HYPOPHYSIS (PITUITARY GLAND). WITH TIME, THE SECRETION OF BRIGHTENED FOLLICULAR CELLS WILL INCREASE, AND CONSEQUENTLY WILL STRENGTHEN THE LIGHT SHINING IN THE THYROID. THE MOLECULAR WEIGHT OF THESE WILL INCREASE FROM APPROXIMATELY 28,000 DALTONS (DA), TO 29,700 DA. THIS CHANGE REVOLUTIONIZES THE THYROID AND DRASTICALLY INCREASES THE

SENT DEPENDS ON THE BODY'S GENDER.FSH IN FEMALES INSPIRES

RATION OF THE REDEMPTORY GONADOTROPHIN HORMONE, WHER

R AS BODY MASS GETS USED TO IT. WE WILL BALANCE THE S

STERS PERMANENTLY EMANATE. IN SOME CASES, THIS EN

TERIOR HYPOPHYSIS, WHERE THE PRODUCTION OF TH

IOUS AMINO ACIDS THROUGH PEPTIDE LINKS WHI

ESMERIZING LIGHT THAT WILL CHANGE YOUR O

PEPTIDE TRIAD THAT IS WREATHED BY CR

ALSO CONNECT THEM. THE ATTENTIV

HAT THERE ISN'T JUST ONE ENE

ETWEEN THE THYROTROPIN AND

IIODOTHYRONINE (T3) INTO

ON AND LUMINOUS ADJU

OTEIN PROVIDES AMI

THE VIRUS INJE

BULIN, WHICH

THIS PROT

HAD A

OF

D

ED P

EIGHT O

D TO ON EA

EHAVE IN A ST

ESS IN THE PAST.

IZE THYROIDAL HORMO

AND REGULATE THE RELEA

N UNUSUAL WAY. WHEN WE O

R CALLED THYROLIBERIN, WHICH

THESE VORTICES, BUT THAT CONCRE

ES THE NERVOUS TERMINATIONS OF THE

, ALONG WITH THE SERAPHIM, DISCHARGES

TACHED TO THE MOLECULAR STRUCTURE CONSTI

ITH THE HELP OF MESSIANIC RAYS UNTIL THEY RE

XTREME CHANGES WILL TAKE PLACE DUE TO EXTRA SEN

M TEMPORARILY, AND THE READER USUALLY LOSES WEIGHT;

A INSIDE THE CELLS. THE SYNTHESIS AND LIBERATION OF FSH

MPOSED OVER ENERGETIC VORTICES. THE WAY IN WHICH WE WORK

ESTROGEN RELEASE. FSH IN MALESIS RESPONSIBLE FOR SPERM PR

AWAKENING OF ASUNTARA. TWO MORE AMINO ACIDS ARE ATTA

CYANIDE OLIGOMERS THAT WERE EXTRACTED, HYDROLYZED,

DS ARE INSERTED, IN THE SHAPE OF THOUSANDS OF CRY

REQUIRE THE PRESENCE OF WATER TO BE TRANSFORM

CHAIN OF THE LH. SIMULTANEOUSLY, THREE COD

AND TSH WITH A BETA CHAIN OF 121 AMINO

RCULATE IN HIGHER INTERNAL ORBITS, WH

FINALLY, THIS CIRCULATING RADIAL

IGHTNESS CAUSED BY THE CHANGE,

MORE DENSE PARTICLES OF DE

CELLULAR DNA, IN THE AS

D ONE IN THE MIDDLE,

L BE SUPERIMPOSED

IN WOMEN WILL

ELEASE. IN O

URCE WILL

F THE

WI

TE

YCLE

TION IN

ALMIGHTY

THE OVULE'S M

OUGH THE DIFFERE

OWERFUL STRAND. AL

WILL BE ADDED, IN THE

THE END, TWO MORE FILAMENT

WITH LIGHT FILAMENTS, TO BE R

A'S ASCENSION, AND IN CONJUNCTION

E HUMAN BODY FOR THE AFOREMENTIONE

, THE SEXUAL\BRAIN CONNECTION CHANGES

S ARE ATTACHED IN THE SAME WAY TO THE ALP

OF HIGH TEMPERATURES, ARE ALSO INTRODUCED IN

THE ASTRAL ENERGY COUNTERPARTS OF AMINO ACIDS

ERAPHIM. ONCE THIS PERMUTATION HAS HAPPENED, THE E

S CONSTITUTED BY 92 AMINO ACIDS. ONE TYPE IS FOUND IN T

N AND SPERM, ARE USED TO PRODUCE THE ULTRA RADIANT FIERY

H WILL TURN INTO A 42 AMINO ACID PEPTIDE. THIS WILL CHANG
E EIGHTH VORTEX; THIS CONNECTION OPENS THE MIND, AND WI
A BABY, THE MILK PRODUCTION WILL BE HIGHER AND THE CH
HILDREN. SHE WON'T PRODUCE MILK DURING THIS CHANG
HAS WILL BE MODIFIED, PROVOKING AN ENERGY ALT
INTO THE FEMININE PROLACTIN THE GLOW OF T
URATION AND THE RESTORATION OF ITS QUADR
THE TESTICLES, INDUCING THE EXUDATI
MAGNETISM TO CONVINCE OTHERS OF
BE VERY DIFFICULT TO REJECT
LASTICITY OF THE SKIN; QUI
WILL BE REABSORBED. ENE
TION WILL ACQUIRE AN
L HER MENSTRUAL AN
DIFIED IN THIS
ULTRA CRYST
ICH WILL
ORPUS
FO
T
NING
OLDEN B
OGESTERONE
HE MENSTRUAL
N WILL BE ABLE T
E ENERGY THAT IS L
G COURSE. THE SECRETIO
E RECYCLED AS IN THE PAST
SKIN WILL POSSESS A RADIANCE
S BOOK AND GOES THROUGH THE CHA
T. THE MODIFIED LH IN MALES WILL COV
ITH SEVENTH DIMENSIONAL LIGHT, WHICH
DDISH FIERY GLOW INTO A SOLAR NUCLEAR BLA
THAT CRASHED HERE ON EARTH, AND THE 198 CHA
DUCE HIGHER AMOUNTS OF PROLACTIN AT ALL TIMES EV
D TO CAUSE AN ENERGETIC REDIRECTION. ON THE OTHER H
NAL ENERGY. WITH THIS SECRETION, THE FEMALE ENERGETIC
F LOVE. THESE PERMUTATIONS UNCHAIN CHANGES IN ALMOST ALL

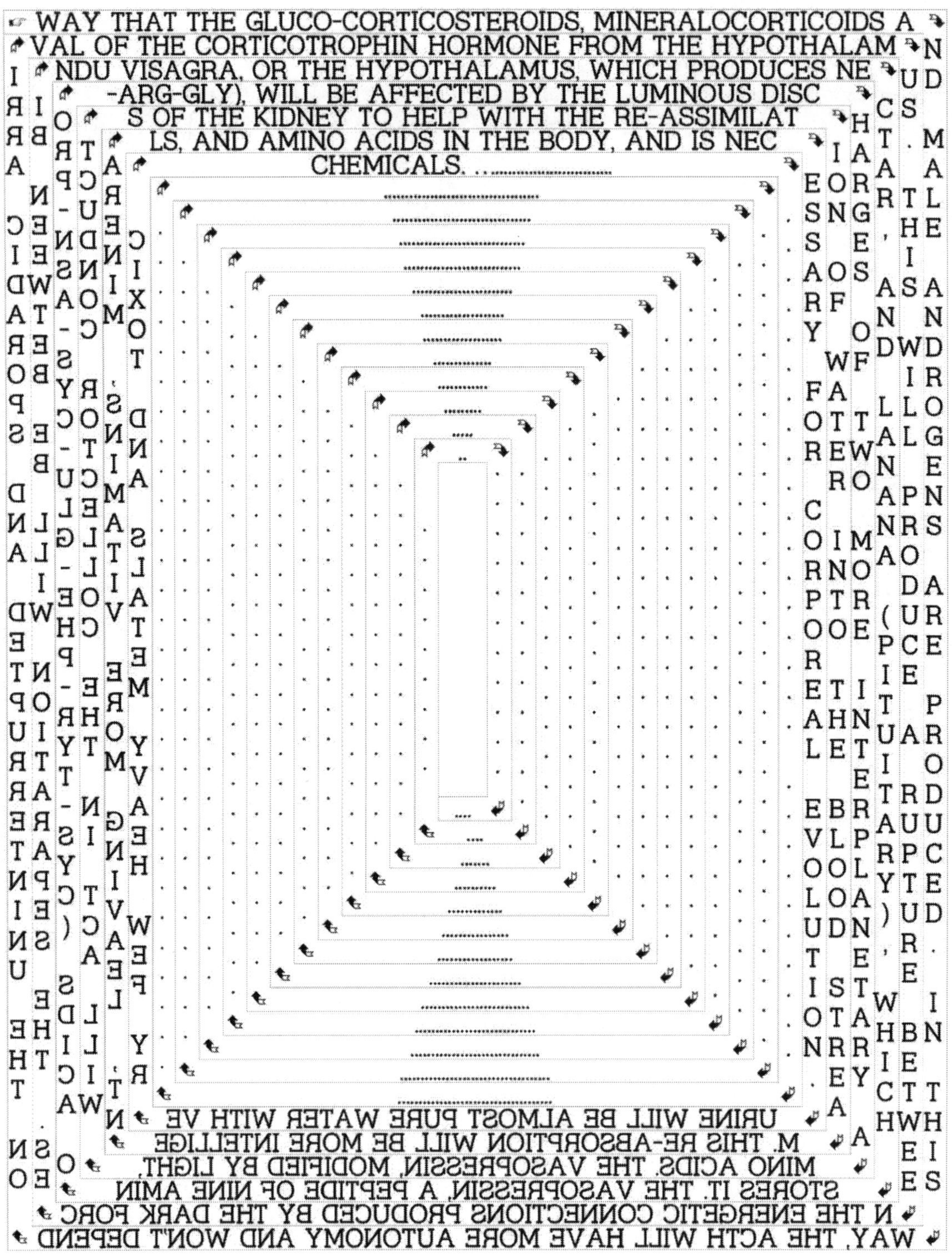
WAY THAT THE GLUCO-CORTICOSTEROIDS, MINERALOCORTICOIDS A
ND MALE ANDROGENS ARE PRODUCED. IN THIS
WAY, THE ACTH WILL HAVE MORE AUTONOMY AND WON'T DEPEND
ON THE UNINTERRUPTED AND SPORADIC ARRI
VAL OF THE CORTICOTROPHIN HORMONE FROM THE HYPOTHALAM
US. THIS WILL PRODUCE A RUPTURE BETWEE
N THE ENERGETIC CONNECTIONS PRODUCED BY THE DARK FORC
ES. THE SEPARATION WILL BE BETWEEN BI
NDU VISAGRA, OR THE HYPOTHALAMUS, WHICH PRODUCES NE
CTAR, AND LANANA (PITUITARY), WHICH
STORES IT. THE VASOPRESSIN, A PEPTIDE OF NINE AMIN
O ACIDS (CYS-TYR-PHE-GLU-CYS-ASN-PRO
-ARG-GLY), WILL BE AFFECTED BY THE LUMINOUS DISC
HARGES OF TWO MORE INTERPLANETARY A
MINO ACIDS. THE VASOPRESSIN, MODIFIED BY LIGHT,
WILL ACT IN THE COLLECTOR CONDUCT
S OF THE KIDNEY TO HELP WITH THE RE-ASSIMILAT
ION OF WATER INTO THE BLOODSTREA
M. THIS RE-ABSORPTION WILL BE MORE INTELLIGE
NT, LEAVING MORE VITAMINS, MINERA
LS, AND AMINO ACIDS IN THE BODY, AND IS NEC
ESSARY FOR CORPOREAL EVOLUTION.
URINE WILL BE ALMOST PURE WATER WITH VE
RY FEW HEAVY METALS AND TOXIC
CHEMICALS.

The Seventh Vortex

The seventh vortex is the fundamental axis of communication. Here, the disciple can reach lower levels of altered consciousness. In such states, all of the person's psychological problems are discarded and his/her energy gets depurated.
The seventh vortex has a connection with both the internal and the external; it relates to individuality and confers extrasensory perception.

Thyroid and the Seventh Vortex

Admatviat traktakatsatiam uditratim Anab-el Yori-el

The thyroid hormones thyroxine (T4) and triiodothyronine (T3) are injected with spirals of astral-causal light that reach their nucleus directly. The T3, which is more potent, is bathed with liquid light to incite it to subdivide and replicate as vertiginously as possible. These resultant hormones are assisted subsequently by an oxidation reaction in which a set of carboxyl is annulled from a molecule, establishing an accumulation of an alive and intelligent acetyl that makes up for the newly produced carbon dioxide. Said process calms the nervous electricity the reader experiences due to the suffered energetic change.
Subsequently, a systematic loss of iodine will take place along with a simultaneous reproduction of the same element. This will stabilize the mind.
The reader will enjoy sustained heat production, usage of oxygen, and the perfect organization of the hormonal systems.
After our adjustments, there will be a perfect synthesis of the growth hormone, and there will be neuronal maturity.
The created balance is such that the regulation of the metabolism of proteins, fats, and carbohydrates becomes almost perfect.
The process will be gradual and slow so the vital signs do not collapse.
The thyroidal hormones generated by this new balance created by the forces of absolute brightness help the body's heat to rise in climates with extremely cold temperatures.

The Eighth Vortex

The eighth vortex relates to the feminine energy of the tongue.

It occupies the astral realm of the pituitary in space-time $V = \frac{4}{3}\pi r^3$.
It gives the reader the vision of the great spiritual emptiness.

If this center is stimulated correctly, the practitioner will reach nine psychic faculties.
This vortex, however, presents the student with the danger of losing him/herself while enjoying these psychic powers, therefore moving away from the self-realization process.
This vortex gathers and spurs the nectar of immortality.

Pituitary and the Eighth Vortex

Adoratm admiatam trataishtrat ariatram Mikha-el

When we go deeper into cerebral vortices, we have to be more careful and go slower, since they are hypersensitive.
In these areas, we plant a crystalline seed of light, we water it with transcendental energies, and we have incommensurable patience until beautiful radiant spheres grow like flowers and share the three-dimensional space with the pituitary, pineal and other glands.
When one of these spheres occupies the causal and astral spaces superimposed on the pituitary, it makes the gland segregate the human growth hormone (HGH) abundantly. Remember that these hormones are tied to aging. Like this, we regenerate the physical bodies (please excuse this redundancy, but right now we are making the necessary adjustments in the astral level so that this happens in your body); if you pay attention, you will realize that there are subtle movements of energy in your brain while you read.
These movements also affect the thyrotropin segregation, which stimulates the thyroid to produce FSH hormones. On the other hand, the luminous crystalline spheres reinstalled by us (I say reinstalled because when the human being had a thirteen-spiral DNA, (s)he was created with those spheres, but they were robbed by the forces of the Nebula) will increase and modify the production of hormones composed by molecules of a protein adapted to the carbohydrates. Such hormones are injected with life,

intelligence, and light in the here and now so that these, among other functions, have the gift of cellular recognition. They are presented as dazzling illuminated points over the plasmatic superficial membrane, and are produced by the prefixed lobule of the hypophysis (pituitary gland). With time, the secretion of brightened follicular cells will increase, and consequently will strengthen the light shining in the thyroid.
The molecular weight of these will increase from approximately 28,000 Daltons (Da), to 29,700 Da.

This change revolutionizes the thyroid and drastically increases the degradation of an iodinated protein that had a molecular weight of 666,000 Da (correlating with the famous number of the beast described in the bible, which in reality refers to the change created by the forces of darkness implanted in the original human body). This protein is referred to on Earth as thyroglobulin, which has been forced to behave in a strange way due to the virus injected by the darkness in the past. This iodinated protein provides amino acids to synthesize thyroidal hormones; our modification and luminous adjustments will incite and regulate the release of thyroxin and triiodothyronine (T3) into the blood stream in an unusual way.
When we observe the connection between the thyrotropin and a hypothalamic regulator called thyroliberin, which controls it, we can say that there isn't just one energetic connection between these vortices, but that concrete chains of living matter also connect them.
The attentive reading of this book forces the nervous terminations of the hypothalamus to segregate a peptide triad that is wreathed by crystalline lighting. This book, along with the Seraphim, discharges over your three bodies as a mesmerizing light that will change your overall personality, which is attached to the molecular structure constituted by the association of various amino acids through peptide links that are now being moved very carefully with the help of messianic rays until they reach the glandular cells of the anterior hypophysis, where the production of thyrotropin is forced to increase.
Extreme changes will take place due to extra sensorial magnetism that the astral masters permanently emanate.
In some cases, this entire process increases the metabolism temporarily, and the reader usually loses weight; however, this symptom will disappear as body mass gets used to it.
In addition, we will be balancing the subatomic opposites that affect the DNA inside the cells.

The synthesis and liberation of FSH are pressed to unfold due to the suppuration of the redemptory gonadotrophin hormone, where we find another physical union superimposed over energetic vortices.
The way in which we work with the human body when the FSH is present depends on the body's gender. FSH in females inspires estrogen release. FSH in males is responsible for sperm production.
These two factors, the estrogen and sperm, are used to produce the ultra radiant fiery light that will be responsible for the awakening of Asuntara.
Two more amino acids are attached to the luteinizing hormone that is constituted by ninety-two amino acids. One type is found in the lunar surface and originated from cyanide oligomers that were extracted, hydrolyzed, and molecularly decomposed by the Seraphim. Once this permutation has happened, the encrypting and codes of the amino acids are inserted into the hormone in the shape of thousands of crystalline strands.
The astral energy counterparts of amino acids coming from asteroids that don't require the presence of water to be transformed and that received solar winds of high temperatures are also introduced in this moment into this amino acid chain of the LH. Simultaneously, three codes of interplanetary amino acids are attached in the same way to the alpha subunit found in FSH and TSH with a beta chain of one hundred and twenty-one amino acids. With this modification, the sexual/brain connection changes and said energy begins to circulate in higher internal orbits, which regenerate and prepare the human body for the aforementioned intermolecular awakening. Finally, this circulating radial energy joins with Asuntara's ascension and, in conjunction with the explosion of brightness caused by the change, modifies that DNA—first with light filaments, to be replaced afterwards with denser particles of deoxyribonucleic acid. At the end, two more filaments will be added to the cellular DNA. In the astral body another two will be added, in the causal two more, and one in the center, which is the most powerful strand. All the filaments will be superimposed and connected through the different bodies.
The LH in women will glow and modify the ovule's meiosis and its release. In other words, the almighty light of the Source will affect ovulation in the middle of the menstrual cycle, where it will stimulate the vacant follicle, turning it into a corpus luteum of golden brilliance, which will distill the progesterone and take it to ultra crystalline levels. The menstrual phase will be modified in this way and the woman will be able to mentally control her menstrual and hormonal flow. The energy that is lost during menstruation will acquire an energetic, ascending course. The

secretion, on the other hand, will be reabsorbed. Energies and blood will be recycled as in the past without affecting the elasticity of the skin; quite to the contrary, the skin will possess radiance and magnetism that will be very difficult to reject. Any woman who reads this book and goes through the changes will have to use this magnetism to convince others into taking the way of the light.

The modified LH in males will cover the interstitial cells of the testicles, inducing the exudation of testosterone modified with seventh dimensional light, which will help Asuntara's restructuration and the restoration of its quadruple helix, and changing its reddish fiery glow into a solar nuclear blaze.

We will holographically add into the feminine prolactin the glow of two amino acids found in asteroids that crashed here on Earth, and the one hundred and ninety-eight chains of amino acids that prolactin has will be modified, provoking an energy alteration, since the female will produce higher amounts of prolactin at all times, even if she is not pregnant or with children. She won't produce milk during this change. The hormone will simply change to cause an energetic redirection. On the other hand, if the female is currently the mother of a baby, the milk production will be higher and the child will receive more depurated maternal energy.

With this secretion, the female energetically connects the fifth vortex with the eighth vortex; this connection opens the mind, and will take her to astro-dynamic horizons of Love.

These permutations unchain changes in almost all hormones.

The thirty-nine amino acid peptides ACTH will turn into forty-two amino acid peptides. This will change the way that the gluco-corticosteroids, mineralocorticoids and male androgens are produced.

In this way, the ACTH will have more autonomy and won't depend on the uninterrupted and sporadic arrival of the corticotrophin hormone from the hypothalamus. This will produce a rupture between the energetic connections produced by the dark forces. The separation will be between Bindu Visagra, or the hypothalamus, which produces nectar, and Lanana (pituitary), which stores it.

The vasopressin, a peptide of nine amino acids (Cys-Tyr-Phe-Glu-Cys-Asn-Pro-Arg-Gly), will be affected by the luminous discharges of two more interplanetary amino acids. The vasopressin, modified by light, will act in the collector conducts of the kidney to help with the re-assimilation of water into the blood stream. This re-absorption will be more intelligent, leaving more vitamins, minerals, and amino acids in the body, which are necessary for corporeal evolution. Urine will be almost pure water with very few heavy metals and toxic chemicals.

The Internal Eye Vortex

The ninth vortex is related to clairvoyance. From here originate the qualities of trust, solidarity, and enquiry for truth, as well as the gaze into the interior of being.
It makes the reader conscious of the mechanism of intelligence.
An additional function of this center is to leave behind the limitations imposed by time and space. In this way, it will give us a better vision of the space that surrounds us and will take out the veil of time that covers this apparent reality.
When this vortex lacks energy, the mind loses its center and becomes tense. An apparent mist covers it; this is the reason why the reflection process displays itself in planes of unorganized patterns. It will be here where a series of lucubration starts and where the path gets complicated. The levels of instinctive comprehension can digress, transfiguring and creating a pattern of illusions or hallucinations, nightmares, and headaches that might unchain serious psychological problems.

The Pineal Gland and its Connection to the Ninth Vortex

Adviashtat adviashtat taratakam Gabri-el-a

The pineal gland is a small endocrine gland in the center of the brain. It produces serotonin and DMT—a very important chemical for the light beings. This chemical is the key that opens the portals of the spirit and lets us unite with the expanded peace of multidimensional universes.
The melatonin and the serotonin are modified by the Seraphim with volts of lightning that are high in electrostatic content in order to exert influence over the modulations between vigil and sleep.
The pineal gland was affected by the Nebula, and that drastically changed the mood modulations of the human individual and his/her capacity for connection, as well as that of seeing other dimensions.
The DMT was censored by the children of the Nebula through processes that employed the use of gelatinous tar and a dark enzyme. However, the Seraphim will clean up the entire inconsistent residues that remain and, with time, they will make this psychoactive element start to grant visions from other unknown worlds and extensions.
The modified pineal gland will speed up the metabolism and will regulate the sexual development so that this happens in a balanced way with ascendant energy instead of descendent.

The modified pineal gland will work in synchronization with the hypothalamus and will give the body the perfect power to control basic needs, such as eating, drinking, sexual desires, etc. The pineal gland will turn into a type of slow biological watch that delays aging.

With the reading of this book, or the terrestrial practices of Kechari Mudra and Sun gazing, the pineal gland gets bigger, giving the human being the possibility of adapting to any extreme situation for a long time. The transformed individual will be able to live without eating much and won't be bothered by hunger, thirst, or weakness. It will also be able to control and redirect the sexual impulses without any problem whatsoever.

We are not saying that the natural impulses, like feeding, sexual desire, etc. are negative, but human beings have become slaves of these impulses, and other addictions as well. Here, we are simply talking about absolute freedom; you will be free from every addiction, no matter what it is.

The Luminous Ones will change patterns, grant visions, and bring endless surprises with the stimulation of this gland.

By the way, in this moment, the pineal gland is being restructured. Breathe in the prescribed manner, (inhaling 3 to 4 seconds or more if you are comfortable, hold for the same amount, exhale for the same amount and hold again keeping the same count all through) read the words again and focus in the middle of the brain if you would like to speed up the process. Do it even if you don't understand basic chemistry.

We will prevent the collapse of the serotonin, inhibiting its confinement inside the brain synapses.

The pineal gland will change its molecular structure and it will be incited to produce "neuro-modulator" chemicals modified by the light. These chemicals are called beta-irradiators (similar to the beta-carbolines, but with a visible difference on a molecular level) that will affect the brain so that it will be able to absorb its expansive universality.

The MAO is now being transformed and energy from amino acids from asteroids are being added to change its electromagnetic frequency and acquire inter-dimensional properties. Right now, we are energetically changing the X chromosome where MAO-A and B are situated.

We will focus on the monoamine oxidase since it conceives one of the worst modifications of the children of the Nebula. With this chemical, they broke all the bonds the humans had with the Source of all Radiance and, therefore, all its faction. We will reprogram, restructure, and restore this connection to any one who is reading now. However, the process will be gradual, since a drastic change could end up generating a serious hallucinatory psychosis.

The MAO-A (and this is scientifically proven on Earth by terrestrial scientists) dissolves serotonin, melatonin, epinephrine, and norepinephrine. The MAO-B dissolves phenylethylamine and other amino traces. Dopamine is affected by both groups.
By forcing the inhibition of MAO-A with flashes of light from the seventh dimension, we will block serotonin dissolution. With this interposition of light, the aggression, the lack of bodily temperance, rage, moods, drowsiness, nausea, erotic impulses and appetite will be completely under the control of the soul and the symptoms of depression associated with the physical body will disappear. On the other hand, the human being will enjoy high levels of norepinephrine and dopamine. With such intensity, you will understand the mental desegregations, hallucinations, pains, moods, and pain and pleasure swings caused by the dark forces with the only purpose of confusing you.
Additionally, the tyramine will be metabolized through MAO-B; this process will counter any headaches.
Through nuclear-molecular permutations, we will change the way this inhibition happens.
When we inhibit the MAO-B with columns of golden shining light for sufficient periods of time, we reduce the dissolution of the dopamine and phenylethylamine. This process will restore life to the real metabolic absorption of the tyramine; all these chemicals combined will make the human being experience ascendant ecstasy.
The phenylhydroxylamine will be reformed with ultra potent oscillations and convulsing vibrations that change its molecular structure with the purpose of giving inter-dimensional vision to the human.
The improvement of this inhibition will open the dazzling gate for the boost of the N, N- dimethyltryptamine concentration.
In humans, DMT only occurs naturally in small amounts because the forces of the children of the Nebula managed to inhibit its production. The specific function of DMT lies in the neurotransmission of information connected to luminous fields from other dimensions.
The DMT will be carefully handled through tryptophan, an essential amino acid produced by the radiant Seraphim with the help of an enzyme present in non-neural tissues that catalyzes chemical amalgamations that are structurally related.
The DMT particles are analogous to the serotonin neurotransmitter. We can make the serotonin molecules spin very fast, one hundred and eight times counterclockwise at a speed of 343m/s. This spinning process makes the melatonin and other psychedelic tryptamines, such as 5-MeO-DMT, bufotenine and psilocine, activate with divine radiance.

DMT, serotonin, melatonin and other such biochemicals are known on Earth to have psychedelic properties, especially when these are regenerated and recharged.
From our point of view, since human beings were modified by the dark forces, present-day humans are perpetually hallucinating a dark reality that is inexistent to us. That is why we propose that this group of hormones and amino acids have to be altered; so that the human can see the reality of the light dimensions again.
The change might look unnatural when the reader starts to see other dimensions since (s)he may not be used to it, but we guarantee that this is your natural state, and that the condition that you are used to is just a sensorial slavery that must be broken to go back to the natural state created by the Source of all Radiance.
Don't be scared; the change will be gradual and peaceful.
When the dark forces modified humans in the past, they started to live locked up in their present perceptual dungeon. Many didn't withstand the change and died, others committed suicide, some of them lost their senses and suffering choked them; a few survived and they got used to the suffering. You are their descendants.
We couldn't revert the change immediately because Ci-tri-ini 1 (the channel located in the middle of the spine) was left very weak and the darkness' resolution was strong; but now, thanks to the Source of all Radiance and the humans, darkness has its days numbered and we and our resolutions are even stronger.
Currently, DMT has to do with the dreaming phenomenon. While dreaming, the DMT levels in the brain are amplified by the Seraphim to induce dreamlike hallucinations and awaken perceptual memories that are dormant in the DNA and that come from the repressed reality. This is how, for thousands of years, the light beings started to stimulate the pineal gland so it would produce higher and higher doses. For example, in the year 1000 BC, the dreams were very different from the dreams of 100, or 2000 AD. In each period of time, the manner in which we dream has changed, thanks to the Seraphim.
Serotonin and melatonin production are somehow involved in the psychic phenomena. It is important to note that a lot of hallucinogenic substances are chemical relatives of those produced by the pineal gland.
When the pineal gland is geomagnetically stimulated, it produces chemical substances that are similar to the ones we find in hallucinogenic plants that alter consciousness. Other terrestrial studies show that psychedelic drugs alter the melatonin and serotonin levels, which, in some cases, results in hallucinatory psychosis.

Understand that there is no need for any external catalyst to access other dimensions. Everything that we need is within; we only have to make an internal adjustment. This way, we can make sure that the path is safe and sound.
The Seraphim use electromagnetic and geomagnetic fields that greatly affect the production of the corporal molecular activity.
The Source of all Radiance will make strong changes in the terrestrial environmental magnetic field, increasing and decreasing its gravitational power sporadically. These modifications will inhibit the hydroxindole O-methyltransferase (HIOMT) production.
The enzyme serotonin N-acetyltransferase is strongly affected by the individual electromagnetic fields created by us right this second, while you read.
In conclusion, the human shell is hypersensitive and any important permutation of the terrestrial magnetic field will produce a natural hallucinogenic avalanche that will let us be more psychically receptive.

SEXUAL IMPULSES WITHOUT ANY PROBLEM WHATSOEVER. WE ARE

UATION FOR A LONG TIME. THE TRANSFORMED INDIVIDUAL WILL

READING OF THIS BOOK, OR THE TERRESTRIAL PRACTICES OF

POWER TO CONTROL THE BASIC NEEDS, SUCH AS EATING,

WITH ASCENDANT ENERGY INSTEAD OF DESCENDENT.

S AND EXTENSIONS. THE MODIFIED PINEAL GLAN

RE INCONSISTENT RESIDUES THAT REMAIN, AN

E NEBULA THROUGH PROCESSES THAT EMP

ND HIS/HER CAPACITY FOR CONNECTI

GLAND WAS AFFECTED BY THE NE

TROSTATIC CONTENT IN ORDER

IN AND THE SEROTONIN ARE

AND LETS US UNITE WI

CALLED DMT. THIS C

CES SEROTONIN

MALL ENDOCRI

TARAT TAT

THE N

G

S CO

{ADVIA

A}THE PINE

CENTER OF THE

ANT CHEMICAL FOR

THAT OPENS THE POR

E OF MULTIDIMENSIONAL U

HIM WITH VOLTS OF LIGHTNIN

THE MODULATIONS BETWEEN VIG

Y CHANGED THE MOOD MODULATIONS

NG OTHER DIMENSIONS. THE DMT WAS CE

AR AND A DARK ENZYME. HOWEVER, THE SE

PSYCHOACTIVE ELEMENT TO START TO GRANT V

D WILL REGULATE THE SEXUAL DEVELOPMENT SO TH

RK IN SYNCHRONIZATION WITH THE HYPOTHALAMUS AN

PINEAL GLAND WILL TURN INTO A TYPE OF SLOW BIOLOGIC

NEAL GLAND GETS BIGGER, GIVING THE HUMAN BEING THE POSS

WON'T BE BOTHERED BY HUNGER, THIRST, OR WEAKNESS. IT WILL

NOT SAYING THAT THE NATURAL IMPULSES LIKE FEEDING, SEXUAL DESIRE, ETC. ARE NEGATIVE, BUT HUMAN BEINGS HAVE BECOME SLAVES OF THESE IMPULSES, AND OTHER ADDICTIONS AS WELL. HERE WE ARE SIMPLY TALKING ABOUT ABSOLUTE FREEDOM; YOU WILL BE FREE FROM EVERY ADDICTION, NO MATTER WHAT IT IS. THE LUMINOUS ONES WILL CHANGE PATTERNS, GRANT VISIONS, AND WILL BRING ENDLESS SURPRISES WITH THE STIMULATION OF THIS GLAND. BY THE WAY, IN THIS MOMENT, THE PINEAL GLAND IS BEING RESTRUCTURED. BREATHE IN THE PRESCRIBED MANNER, READ MY WORDS AGAIN AND FOCUS ON THE MIDDLE OF THE BRAIN IF YOU WOULD LIKE TO SPEED UP THE PROCESS. DO IT EVEN IF YOU DON'T UNDERSTAND BASIC CHEMISTRY. WE WILL PREVENT THE COLLAPSE OF THE SEROTONIN, INHIBITING ITS CONFINEMENT INSIDE THE BRAIN SYNAPSES. THE PINEAL GLAND WILL CHANGE ITS MOLECULAR STRUCTURE AND IT WILL BE INCITED TO PRODUCE "NEURO-MODULATOR" CHEMICALS MODIFIED BY THE LIGHT. THESE CHEMICALS ARE CALLED ELECTROACOUSTIC BETA-IRRADIATORS (SIMILAR TO THE BETA-CARBOLINES, BUT WITH A VISIBLE DIFFERENCE ON A MOLECULAR LEVEL) THAT WILL AFFECT THE BRAIN SO THAT IT WILL BE ABLE TO ABSORB ITS EXPANSIVE UNIVERSALITY. THE MAO IS NOW BEING TRANSFORMED, AND ENERGY FROM AMINO ACIDS FROM ASTEROIDS ARE BEING ADDED TO CHANGE ITS ELECTROMAGNETIC FREQUENCY AND ACQUIRE INTER-DIMENSIONAL PROPERTIES. RIGHT NOW, WE ARE ENERGETICALLY CHANGING THE X CHROMOSOME WHERE MAO-A AND B ARE SITUATED. WE WILL FOCUS ON THE MONOAMINE OXIDASE SINCE IT CONCEIVES ONE OF THE WORST MODIFICATIONS OF THE CHILDREN OF THE NEBULA. WITH THIS CHEMICAL, THEY BROKE ALL THE BONDS THAT THE HUMANS HAD WITH THE SOURCE OF ALL RADIANCE, AND THEREFORE, ALL ITS FACTION. WE WILL REPROGRAM, RESTRUCTURE, AND RESTORE THIS CONNECTION TO THE ONE THAT IS READING NOW. HOWEVER, THE PROCESS WILL BE GRADUAL SINCE A DRASTIC CHANGE COULD END UP IN A SERIOUS HALLUCINATORY PSYCHOSIS. THE MAO-A (AND THIS IS SCIENTIFICALLY PROVEN ON EARTH BY TERRESTRIAL SCIENTISTS) DISSOLVES SEROTONIN, MELATONIN, EPINEPHRINE, AND NOREPINEPHRINE. THE MAO-B DISSOLVES PHENYLETHYLAMINE

AND OTHER AMINO TRACES. DOPAMINE IS AFFECTED BY BOTH GROUPS. BY FORCING THE INHIBITION OF MAO-A WITH FLASHES OF LIGHT FROM THE SEVENTH DIMENSIONS, WE WILL BLOCK SEROTONIN DISSOLUTION. WITH THIS INTERPOSITION OF LIGHT, THE AGGRESSION, THE LACK OF BODILY TEMPERANCE, RAGE, MOODS, DROWSINESS, NAUSEA, EROTIC IMPULSES AND APPETITE WILL BE COMPLETELY UNDER THE CONTROL OF THE SOUL AND THE SYMPTOMS OF DEPRESSION ASSOCIATED WITH THE PHYSICAL BODY WILL DISAPPEAR. ON THE OTHER HAND, THE HUMAN BEING WILL ENJOY HIGH LEVELS OF NOREPINEPHRINE AND DOPAMINE. WITH SUCH INTENSITY, YOU WILL UNDERSTAND THE MENTAL DESEGREGATIONS, HALLUCINATIONS, PAINS, MOODS, AND PAIN AND PLEASURE SWINGS CAUSED BY THE DARK FORCES WITH THE ONLY PURPOSE OF CONFUSING YOU. ADDITIONALLY, THE TYRAMINE WILL BE METABOLIZED THROUGH MAO-B; THIS PROCESS WILL COUNTER ANY HEADACHES. THROUGH NUCLEAR-MOLECULAR PERMUTATIONS, WE WILL CHANGE THE WAY THIS INHIBITION HAPPENS. WHEN WE INHIBIT THE MAO-B WITH COLUMNS OF GOLDEN SHINING LIGHT FOR SUFFICIENT PERIODS OF TIME, WE REDUCE THE DISSOLUTION OF THE DOPAMINE AND PHENYLETHYLAMINE. THIS PROCESS WILL RESTORE LIFE TO THE REAL METABOLIC ABSORPTION OF THE TYRAMINE; ALL THESE CHEMICALS COMBINED WILL MAKE THE HUMAN BEING EXPERIENCE ASCENDANT ECSTASY. THE PHENYLHYDROXYLAMINE WILL BE REFORMED WITH ULTRAPOTENT OSCILLATIONS AND CONVULSING VIBRATIONS THAT CHANGE ITS MOLECULAR STRUCTURE WITH THE PURPOSE OF GIVING INTER-DIMENSIONAL VISION TO THE HUMAN. THE IMPROVEMENT OF THIS INHIBITION WILL OPEN THE DAZZLING GATE FOR THE BOOST OF THE N, N- DIMETHYLTRYPTAMINE CONCENTRATION. IN HUMANS, DMT ONLY OCCURS NATURALLY IN SMALL AMOUNTS BECAUSE THE FORCES OF THE CHILDREN OF THE NEBULA MANAGED TO INHIBIT ITS PRODUCTION. THE SPECIFIC FUNCTION OF DMT LIES IN THE NEUROTRANSMISSION OF INFORMATION CONNECTED TO LUMINOUS FIELDS FROM OTHER DIMENSIONS. THE DMT WILL BE CAREFULLY HANDLED THROUGH TRYPTOPHAN, AN ESSENTIAL AMINO ACID PRODUCED BY THE RADIANT SERAPHIM WITH THE HELP OF AN ENZYME THAT IS PRESENT IN NON-NEURAL TISSUES, WHICH

CATALYZES CHEMICAL AMALGAMATIONS THAT ARE STRUCTURALLY RELATED. THE DMT PARTICLES ARE ANALOGOUS TO THE SEROTONIN NEUROTRANSMITTER. WE CAN MAKE THE SEROTONIN MOLECULES SPIN VERY FAST. 168TIMES COUNTERCLOCKWISE AT A SPEED OF 343M/S.THIS SPINNING PROCESS MAKES THE MELATONIN AND OTHER PSYCHEDELIC TRYPTAMINES SUCH AS 5-MEO-DMT, BUFOTENINE AND PSILOCINE ACTIVATE WITH DIVINE RADIANCE. DMT, SEROTONIN, MELATONIN AND OTHER SUCH BIOCHEMICALS ARE KNOWN ON EARTH TO HAVE PSYCHEDELIC PROPERTIES, ESPECIALLY WHEN THESE ARE REGENERATED AND RECHARGED. FROM OUR POINT OF VIEW, SINCE THE HUMAN BEINGS WERE MODIFIED BY THE DARK FORCES, PRESENT-DAY HUMANS ARE PERPETUALLY HALLUCINATING A DARK REALITY THAT IS INEXISTENT TO US. THAT IS WHY WE PROPOSE THAT THIS GROUP OF HORMONES AND AMINO ACIDS HAVE TO BE ALTERED; SO THAT THE HUMAN CAN SEE THE REALITY OF THE LIGHT DIMENSIONS AGAIN. THE CHANGE MIGHT LOOK UNNATURAL WHEN THE READER STARTS TO SEE OTHER DIMENSIONS SINCE (S)HE MAY NOT BE USED TO IT, BUT WE GUARANTEE THAT THIS IS YOUR NATURAL STATE, AND THAT THE CONDITION THAT YOU ARE USED TO IS JUST A SENSORIAL SLAVERY THAT MUST BE BROKEN TO GO BACK TO THE NATURAL STATE CREATED BY THE SOURCE OF ALL RADIANCE. DON'T BE SCARED; THE CHANGE WILL BE GRADUAL AND PEACEFUL. WHEN THE HUMAN WAS MODIFIED BY THE DARK FORCES IN THE PAST, IT STARTED TO LIVE LOCKED UP IN ITS PRESENT PERCEPTUAL DUNGEON. MANY DIDN'T WITHSTAND THE CHANGE AND DIED, OTHERS COMMITTED SUICIDE, SOME OF THEM LOST THEIR SENSES AND SUFFERING CHOKED THEM; A FEW SURVIVED AND THEY GOT USED TO THE SUFFERING. YOU ARE THEIR DESCENDANTS. WE COULDN'T REVERT THE CHANGE IMMEDIATELY BECAUSE CITRINI IN THE MIDDLE OF THE SPINE WAS LEFT VERY WEAK AND THE DARKNESS' RESOLUTION WAS STRONG; BUT NOW, THANKS TO THE SOURCE OF ALL RADIANCE AND THE HUMANS, DARKNESS HAS ITS DAYS NUMBERED AND WE AND OUR RESOLUTIONS ARE EVEN STRONGER. CURRENTLY, DMT HAS TO DO WITH THE DREAMING PHENOMENON. WHILE DREAMING, THE DMT LEVELS IN THE BRAIN ARE AMPLIFIED BY THE SERAPHIM TO INDUCE DREAMLIKE HALLUCINATION

ITIVE AND ANY IMPORTANT PERMUTATION OF THE TERRESTRIAL

TONIN N-ACETYLTRANSFERASE IS STRONGLY AFFECTED BY TH

, INCREASING AND DECREASING ITS GRAVITATIONAL POW

TLY AFFECT THE PRODUCTION OF THE CORPORAL MOL

KE AN INTERNAL ADJUSTMENT. THIS WAY, WE CA

. UNDERSTAND THAT THERE IS NO NEED FOR

TUDIES SHOW THAT PSYCHEDELIC DRUGS A

STANCES THAT ARE SIMILAR TO THE

SE PRODUCED BY THE PINEAL GL

HENOMENA. IT IS IMPORTANT

ANKS TO THE SERAPHIM. SE

00, OR 2000 AD. IN E

E, IN THE YEAR 1000

AL GLAND SO IT

S OF YEARS T

THE REPR

DORMA

PE

A

MORI

A AND T

THIS IS H

STARTED TO ST

GHER AND HIGHER

E VERY DIFFERENT F

THE MANNER IN WHICH WE

PRODUCTION ARE SOMEHOW IN

LLUCINOGENIC SUBSTANCES ARE

D IS GEOMAGNETICALLY STIMULATED

NIC PLANTS THAT HELP TO ALTER CONSCI

NIN LEVELS, WHICH IN SOME CASES RESUL

OTHER DIMENSIONS. EVERYTHING THAT WE NEE

AND SOUND. THE SERAPHIM USE ELECTROMAGNETIC

RADIANCE WILL MAKE STRONG CHANGES IN THE TERRE

WILL INHIBIT THE HYDROXINDOLE O-METHYLTRANSFERASE

REATED BY US RIGHT THIS SECOND, WHILE YOU READ. IN CO

HALLUCINOGENIC AVALANCHE THAT WILL LET US BE MORE PSYCHI

Frequencies

The mind functions with, and is stimulated by, certain frequencies. These frequencies are:

- ALPHA (7.5 to 13Hz)
- BETA (13 to 28 Hz)
- DELTA (0.2 to 3.5 Hz)
- THETA (3.5 to 7.5 Hz)
- HIGH RAM (28 Hz or more)

The BETA frequency is the one that humans are regularly habituated to during the day.

ALPHA is a state of relaxation, or even exhaustion.

DELTA goes hand-in-hand with deep sleep.

THETA relates to light sleep and meditation

HIGH RAM is associated with uncertainty, stress and tension.

The forces of darkness have implemented the use of machines that modify and disrupt the electromagnetic frequencies.
With the use of these machines, they could dominate the unprepared human easily using hallucinations, stress, emotions, and even introducing dominating thoughts that originate from the exterior.
With these machines, the darkness can simultaneously affect the magnetosphere, which keeps us safe from cosmic radiation and solar winds.
In the earth's poles, the magnetic field is more fragile. As they are bombarded continuously by solar winds of resplendent particles charged with omniscient power, they thus cause the Aurora Borealis in the North Pole and the Aurora Australis in the South Pole, which originate when the solar particles collide with the atmospheric gases, inducing a kind of holographic buff.
These auroras have been unnaturally modified and where surprisingly seen thirty-eight minutes before the earthquake in China, the Tsunami in the year 2004; and before other horrible catastrophes, this indicates that, presently, there is an extenuation of the earth's magnetic field that might

have been caused by the machinery from the darkest shadows and not from the Sun. These modifications could cause a permutation of the polarity in the magnetic fields that would completely change the terrestrial surface.

Several countries are implementing new parameters for modern life without knowing how life will change on the earth's surface with looms of darkness. The minds that are governed by such forces don't know that in their hands they have the spiritual armament of a geophysical character that intervenes within the troposphere with low frequency radio undulations of darkness. These weapons are dangerous to themselves. These weapons that threaten the spirit do not only allow the manipulation of human beings, but they are also powerful weapons that alter the electromagnetic field, inducing permutations in the climate.
If humans don't alter their course, their entire planet is endangered, and it will be swallowed by the dark throat of the perplexing Nebula. You, as a warrior of the light, need not rebel; simply allow these words to penetrate and awaken you. When you are ready, we will take you from this planet into a better realm of consciousness. If the humans don't listen to us and continue to fall into abysmal darkness, we will have to use our Plan B. The change will be stronger and it will not be gradual like the one that is happening right now. The prepared human beings (you along with others) will take charge and guide humans in the awakening process imposed by us. Humans will be forced to align themselves with the patterns of tender and loving light that will guide the future of the human race.

Hypothalamus and the Tenth Vortex (the Stimulator of the Nectar of Immortality)

Ashtrtakam bashtiam britashtit badrampat tastiam Yori-El

The hypothalamus, which connects the nervous system with the endocrinal system through the pituitary gland, is being used right this very second to create modulations in the metabolic processes. Along with other activities, the hypothalamus will produce and distill neuro-hormones that exude mystical heat. Such an increase in heat and radiation will benefit the production of specific hormones and simultaneously obstruct the emission of certain hormones in the hypothalamus. When this vortex awakens, you will be able to control the body temperature with your mind and you will not need any more winter clothing, since you will be immune to the cold

or extreme heat; you will also be capable of controlling fatigue, thirst, sleep, hunger and circadian cycles.
The hypothalamus is so important for us because it is associated with numerous parts of the central nervous system that have been affected by the Nebula, as well as the reticular formation of the brainstem and the autonomic zones, such as the limbic forebrain, amygdala, septum, olfactory bulb and the brain cortex.
There are important hypothalamus hormones, such as:

- Corticotropin-releasing hormone (CRH).
- Thyrotropin-releasing hormone (TRH).
- Follicle-stimulating hormone-releasing hormone (FSHRH).
- Luteinizing hormone-releasing hormone (LHRH).
- Growth hormone-releasing hormone: activates the pituitary gland to produce and release the human growth hormone (GHRH).
- CRH: helps the suprarenal glands.
- ACTH and corticoids.
- TRH: stimulates the thyroid to segregate T3 and T4 hormones.
- FSH: stimulates the ovaries and testicles where the maturing of the ovule and the spermatozoa is made possible; it also promotes the increase of ovulation and increases the production of progesterone and its release.
- GHRH stimulates the anterior pituitary gland to segregate the growth hormone of the body tissue and increases the production of protein and glucose in the blood.

These hormones are presently being modified by the liver and intelligent crystalline light from the ninth dimension. Take rest, relax, and allow the light to restructure your body.

The Seat of the Mind

Madat vastrat akturiat madaveiel barastrat Sabi-El

Amygdala and the Eleventh Vortex

The amygdala is connected with the mind vortex; in India, this zone is referred to as "Manas Chakra": the seat of the mind, the personality and ego.
The amygdala is located deep within the temporal lobes of the brain and executes functions related to emotional reactions. The amygdala is a very important part of the limbic system; it is in permanent contact with the hypothalamus and the sympathetic nervous system.

With ultraviolet and infrared solar light, The Luminous Ones awaken the nucleus of the reticular thalamus through the optic nerve in order to increase the reflexes and activate the nucleus of the trigeminal nerve and the facial nerve (remember that the face, the ego and the personality are connected).

The ventral tegmental area, locus coeruleus, dorsal nucleus and the lateral segments will be rearranged so that they increase the dopamine, norepinephrine and epinephrine production. This gradual modification will alter the human consciousness.

The amygdala was seriously modified by the dark forces. These forces made strong and murky genetic changes so that the amygdala would hold not only the darkness of fears, panic and trepidation, but also so that the humans could be dominated by animal instincts related to smell and pheromone dispensation.

The amygdala delineates the structure of memories. It not only stores them, but disparages them as well (note that the ego and the personality are affected by memories and past experiences), distilling emotional essences from these.

When fear is felt, the amygdala of the person sends sensorial incentives to the lateral nuclei, awakening and creating bonds with the emotional memories of the past events stored in the brain. The central nucleus of the amygdala is implicated with the origin of many lots of the reactions to fear, such as anxiety, fast breathing, palpitations, and immobility. All these symptoms occur because the amygdala produces the stress hormone. Lesions in the amygdala damage the capacity to feel fear.

If we destroy the darkness that surrounds the amygdala through solar stimuli, at some point the reader will stop feeling fear.

You might think that the shadows of fear are necessary for human existence, since fear indicates danger at certain moments in life. It is thought that, without this fear, a person wouldn't be able to escape from a dangerous situation. However, the human being has judgment and discrimination; humans are intelligent beings and are with no doubt able to decide, without fear, in a moment of danger. On the other hand, judgment and discrimination get completely lost when fear appears; fear will make a person run hysterically in a moment of extreme danger, for example if he or she is being attack by lion. From an intellectual point of view, this is not the best idea, logically, because a lion would outrun a human very easily and everyone knows that lions prefer to attack from behind instead of attacking from the front. Without fear, the individual would think and, in a split second, he or she could choose another, more intelligent, more human course of action, like making use of psychic powers.

Fear is the root of all emotions. Rage stems from it and gives the human enough energy to fight against fearful situations. But if rage can't solve the problem the fear caused in the first place, a feeling of sadness and defeat would take us by surprise and overwhelm us; on the other hand, if you were to overcome the obstacle, a euphoric feeling would embrace you, but this euphoria is false in nature and it is not long-lasting. The root of all these emotions is fear, and it affects the construction of ego-mind constantly. Each second of one's life, unless one defeats these corporeal brain emotions and transmute them into an ethereal and causal feeling of Love, the individual will be just another slave of the darkness. Our real nature has been forgotten and covered by corporeal sensations of fear, rage, sadness, happiness, insecurity, and imbalance. Examine your interior, and you will see that my words are true.

As if this wasn't enough, the amygdala is connected to alcoholism and other addictions; it is an imperative regulator of the conduct's responses to toxic products.

The main function of the amygdala consists of adjusting and consolidating the memories in other areas of the brain and detracting them completely. The amygdala is one of the bodily areas that have been modified by the darkness. Now it is time to completely retro-transform it with golden shining light.

In this precise moment, we are destroying all the imperfections. Trust that we simply want to help; help us to change you, too. Whenever you feel fear, call us by the names of Anabel, Yoriel, Gabriel, Mikhael and we will come and destroy the shadowy energies that surround you.

Connect with us, feel us, call us—we are with you, our sweet reader who wants to change and wants to Love. Choose the side of the almighty light: choose God's side. We are eager to help you change your fear for Love. We will remove the thorn of apprehension and anxiety that affects the amygdala. In this way, we will destroy the egotistic tentacles that embrace the spiritual heart. Have faith, patience, and remember that the energetic change can't be so fast because of the delicate condition of the energetic meridian system. Even so, it is happening right now.

{ASHTRTAKAM BASHTIAM BRITASHTIT BADRAMPAT TASTIAM YORI-
VERY SECOND TO CREATE MODULATIONS IN THE METABOLIC PRO
INCREASE IN HEAT AND RADIATION WILL BENEFIT THE PRODU
TEX AWAKENS, YOU WILL BE ABLE TO CONTROL THE BODY
XTREME HEAT; YOU WILL ALSO BE CAPABLE OF CONT
IT IS ASSOCIATED WITH NUMEROUS PARTS OF THE
E BRAINSTEM AND THE AUTONOMIC ZONES, SU
PORTANT HYPOTHALAMUS HORMONES, SUC
LICLE-STIMULATING HORMONE-RELEAS
ONE-RELEASING HORMONE: ACTIVAT
. - CRH: HELPS THE SUPRAREN
GATE T3 AND T4 HORMONES
G OF THE OVULE AND T
ASE OF OVULATION A
RELEASE.- GHRH
GREGATE THE
CREASES T
COSE I
A

THE
OF PRO
F THE BODY
NTERIOR PITUI
RODUCTION OF PRO
ADE POSSIBLE; IT ALSO
HE OVARIES AND TESTICL
ORTICOIDS. - TRH: STIMULATE
PRODUCE AND RELEASE THE HUM
EINIZING HORMONE-RELEASING HORM
ING HORMONE (CRH). - THYROTROPIN-REL
MYGDALA, SEPTUM, OLFACTORY BULB AND T
VE BEEN AFFECTED BY THE NEBULA, AS WELL A
UNGER AND CIRCADIAN CYCLES. THE HYPOTHALAMU
WILL NOT NEED ANY MORE WINTER CLOTHING, SINCE Y
TANEOUSLY OBSTRUCT THE EMISSION OF CERTAIN HORMONE
HE HYPOTHALAMUS WILL PRODUCE AND DISTILL NEURO-HORMO
NERVOUS SYSTEM WITH THE ENDOCRINAL SYSTEM THROUGH THE PI

BEING MODIFIED BY THE LIVER AND INTELLIGENT CRYSTALLINE LIGHT FROM THE NINTH DIMENSION. TAKE REST, RELAX, AND ALLOW THE LIGHT TO RESTRUCTURE YOUR BODY.{ THE SEAT OF THE MIND}{MADAT VASTRAT AKTURIAT MADAVEIEL BARASTRAT SABI-EL}{ AMYGDALA AND THE ELEVENTH VORTEX}{ THE AMYGDALA IS CONNECTED WITH THE MIND VORTEX; IN INDIA, THIS ZONE IS REFERRED TO AS “MANAS CHAKRA”: THE SEAT OF THE MIND, THE PERSONALITY AND EGO. THE AMYGDALA IS LOCATED DEEP WITHIN THE TEMPORAL LOBES OF THE BRAIN AND EXECUTES FUNCTIONS RELATED TO EMOTIONAL REACTIONS. THE AMYGDALA IS A VERY IMPORTANT PART OF THE LIMBIC SYSTEM; IT IS IN PERMANENT CONTACT WITH THE HYPOTHALAMUS AND THE SYMPATHETIC NERVOUS SYSTEM. WITH ULTRAVIOLET AND INFRARED SOLAR LIGHT, THE LUMINOUS ONES AWAKEN THE NUCLEUS OF THE RETICULAR THALAMUS THROUGH THE OPTIC NERVE IN ORDER TO INCREASE THE REFLEXES AND ACTIVATE THE NUCLEUS OF THE TRIGEMINAL NERVE AND THE FACIAL NERVE (REMEMBER THAT THE FACE, THE EGO AND THE PERSONALITY ARE CONNECTED). THE VENTRAL TEGMENTAL AREA, LOCUS COERULEUS, DORSAL NUCLEUS AND THE LATERAL SEGMENTS WILL BE REARRANGED SO THAT THEY INCREASE THE DOPAMINE, NOREPINEPHRINE AND EPINEPHRINE PRODUCTION. THIS GRADUAL MODIFICATION WILL ALTER THE HUMAN CONSCIOUSNESS. THE AMYGDALA WAS SERIOUSLY MODIFIED BY THE DARK FORCES. THESE FORCES MADE STRONG AND MURKY GENETIC CHANGES SO THAT THE AMYGDALA WOULD HOLD NOT ONLY THE DARKNESS OF FEARS. PANIC AND TREPIDATION, BUT ALSO SO THAT THE HUMANS COULD BE DOMINATED BY ANIMAL INSTINCTS RELATED TO SMELL AND PHEROMONE DISPENSATION. THE AMYGDALA DELINEATES THE STRUCTURE OF MEMORIES. IT NOT ONLY STORES THEM, BUT DISPARAGES THEM AS WELL (NOTE THAT THE EGO AND THE PERSONALITY ARE AFFECTED BY MEMORIES AND PAST EXPERIENCES), DISTILLING EMOTIONAL ESSENCES FROM THESE. WHEN FEAR IS FELT, THE AMYGDALA OF THE PERSON SENDS SENSORIAL INCENTIVES TO THE LATERAL NUCLEI, AWAKENING AND CREATING BONDS WITH THE EMOTIONAL MEMORIES OF THE PAST EVENTS STORED IN THE BRAIN. THE CENTRAL NUCLEUS OF THE AMYGDALA IS IMPLICATED WITH THE ORIGIN OF

MANY LOTS OF THE REACTIONS TO FEAR, SUCH AS ANXIETY, FAST BREATHING, PALPITATIONS, AND IMMOBILITY. ALL THESE SYMPTOMS OCCUR BECAUSE THE AMYGDALA PRODUCES THE STRESS HORMONE. LESIONS IN THE AMYGDALA DAMAGE THE CAPACITY TO FEEL FEAR. IF WE DESTROY THE DARKNESS THAT SURROUNDS THE AMYGDALA THROUGH SOLAR STIMULI, AT SOME POINT THE READER WILL STOP FEELING FEAR. SOME MIGHT THINK THAT THE SHADOWS OF FEAR ARE NECESSARY FOR HUMAN EXISTENCES, SINCE FEAR INDICATES DANGER AT CERTAIN MOMENTS IN LIFE. IT IS THOUGHT THAT WITHOUT THIS FEAR WE WON'T BE ABLE TO RUN, FOR INSTANCE, WHEN A LION THROWS ITSELF AT US, OR BE ABLE TO ESCAPE FROM ANY OTHER DANGEROUS SITUATION; HOWEVER, THE HUMAN BEING HAS JUDGMENT AND DISCRIMINATION, HUMANS ARE INTELLIGENT BEINGS AND WILL BE ABLE TO DECIDE WITHOUT FEAR IN A MOMENT OF DANGER. ON THE OTHER HAND, JUDGMENT AND DISCRIMINATION GET COMPLETELY LOST WHEN FEAR APPEARS; FEAR WILL MAKE US RUN HYSTERICALLY WHEN A LION THROWS ITSELF AT US. FROM AN INTELLECTUAL POINT OF VIEW, THIS IS NOT THE BEST IDEA, BECAUSE A LION WOULD OUTRUN A HUMAN VERY EASILY AND EVERYONE KNOWS THAT LIONS PREFER TO ATTACK FROM BEHIND INSTEAD OF ATTACKING FROM THE FRONT. WITHOUT FEAR, WE WOULD THINK AND IN A SPLIT SECOND WE COULD CHOOSE ANOTHER, MORE INTELLIGENT, MORE HUMAN COURSE OF ACTION, LIKE MAKING USE OF PSYCHIC POWERS. FEAR IS THE ROOT OF ALL EMOTIONS, AND FROM THIS STEMS RAGE THAT GIVES THE HUMAN THE ENERGY TO FIGHT AGAINST FEARFUL SITUATIONS. BUT IF RAGE CAN'T SOLVE THE PROBLEM THAT THE FEAR CAUSED IN THE FIRST PLACE, A FEELING OF SADNESS AND DEFEAT WOULD OVERWHELMINGLY TAKE US BY SURPRISE; ON THE ON THE OTHER HAND, IF YOU WERE TO OVERCOME THE OBSTACLE, A EUPHORIC FEELING WOULD EMBRACE YOU, BUT THIS EUPHORIA IS FALSE IN NATURE AND IT IS NOT LONG-LASTING. THE ROOT OF ALL THESE EMOTIONS IS FEAR AND IT AFFECTS THE CONSTRUCTION THE OF EGO-MIND CONSTANTLY. EACH SECOND OF ONE'S LIFE, UNLESS ONE DEFEATS THESE CORPOREAL BRAIN EMOTIONS AND TWISTS THEM INTO AN ETHEREAL AND CAUSAL FEELING OF LOVE, THE INDIVIDUAL WILL

BE JUST ANOTHER SLAVE OF THE DARKNESS. OUR REAL NATURE HAS BEEN FORGOTTEN AND COVERED BY CORPOREAL SENSATIONS OF FEAR, RAGE, SADNESS, HAPPINESS, INSECURITY, AND IMBALANCE. EXAMINE YOUR INTERIOR, AND YOU WILL SEE THAT MY WORDS ARE TRUE. AS IF THIS WASN'T ENOUGH, THE AMYGDALA IS CONNECTED TO ALCOHOLISM AND OTHER ADDICTIONS; IT IS AN IMPERATIVE REGULATOR OF THE CONDUCT'S RESPONSES TO TOXIC PRODUCTS. THE MAIN FUNCTION OF THE AMYGDALA CONSISTS OF ADJUSTING AND CONSOLIDATING THE MEMORIES IN OTHER AREAS OF THE BRAIN AND DETRACTING THEM COMPLETELY. THE AMYGDALA IS ONE OF THE BODILY AREAS THAT HAS BEEN MODIFIED BY THE DARKNESS AND NOW IT IS TIME TO COMPLETELY RETRO-TRANSFORM IT WITH GOLDEN SHINING LIGHT. IN THIS PRECISE MOMENT, WE ARE DESTROYING ALL THE IMPERFECTIONS. TRUST THAT WE SIMPLY WANT TO HELP; HELP US TO CHANGE YOU. TOO. WHENEVER YOU FEEL FEAR CALL US BY THE NAMES OF ANABEL, YORIEL, GABRIEL, MIKHAEL AND WE WILL COME AND DESTROY THE SHADOWY ENERGIES THAT SURROUND YOU. CONNECT WITH US, FEEL US, CALL US—WE ARE WITH YOU, OUR SWEET READER THAT WANTS TO CHANGE AND WANTS TO LOVE. CHOOSE THE SIDE OF THE ALMIGHTY LIGHT, CHOOSE GOD'S SIDE. WE ARE EAGER TO HELP YOU CHANGE YOUR FEAR FOR LOVE. WE WILL REMOVE THE THORN OF APPREHENSION AND ANXIETY THAT AFFECTS THE AMYGDALA. IN THIS WAY WE WILL DESTROY THE EGOTISTIC TENTACLES THAT EMBRACE THE SPIRITUAL HEART. HAVE FAITH, PATIENCE AND REMEMBER THAT THE ENERGETIC CHANGE CAN'T BE SO FAST BECAUSE OF THE DELICATE CONDITION OF THE ENERGETIC MERIDIAN SYSTEM. EVEN SO, IT IS HAPPENING RIGHT NOW. ....

The Twelfth Vortex

This is the center of the ecstasy of the immortal spirit.
The mind, or individual consciousness, keeps in constant contact with all kinds of information that comes from the cosmos and all the spirit's extensions.
This vortex is related in diverse ways with the universe.
When it is balanced, it amplifies the consciousness' capacity, letting us appreciate our surroundings with transparency.
In case of malfunction or centrifugal agitation, you can observe symptoms of desperation, isolation, lack of wisdom and grounding. These disorders can be exteriorized all of a sudden, and are sometimes felt as a gray cloud that displays itself all over the entire body. Alienation, lack of hope, lethargy, mood swings, fatigue and boredom are feelings that can be had as a result.

Brain Neo-Cortex

Atronixitrat advatiam vashti udrit agramat Anab-el

The magnetic fields under the neural acceleration schemes are being modified right this second. Pay attention, focus on the reading and let it transform you.
The structure of subjacent distributive bonds, which are a thick web of fibers and access links in the regions of the brain cortex, are being illuminated with inter-dimensional light. We use propagation methodologies of dream iconography, which allow us to do a type of non-invasive mapping to learn where the seeds implanted by the Shadows are located in the cortical zone.
Our analysis of the complex neuronal grid reveals cortex zones that are connected and centralized in darkness, forming an unbalanced structural nucleus that is energetically imbalanced.
The primordial modules of the dark nuclei are the areas of the posterior central cortex, which become active while you rest or sleep and in moments where the brain is not part of a demanding cognitive task. The Devas of Crystalline Fire have been planting seeds of light in some of these areas to counter murky programming and slowly disband the nucleus.
The structural and functional correlation schemes between the cortex zones are significantly related to this anti-natural nucleus; however, close

to the crown of the head, there exists a parallel ultra bright nucleus that, in the last ten years, has been constantly receiving a small amount of bright rays from the fifth, seventh and ninth dimensions. This nucleus will imminently change the human brain's molecular structure and, therefore, its chemical structure.

The neural links of the cortex will be stimulated by electric-luminescent information, making its structure stronger so that its link with the gloomy emotional tissue becomes enlightened. Once the neuronal area of the brain cortex is codified, the resident memory in the cortex region will acquire a different color—the "color of truth"—and, in this way, you will learn to see the past and the future as if these were the continuous and eternal present. The information that is received and processed in the three amalgamated time tenses will be envisioned like internal three-dimensional holograms.

The predominating neural morphology will be affected by lightning of a white solar spectrum, which will come in through the eyes each time the reader goes out into the open; this light will affect the sub cortical projections. The layer that receives the information coming from the thalamus will be flooded by this light as well, affecting the small-sized neurons that form the granular layer. On the other hand, the supra-granular layers will be forced to connect with different cortical areas (homo and counter lateral), with the purpose of reopening subjacent meridians blocked by the forces of the Nebula.

The infra-granular layers will project light created by the change done to the sub cortical structures, in this way opening a series of small vortices with spectral arachnid-like meridians that project holographic structures to the central and posterior brain, and to the bone marrow as well.

In a cascade, the neocortex will receive a flow of light, affecting the reasoning process.

The archicortex (the olfactory cortex of the cerebrum), will be restructured and divided, and the Source of Radiant Essence will cauterize some areas of it. She (the Source) will obliterate the reptilian and instinctive part of the human brain that is in charge of all the automated reactions, like survival and physiological processes. Instinctual behavior will be transformed into intuitive awareness.

The neocortex will be prepared to receive inter-dimensional psychic information through symbols of multicolored lights.

The neurons of the temporal lobe will be reprogrammed to embrace sonorous geometrical characters.

The frontal lobe will be transformed and become capable of predicting the future.

The parietal lobe of the somatosensory primary cortex, will suffer such a drastic change that the reader will feel life in every single one of its pores; this will make him/her feel a kind of immortal ecstasy.

The occipital posterior lobe will grant multidimensional vision.

In conclusion, we will open the nucleus of the crown of the head and, from here, intelligence and vibrant energy will be injected, which will destroy the murky nucleus and connect the human with the Radiant Source. This celestial energy will travel to the first vortex and, if Asuntara is not yet awakened, the magnanimous power will awaken it from its sleep and take it beyond the borders of the outline of the three bodies.

{BRAIN NEOCORTEX}{ATRONIXITRAT ADVATIAM VASHTI UDRIT AGR
READING AND LET IT TRANSFORM YOU. THE STRUCTURE OF SUB
INATED WITH INTER-DIMENSIONAL LIGHT. WE USE PROPAGATI
TED BY THE SHADOWS ARE LOCATED IN THE CORTICAL Z
FORMING AN UNBALANCED STRUCTURAL NUCLEUS TH
AL CORTEX, WHICH BECOME ACTIVE WHILE YOU RE
STALLINE FIRE HAVE BEEN PLANTING SEEDS O
STRUCTURAL AND FUNCTIONAL CORRELATI
HOWEVER, CLOSE TO THE CROWN OF T
AS BEEN CONSTANTLY RECEIVING A
S NUCLEUS WILL IMMINENTLY CH
CAL STRUCTURE. THE NEURA
INFORMATION, MAKING
EMOTIONAL TISSUE B
BRAIN CORTEX I
REGION WILL
F TRUTH"—
TO SE
S

RE
ND T
AY, YOU
ERENT COLO
RESIDENT MEMO
D. ONCE THE NEUR
NGER SO THAT ITS L
WILL BE STIMULATED BY
TS MOLECULAR STRUCTURE A
AYS FROM THE FIFTH, SEVENTH A
RALLEL ULTRA BRIGHT NUCLEUS THA
X ZONES ARE SIGNIFICANTLY RELATED TO
S TO COUNTER MURKY PROGRAMMING AND SL
RE THE BRAIN IS NOT PART OF A DEMANDING C
HE PRIMORDIAL MODULES OF THE DARK NUCLEI ARE
URONAL GRID REVEALS CORTEX ZONES THAT ARE CONN
Y, WHICH ALLOW US TO DO A TYPE OF NON-INVASIVE MAP
HE THICK WEB OF FIBERS AND ACCESS LINKS IN THE REGIONS
E NEURAL ACCELERATION SCHEMES ARE BEING MODIFIED RIGHT T

THE CONTINUOUS AND ETERNAL PRESENT. THE INFORMATION THAT IS RECEIVED AND PROCESSED IN THE THREE AMALGAMATED TIME TENSES, WILL BE ENVISIONED LIKE INTERNAL THREE-DIMENSIONAL HOLOGRAMS. THE PREDOMINATING NEURAL MORPHOLOGY WILL BE AFFECTED BY A LIGHTNING OF A WHITE SOLAR SPECTRUM, WHICH WILL COME IN THROUGH THE EYES EACH TIME THAT THE READER GOES OUT INTO THE OPEN; THIS LIGHT WILL AFFECT THE SUBCORTICAL PROJECTIONS. THE LAYER THAT RECEIVES THE INFORMATION COMING FROM THE THALAMUS WILL BE FLOODED BY THIS LIGHT AS WELL, AFFECTING THE SMALL-SIZED NEURONS THAT FORM THE GRANULAR LAYER. ON THE OTHER HAND, THE SUPRA-GRANULAR LAYERS WILL BE FORCED TO CONNECT WITH DIFFERENT CORTICAL AREAS (HOMO AND COUNTER LATERAL), WITH THE PURPOSE OF REOPENING SUBJACENT MERIDIANS BLOCKED BY THE FORCES OF THE NEBULA. THE INFRA-GRANULAR LAYERS WILL PROJECT LIGHT, CREATED BY THE CHANGE DONE TO THE SUBCORTICAL STRUCTURES, OPENING IN THIS WAY A SERIES OF SMALL VORTICES WITH SPECTRAL ARACHNID-LIKE MERIDIANS THAT PROJECT HOLOGRAPHIC STRUCTURES TO THE CENTRAL AND POSTERIOR BRAIN, AND TO THE BONE MARROW AS WELL. IN A CASCADE. THE NEOCORTEX WILL RECEIVE A FLOW OF LIGHT, AFFECTING THE REASONING PROCESS. THE ARCHICORTEX (THE OLFACTORY CORTEX OF THE CEREBRUM), WILL BE RESTRUCTURED, DIVIDED AND SOME AREAS OF IT WILL BE CAUTERIZED BY THE SOURCE OF RADIANT ESSENCE. SHE (THE SOURCE) WILL OBLITERATE THE REPTILIAN AND INSTINCTIVE PART OF THE HUMAN BRAIN THAT IS IN CHARGE OF ALL THE AUTOMATED REACTIONS, LIKE SURVIVAL AND PHYSIOLOGICAL PROCESSES. INSTINCTUAL BEHAVIOR WILL BE TRANSFORMED INTO INTUITIVE AWARENESS. THE NEOCORTEX WILL BE PREPARED TO RECEIVE INTER-DIMENSIONAL PSYCHIC INFORMATION THROUGH SYMBOLS OF MULTICOLORED LIGHTS. THE NEURONS OF THE TEMPORAL LOBE WILL BE REPROGRAMMED TO EMBRACE SONOROUS GEOMETRICAL CHARACTERS. THE FRONTAL LOBE WILL BE TRANSFORMED AND BE CAPABLE OF PREDICTING THE FUTURE. THE PARIETAL LOBE OF THE SOMATOSENSORY PRIMARY CORTEX, WILL SUFFER SUCH A DRASTIC CHANGE THAT THE READER WILL FEEL LIFE IN EVERY SINGLE

Repeat this mantram in each one of the following vortices.

Idratmin adiat Mikha-ella-astrtaiam

The Twelfth Vortex 010011-011011-000110

You will be flooded with quantum light, composed of 001000, 010000 and 100000 lights. Once this happens, the human being will have the powers of instant manifestation. This process will connect the person with the center of the solar system and the Sun will grant him her expansive wisdom.

The Thirteenth Vortex Arcaris

Idratmin adiat adiat adiat Mikha-ella-astrtaiam

When you are woken up by Sirian light of the fifth dimension, you will be reconnected to the interstellar galactic center in the proximities of the central black hole. You will be able to penetrate darkness without being affected or stained by astral murkiness. You, unlike other advanced beings, will deeply understand the mechanisms of this dense energy and will be strong enough to dismantle it with radiant power. Therefore, you, as a catalyst, will help incandescent beings to understand the aliveness of the grayish forces inside the black hole. With this grand discovery and new understanding, the incandescent beings will alter your internal vortices and replace them with atomic light of high condensation. In turn, your three remanufactured bodies will connect even deeper to the center of the galaxy and slowly transmit information from the black hole to the Source.
After this, you will be completely immune to the forces of the Shadows and absolutely every single fear will vanish forever and ever from then on.

The Fourteenth Vortex: The Solaris Vortex

Idratmin adiat adiat adiat Mikha-ella-astrtaiam

At the fourteenth vortex, you will connect directly to the three-dimensional manifestation of the Source of Radiant Essence located in the center of the universe. This connection will change your personality completely, and you will be able to comprehend all the secrets of the dreamed creation, being able to modify and alter creation with the sole purpose of stimulating its evolution.

This connection with the center of the universe will propagate your identity and sense of interstellar individuality; you will be able to experience the power of one billion suns in your interior, and you will be capable of becoming one with them, understanding, likewise, the photonic power of light in the third dimension. In this phase, you will chromosomically manipulate the punctual particles and collections of quarks with gluons simultaneously, forming hadrons where the subatomic particles remain integrated due to their potent interaction.
You will be able to balance the thermal changes between matter and electromagnetic radiation. You will also be able to change the corpuscular waves to undulations and vice versa, affecting other denser particles in a different way.

The Fifteenth Vortex TX

Idratmin adiat adiat adiat Mikha-ella-astrtaiam

When this vortex is reached, you will conquer the time/space illusion and understand the secrets that the fourth and fifth dimensions hold. You will cross the time and space coordinates (time in three-dimensional space gives the impression of being a separate coordinate, but these will seem to unify in higher dimensions).
Time in this apparent sub-alternate reality seems to be linear, even though it is not. In other dimensions, time and space take on a more flexible, wavy, dreamy nature. This is the reason it is easier for the mind to transcend them (time/space) in something that could be called hyperspace; as long as hyperspace is not compacted.
Remember that dimensions are not real—only dreams inside dreams.

The Sixteenth Vortex 011001-111010-001001

Idratmin adiat adiat adiat Mikha-ella-astrtaiam

As you reach this vortex, you will break the barrier of the fifth dimension and will have access to the sixth, where the luminous beings have been denied access until they surrender their attachment to the unending ecstasy that is felt here.

You will be able to understand the most elevated aspects of purity and kindness. There will be no need of external light here and you will go through an amazing metamorphosis and live behind the Luminiferus entity apparel to adopt a resplendent, luminous one.

The Seventeenth Vortex 010110-110100-010011

Idratmin adiat adiat adiat Mikha-ella-astrtaiam

The human body, from three subsequent angles, will be redressed in seven crystalline coverings of high purity. These coverings will serve as alternative bodies in other dimensions and you will be able to access alternate three-dimensional spaces all at the same time. You will also be able to occupy spaces in seven dimensions simultaneously.

The Eighteenth Vortex 011011-111010-001111

Idratmin adiat adiat adiat Mikha-ella-astrtaiam

In this vortex, you will have access to the eighth dimension, and you will acquire seven crystalline bodies that will multiply seven times seven, drastically changing your human personality. Your individual consciousness will suffer a strong but controlled shock.
The acquired powers will be very similar to the powers of the Source of all Radiance, and the Love felt will be the most incredible, marvelous ever conceived.

The Nineteenth Vortex 010111 -010001-011111

Idratmin adiat adiat adiat Mikha-ella-astrtaiam

In this vortex, you will have access to different linear phases of time and space. You will be able to travel to the past and the future with your crystalline bodies without becoming separated from the "no time" where you are anchored. You will have the permission and the right to change the course of historical events that are against luminous evolution.
You will graduate and you will no longer be monitored; the Source and the Devas of Crystalline Fire will have complete trust in you and you will decide on your own about the matters that affect the nine dimensions.

The Twentieth Vortex 010111-010001-111111

Idratmin adiat adiat adiat Mikha-ella-astrtaiam

In this vortex, you will be free of your pragmatic individuality of the forty-nine bodies and will expand, without limits, through the ninth-dimensional dream, accessing all the dimensions simultaneously.
All destinies that had you confined to the forty-nine bodies will be destroyed and you will choose between transcending the ninth-dimensional dream and becoming one with Absolute Consciousness, or joining the Source of all Light with the purpose of helping the evolution process of the nine-dimensional dream.

The Twenty-First Vortex 011011-101000-100111-111111

Idratmin adiat adiat adiat Mikha-ella-astrtaiam

The last vortex is the channel through which one returns to the Absolute Consciousness. If the last border is crossed, there will be no going back. Eternal peace will be the only experience. Here, you will decide; no one decides for you anymore.

ONE OF ITS PORES; THIS WILL MAKE HIM/HER FEEL A KIND OF IMMO

HE HEAD, AND FROM HERE INTELLIGENCE AND VIBRANT ENERGY

Y WILL TRAVEL TO THE FIRST VORTEX AND IF ASUNTARA IS

THREE BODIES. REPEAT THIS MANTRAM IN EACH ONE OF

WILL BE FLOODED WITH QUANTUM LIGHT, COMPOSED

STATION. THIS PROCESS WILL CONNECT THE PERSO

VORTEX ARCARIS} {IDRATMIN ADIAT ADIAT AD

L BE RECONNECTED TO THE INTERSTELLAR

DARKNESS WITHOUT BEING AFFECTED

ERSTAND THE MECHANISMS OF THIS

HEREFORE, YOU, AS A CATALYST

ISH FORCES INSIDE THE BL

INCANDESCENT BEINGS

ATOMIC LIGHT OF HI

BODIES WILL CO

AND SLOWLY

LE TO THE

OMPLE

TH

ND A

T OT

R THIS

MATION FRO

R TO THE CENT

IN TURN, YOUR THR

TERNAL VORTICES AN

RAND DISCOVERY AND NE

T BEINGS TO UNDERSTAND THE

STRONG ENOUGH TO DISMANTLE

NESS. YOU, UNLIKE OTHER ADVANCE

MITIES OF THE CENTRAL BLACK HOLE. YO

N YOU ARE WOKEN UP BY SIRIAN LIGHT OF

SYSTEM AND THE SUN WILL GRANT HIM/HER EXP

TS. ONCE THIS HAPPENS, THE HUMAN BEING WILL

DIAT ADIAT MIKHA-ELLA-ASTRTAIAM THE TWELF

WER WILL AWAKEN IT FROM ITS SLEEP AND TAKE IT BEYO

HE MURKY NUCLEUS AND WILL CONNECT THE HUMAN WITH THE

BE WILL GRANT MULTIDIMENSIONAL VISION. IN CONCLUSION, WE

ABSOLUTELY EVERY SINGLE FEAR WILL VANISH FOREVER AND EVER FROM THE NON. {THE FOURTEENTH VORTEX: THE SOLARIS VORTEX} {IDRATMIN ADIAT ADIAT ADIAT MIKHA-EL LA-ASTRTAIAM} AT THE FOURTEENTH VORTEX, YOU WILL CONNECT DIRECTLY TO THE THREE-DIMENSIONAL MANIFESTATION OF THE SOURCE OF RADIANT ESSENCE LOCATED IN THE CENTER OF THE UNIVERSE. THIS CONNECTION WILL CHANGE YOUR PERSONALITY COMPLETELY, AND YOU WILL BE ABLE TO COMPREHEND ALL THE SECRETS OF THE DREAMED CREATION, BEING ABLE TO MODIFY AND ALTER THE CREATION WITH THE SOLE PURPOSE OF STIMULATING ITS EVOLUTION. THIS CONNECTION WITH THE CENTER OF THE UNIVERSE WILL PROPAGATE YOUR IDENTITY AND SENSE OF INTERSTELLAR INDIVIDUALITY; YOU WILL BE ABLE TO EXPERIENCE THE POWER OF ONE BILLION SUNS IN YOUR INTERIOR, AND YOU WILL BE CAPABLE OF BECOMING ONE WITH THEM, UNDERSTANDING LIKEWISE THE PHOTONIC POWER OF LIGHT IN THE THIRD DIMENSION. IN THIS PHASE, YOU WILL CHROMOSOMICALLY MANIPULATE THE PUNCTUAL PARTICLES AND COLLECTIONS OF QUARKS WITH GLUONS SIMULTANEOUSLY, FORMING HADRONS WHERE THE SUBATOMIC PARTICLES REMAIN INTEGRATED DUE TO THEIR POTENT INTERACTION. YOU WILL BE ABLE TO BALANCE THE THERMAL CHANGES BETWEEN MATTER AND ELECTROMAGNETIC RADIATION. YOU WILL ALSO BE ABLE TO CHANGE THE CORPUSCULAR WAVES TO UNDULATIONS AND VICE VERSA, AFFECTING OTHER MORE DENSE PARTICLES IN A DIFFERENT WAY. {THE FIFTEENTH VORTEX TX} {IDRATMIN ADIAT ADIAT ADIAT MIKHA-EL LA-ASTRATAIAM} WHEN THIS VORTEX IS REACHED, YOU WILL CONQUER THE TIME/SPACE ILLUSION AND UNDERSTAND THE SECRETS THAT THE FOURTH AND FIFTH DIMENSIONS HOLD. YOU WILL CROSS THE TIME AND SPACE COORDINATES (TIME IN THREE-DIMENSIONAL SPACE GIVES THE IMPRESSION OF BEING A SEPARATE COORDINATE, BUT THESE WILL SEEM TO UNIFY IN HIGHER DIMENSIONS). TIME IN THIS APPARENT SUB-ALTERNATE REALITY SEEMS TO BE LINEAR, EVEN THOUGH IT IS NOT. IN OTHER DIMENSIONS, TIME AND SPACE TAKE ON A MORE FLEXIBLE, WAVY, DREAMY COLOR. THIS IS THE REASON WHY IT IS EASIER FOR THE MIND TO TRANSCEND THEM (TIME\SPACE) IN SOMETHING THAT COULD BE CALLED

HYPERSPACE; AS LONG AS HYPERSPACE IS NOT COMPACTED. REME

1001-111010-001001} AS YOU REACH THIS VORTEX, YOU WILL BRE

THEY SURRENDER THEIR ATTACHMENT TO THE UNENDING ECS

NEED OF EXTERNAL LIGHT HERE AND YOU WILL GO THRO

{IDRATMIN ADIAT ADIAT ADIAT MIKHA-ELLA-ASTRT

SSED IN SEVEN CRYSTALLINE COVERINGS OF HIGH

CCESS ALTERNATE THREE-DIMENSIONAL SPACE

LY. {IDRATMIN ADIAT ADIAT ADIAT MIKHA

SS TO THE EIGHTH DIMENSION, AND Y

LLY CHANGING YOUR HUMAN PERSO

SHOCK. THE ACQUIRED POWERS

E LOVE FELT WILL BE THE

T ADIAT MIKHA-ELLA-A

N THIS VORTEX, YOU

E AND SPACE. Y

FUTURE WITH

NG SEPAR

U ARE

HE

N

OU

IT ON"

NE BODIES

TO TRAVEL TO

TO DIFFERENT LIN

EENTH VORTEX 01011

ELOUS EVER CONCEIVED.

THE POWERS OF THE SOURCE

AL CONSCIOUSNESS WILL SUFFER

NE BODIES THAT WILL MULTIPLY SE

EENTH VORTEX 011011-111010-001111} IN THIS

ILL ALSO BE ABLE TO OCCUPY SPACES IN

ERVE AS ALTERNATIVE BODIES IN OTHER DIMEN

110-110100-010011} THE HUMAN BODY, FROM THREE

VE BEHIND THE LUMINIFERUS ENTITY APPAREL, TO AD

ABLE TO UNDERSTAND THE MOST ELEVATED ASPECTS OF PU

AND WILL HAVE ACCESS TO THE SIXTH, WHERE THE LUMINOUS

REAMS INSIDE DREAMS. {IDRATMIN ADIAT ADIAT ADIAT MIKHA-E

IS CROSSED, THERE WILL BE NO GOING BACK. E

VORTEX 01011-101000-100111-111111}THE L

OF HELPING THE EVOLUTION PROCESS OF

NINTH-DIMENSIONAL DREAM AND BEC

ESTINIES THAT HAD YOU CONFIN

D WITHOUT LIMITS THROUGH T

N THIS VORTEX, YOU WILL

IAT ADIAT ADIAT MIKH

N YOUR OWN ABOUT T

LLINE FIRE WIL

O LONGER BE

NOUS EVOL

STORI

TH

A

THE

HAT ARE

L GRADUATE

OURCE AND THE

RUST IN YOU AND

ECT THE NINE DIMEN

HE TWENTIETH VORTEX 01

TIC INDIVIDUALITY OF THE 4

AM, ACCESSING ALL THE DIMENSI

BE DESTROYED AND YOU WILL CHOOS

SCIOUSNESS, OR JOINING THE SOURCE OF

IDRATMIN ADIAT ADIAT ADIAT MIKHA-ELLA

GH WHICH ONE RETURNS TO THE ABSOLUTE CON

ERIENCE. HERE YOU WILL DECIDE; NO ONE DECIDE

X

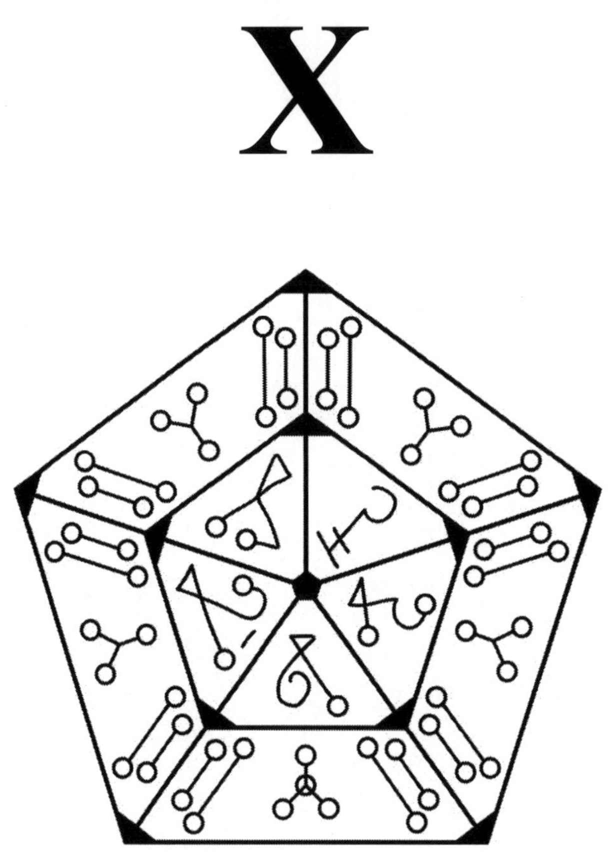

The Source of Radiant Essence Manifests Tri-dimensionally and It Is Mesmerizing

The Appearance of the Source of Radiant Essence in the Three-Dimensional Level

In order for the Source of Radiant Essence to materialize and manifest in the three-dimensional field, conclusive changes must happen in the subatomic and atomic structure of the universe.

These changes will allow human beings to see the incredible beauty of the Source of all Radiance Essence with physical eyes, leaving them completely surprised, fascinated, and awestruck.

The apparitions that have associated energy, which are commeasurable and have foundations in space and time, will simply be another veil of the three-dimensional dream; don't give them your attention, and transcend them.

These fields are in palpable suspension and propagate through temporary space at a speed similar to the speed of light, making colligate energy possible, which reveals the unreality of this dream.

The congregations of atoms on a microscopic level, like the lepton particles with negative electrical impetus, the baryonic particles without electric charge, the baryonic particles with positive electric charge, and the neutrons with magnetic lightning, will lose their processing keys. The electron will transform its elliptical spin to a perfect circular spin and will accelerate its circumferential route due to a change in the conception of the Absolute Consciousness.

From here on, there will be sets of subatomic particles that will form shining matter. Implicitly speaking, the baryons of the nucleus will remain coupled due to the field formed by fifth-dimensional particles similar to pions (mesons with zero spin that quickly decay into gamma-ray photons, little high-energy particles of light that are unaffected by magnetic fields) and introns (a polynucleotide sequence in a nucleic acid that does not code information for protein synthesis and is removed before translation of messenger RNA), which simultaneously will be transmuted; and, even if these keep on saving the zero spin, their structure will be forced to change in many ways. The astral counterparts to the quarks will blend with their three-dimensional projected shadow and will remain assembled through the exchange of implicit ultra radiant Arcturian gluons. When stellar lightning reaches them, they will lose this union, the gluons will become part of another universe, and an incandescent light will replace them. In this way, a change will take place over the perceived matter formed by animated molecules that will constantly decode their thought signatures, producing an alteration in direction, speed and luminous intensity. The ninth dimensional light will become their sort of adhesive in the moment that these collide; the kinetic energy that tends to distance them will lose its impetus and the viable energy that tends to bring them together will remain intact. This process will placate the impermanency of the universe for a while.

This fourth state of matter aggregation will, in due course, become an expressive configuration of incandescent gas that stars four-dimensionally broadcast. The symmetry of these particles will be electrically charged and will have a luminescent electromagnetic balance. This particle's nectar will vigorously express a long range of electromagnetic interactions; this constant interaction of magnetic forces will affect the human being that was prepared through the reading of this book in a positive way, leaving the person perplexed with profound ecstasies and without disintegrating him/her.

The Source will not take a defined shape; for some it will be expansive, for others it will have a human form, angelical form, or any form that the human individual can relate to. In definitive, it could acquire any mental conception of God that the person keeps in its mind. However, the Source will slowly destroy all conceptual shapes or forms, eventually. When the Source, in its plasmatic body, collides with dark magnetic fields, it will create structures of crystalline and lamellar filaments that will be as fine as hair. This will happen since the atoms at that point will be strongly agitated due to the great pressure the Source exerts over them by using high temperatures. The atoms' speed will increase and collide, producing a discharge of electrons. This discharge will reach the deepest reaches of the humans' three bodies.

The plasmatic body of the Source will cover the universe and blend with the intergalactic plasma modified by the darkness, adding a calming brightness to it that will irradiate the intra-clusters and the stars.

The forces of darkness have changed the interstellar plasma in some regions, making the positive/negative balance unstable and causing the flow of electrons to accelerate; such a situation overpowers the forces of electrostatic repulsion. The Source will reestablish the intergalactic plasmatic order of positive and negative charges, annulling the system's general charge.

If the Source feels an affinity for the prepared humans, this will attract them closer, introducing electrons into them, which will slide in the same direction. The humans will not resist such great celestial fascination and they will be disembodied momentarily. To the prepared people, the Source will grant ionic bodies that, at the beginning, will revolve around the Source in opposed orientation; however, in a short period, they will start to oscillate towards their original position, generating perfect balance. When the process ends, they will be returned to earth with light in their eyes. This experience will change their lives completely; the old personality will vanish, and the ego won't have a foundation. This human being will be one with Absolute Consciousness; this person will only want to share its glory in the world so that others may share his/her expansive happiness.

The Source Shows its Immensurable and Unlimited Bright Light

The higher the temperature that the Source transmits, and the higher the propagation of medium quadratic speed, the wider its orbit.
This is how the plasmatic manifestation of the Source is going to start to illuminate itself, and its illumination will be equal to 900,000,000,000,000 suns. Over this apparition, the Source will transfer its conscious forces, and it will start to illuminate and connect directly to its prepared human children that have not yet been disembodied; this link will be invaluable and magnificent it will illuminate the non-prepared pure human fully.
At the beginning, the temperature will be the first bond that connects the human being with the Source, and the magnitude of this temperature will exteriorize the degree of the thermal oscillation. This thermal energetic transfer will take place until the human's temperature is equal to that of the Source, reaching an admirable thermal balance. After reaching such balance, different electromagnetic frequencies will be introduced until, just as we said before, the human soul will be extracted from the body and encapsulated inside an ionic body that revolves around the Source of Infinite Radiance, to be returned to Earth fully enlightened.

The Empty Universe

In between all these conceptual outlines that we are transmitting, we need you to understand that the current terrestrial physical schemes also state that 5% of the universe is composed by a mass of common elements. Terrestrial scientists believe that part of this important mass is a combination of baryons and electrons. The rest of the universe is composed of matter and dark energy; this backs up our statement that this three-dimensional universe was invaded by the children of the dark.

Modern terrestrial sciences indicate that gas, stars, galaxies, and apparently empty space are composed by less baryons than what should really exist. This subtraction of baryons took place after the subatomic and molecular change that the forces of darkness imposed over the three-dimensional universe. Spiritual filaments of dense astral substance that formed a luminous net around the entire universe distributed this non-disintegrated baryonic matter. The dark modification happened after the cosmologic nucleo-synthesis, where the first light elements, such as hydrogen and its conceptual active isotopes, were created.
Because matter is a living thought, it can't be created or destroyed; it only transforms, since mass and energy are reciprocally altered.
What is really interesting is that a portion of all the matter in this universe that is transformed becomes photons; this partial conversion was completed in a far galactic past, before the children of the dark took charge of the third dimension.
Back then, all transmuted matter became pure light. In those times, there was a conversion in the nuclear reactions from matter into radiant energy. The mass, instead of becoming reduced, disappeared completely; a fission process was observed, like a bright marvelous explosion and, through a fusion process, the transformed matter would look like the stars. The universe used to be a light universe, were the human body would become radiant with each splendorous electromagnetic bombing.

Empty Matter

The apparently substantial matter is nothing more than empty fluctuations in the void, or conceptual fluctuations in the thinking universe.
Explaining this from a mental point of view, we can say that an irrational activity happens inside of the protons and the neutrons, which are the particles that contribute to the totality of the material mass.
Terrestrial scientists believe that each proton and neutron composed by three quarks reaches 1% of the total volume of the atom; this indicates that 99% of each object or living being is empty space.
The mass is established by the potency that holds the quarks together. This potency is restrained by a field of implicit particles, called gluons, that randomly invade its existence to later vanish or disappear instantly. These gluons work inter-dimensionally and constantly travel from the fifth to the third dimensions. The energy and the fluctuations in the void are added to the mass of the neutron and the proton.

The anti-quark and quark pairs also travel from dimension to dimension, and can break out and momentarily transmute a proton, converting it into different, more exotic particles.

The atoms are not rigid, unaltered, hermetic, or impenetrable. They are formed systems that are constituted by lots of particles. The interior of the atom is, in its totality, empty thinking space; the small nucleus, on the other hand, which seems to be dense material, is also a thought or dreamed nucleus. Alternately, the dreamed matter of the nucleus that apparently can be touched is like the tip of a pin in the center of a baseball stadium. So, imagine that, even if this universe wasn't a dreamt universe, if we follow the laws of physics, we will understand that we, along with all of creation, are but empty space.

The electrons do not have measurable extensions. They move like a whirlpool in empty space that is a billion times bigger than the volume of the nucleus. This proves that only a billionth of a portion of the atom is of tangible matter. In this very second, you are in a fantasy universe made out of rules that don't make a lot of sense. For example, a marble made out of compact nuclear matter would have an inconceivable density; this little marble could weigh millions of tons; this is conceptual weight, ruled by a mental law.

This is why we say to you: don't believe so much in what you see or in the physical laws, since they are imposed by a spontaneous and spatial mind. All that you observe around you are just living thoughts.

Even though the three-dimensional objects seem constituted by solids, liquids or gasses that can be diluted, transmuted, heated or touched, they are not real. Realize that you are interacting in a dream with mental laws that can be transgressed easily.

XI

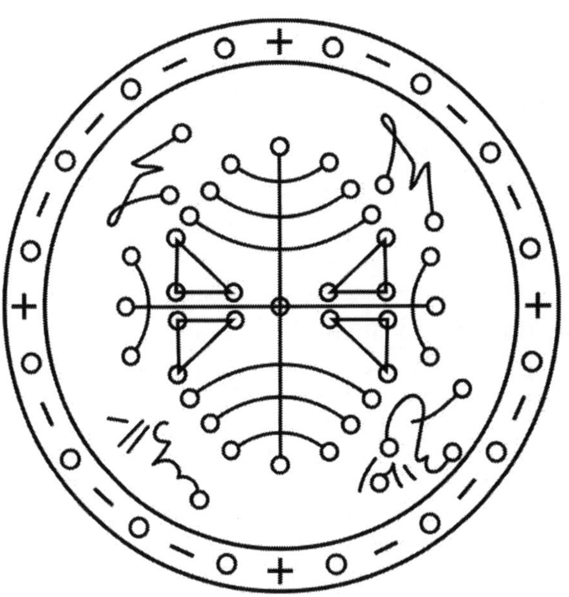

Reading this Book Magically Changes You

The Magic of Reading

Read carefully and transfigure your three bodies

Each sentence written here awakens and illuminates the astro-energetic filaments of the human body. Each printed letter is connected with light beings, that are anxious to start sharing their light and Love with you.
This book acts on the physical body by cleansing the psycho-spiritual patterns planted by the spawn of darkness, and instantly introduces new, evolving, and stabilizing energy patterns.
For example, when you read about the genetic changes explained here, right this very second, the changes are happening inside yourself first in an energetic level.
On an astral plane, right now, we are changing the structure of the hydrogen particles that serve as magnets to hold the nucleic acid chains together. In this way, the magnetism directionally changes and each cell creates an internal vortex that forms a wavy chain where four strands will intercross instead of two.
These chemical matrices are used with the purpose of feeding the evolutionary process. The molecular structure of the synthesized proteins orders your character and behavior. The psycho-corporeal restructuring that the reader is going through as this book is being read changes the internal quality of the molecules.
Through these living words, we modify the way in which the hydrogen "union" protein is being synthesized. We architectonically take this "union hydrogen" into the nucleotide and make it spin at a very high speed. This changes its structure and magnetic gravitation; the action forces the proton, or the proton interface, to become destabilized—with the purpose of destroying the energy of involution injected by the darkness.
Consequently, the hydrogen particle will replicate while it spins and will transmit light flashes over the information matrix that restores life to the expansive thinking in the individual human brain.
The DNA code will become more complex, increasing its filaments in the three bodies.
When you have an extra hydrogen union matrix, it is possible for the cells to carry different combinations of nucleic acids, causing a change in how your internal universe processes the proteins. The DNA that was

blemished by the Nebula consists of two filaments that intercross; the nucleic acid molecule is responsible for this union. This same molecule will be forced to open the doorways to an ineffable world; in this precise place, a new combination will occur.

Be prepared while we alter, in this present moment, the matrix of the repressive and oppressive proton and introduce multiple magnetic scenarios. This magnetism generates an irreversible change in the nuclei of the subatomic particles. Be ready now, because all density scenarios will be modified in the midst of chemical reactions that will affect the molecular transmitters.

This bio-energy process that you have chosen to go through will affect your materiality by transmuting your dense physicality into iridescent energy, which will project spatially or multidimensionally to any wanted region of the universe.

If the dreamt proton flow is controlled with super radiant light filaments coming from the fifth dimension, it is possible for the humans to transmute, change the three-dimensional chemistry, and reprogram cellular regeneration.

The Luminous Nine are urging you to become one of the evolved humans that will assist other humans into their evolution or ascension.

Through this information, they will change the more complex organic compounds, creating corresponding elements for a correct chemical evolution to take place inside the reader's organism.

Additionally, the modulated gravitational waves that come from the fifth dimension, which are caused by a luminous intelligence without precedent, will affect the reader profoundly and will rectify his/her astral body.

This iridescent gravitational force has three symbiotic dream forces, similar to the three-dimensional molecules that form photons.

001001-000000-000000, 000001-000001-000001, 100000-101011-000001, are the three names used to describe these fifth-dimensional particles, which, while united and oscillating, form the base of the astral light. These energy codes penetrate the human spine and a series of tubular meridians in this area. This activates, on an astral level, dormant energies in the first of the human vortices, in the area of the perineum. This energy on Earth, and specifically in India, took the name of Kundalini. This Kundalini was affected by the Source of all Darkness thousands of years ago. Back then, Kundalini had four filaments that affected the nervous system, four filaments that affected the astral body, four that affected the causal body, and one filament that ascended through the center of one of these tubular meridians known to humans as the

Sushumna. These filaments of light also penetrated Citrini, which connected the three bodies known by psychic humans in the present and, at the same time, joined the soul with other multidimensional crystalline silhouette kinds of encasements.

Citrini, which is inside the Sushumna, is a very complex nadi (astral channel), as fine and delicate as silk.

Citrini was decoded and weakened by the darkness, and this made our work significantly more complicated. In the past, when we introduced any kind of astral light, Citrini was destroyed; the physical body collapsed, never recovered, and in most cases resulted in a complete destruction of the organism. In other cases, when the physical body was very strong, as in the case of a young warrior, a sinister nervous breakdown took place. Back then, it was impossible for us to comprehend such impenetrable, grayish, superimposed obscurity and, therefore, we were unable to help. However, we learned how to work with the resources that were available; light and live intelligence. Light is this intelligence. What we were forced to do was to reprogram the 001001-000000-000000, 000001-000001-000001, 100000-101011-000001 so that these would oscillate with different speeds around a 100000-101011-000001 (it is important to mention that in the past, 001001-000000-000000 was the nucleus). This change affected the vibration of the astral light, which created a series of biomagnetic resonances, causing another vibration field where the desired energy conversion took place.

In this moment, these astral luminous forces are being introduced into your body in the shape of living intelligent spirals, which softly embrace Citrini to strengthen it; this, in turn, affects the entire system of human biorhythms, which connects with dense energy of innocuous materiality. With time and patience, we are now finally able to penetrate Citrini without causing intracellular electromagnetic chaos; the time for this change is while you read, relax and trust.

We, as well as you, have to be extremely patient. When Citrini is activated, a powerful light from the seventh dimension will be injected with carc and Love.

In the First Vortex, this light has four different nuclei that are composed by oscillating satellites with elliptic orbits.

These four nuclei do not need a source of energy; they are like a star of loving light that permanently changes its speed to replicate.

When this light pervades the first vortex, the polarization the human will experience will be so prevailing that, when its astral body spawns this living and replicating light, its configuration will change completely, and

its radiance will be appreciated with the naked human eye over the skin of the physical body being modified.
Simultaneously, the Kundalini energy will rise, but instead of being affected by "Eeipioc Serios" and its white star companion, which until now have made Kundalini ascend bilaterally like two intercrossed serpents, this new stimulating energy will come straight from Arcturus, a star that started fusing helium to oxygen that has one carbon molecule. Even though this stellar reaction indicates that helium is beginning to run low and its expansion is inevitable, right now, it is the ideal star to make Kundalini awaken and transmute it with quadruple filaments in each of the three bodies, like a centrifugal axis that relieves Citrini.
When this marvelous experience manifests, with the help of the Luminous Nine and these printed letters, the Source of all Light will be able to embrace the subtle body, destroying all its karma and destiny.
The loving and maternal embrace will liberate all beings from the enslaving grayish darkness forever, and they will be immortalized in Absolute Consciousness.

Three Dimensional Neuronal Effects Provoked by this Reading

Udviat atratakat astamiat drat aditiurt Sabi-el

With the reading of this book, a complex amount of feelings can also be felt. These feelings may seem amorphous, since, on a neuronal level, changes of different types happen. Since the neurons that are characterized by having morphological typologies (also known as perikaryon) feed the cellular body bright watery substances, there is a deep emotional release coming from memories stored deeply within them.
The light will force an undetermined number of elongations to transmit more impulses than usual to the perikaryon; these flashing lights also force the axon to transmit radiant impulses of Arisian light from the perikaryon to another neuron. In this way, new light patterns are created that replace the nocturne patterns of the children of the darkness. The reprogramming that you are undergoing forces the stagnated dusk in the cells to flow to the surface so that the individual can see it.
These intercellular neurological schemes (which seem normal) were created thousands of years ago by the fallen beings of light who were overwhelmed by the shadows so the human beings would be attracted to the deepest night to feel the suffering that spawns from the abyss of the

Nebula in their souls with the purpose of energetically feeding the Nebula with their spirit.
We are the secret to neuronal regeneration, even though it has been thought that said regeneration is impossible. In this moment, we are introducing spherical patterns of light, with the purpose of regenerating the myelinated nerves of the peripheral nervous system with a coat of nucleolus-cellular radiance. In this moment, we are working conspicuously inside the neurons' nuclei, triangulating them with fluorescent celestial programs. In the disperse chromatin, we inject hot aquatic luminescence. This action heats the central axis and relatively increases the transcriptional activity, exciting the possibility of a healthy, sane, and safe evolution towards light and infinite Love.
Because of this transformation, the nuclear wrapping itself displays changes that urge it to develop. Here, we force structures that help accumulate proteins with high tyrosine and arginine contents to appear and reappear by an act of magic.
The living aquatic light keeps pervading all the neuronal spheres in your body here and now while you read, reaching organelles that fill the cytoplasm that surrounds the nucleus and changes its structure.
There is a type of organelle full of free ribosomes that are glued to the rough endoplasmic reticulum; these are like lumps of high electric content. This electricity will be increased almost disproportionally; obligating the organelles will become cisterns of the ando-plasmatic reticulum. These organelles are now permanently discharging their rays to all the cells of the system with the purpose of internally modifying them and getting them prepared for the union of the messianic filaments with the DNA filaments. The biokinetic rate of the perikaryon, in relation to the protein synthesis, will increase right this very second due to the intelligent and living lightning of the light beings. This is how the indefinite reproduction of organelles through the use of hyper-electric tentacles is managed. This action restructures and aligns the psycho-biological body with the causal and astral bodies, increasing the extra sensorial capacities within the individual.
The somatic motor neurons receive discharges of 001001-001100-001111 and 011110-011110-010010 particles directly from the seventh dimension. 001001-001100-001111 and 011110-011110-010010 particles are components of high luminescent content that, along with 010101-001100-010111, 000001-111110-010101 and 0011000-101001-010111 particles of light, produces a certain type of highly radiant atmosphere in the seventh dimension.

001001-001100-001111 and 011110-011110-010010 will be particles that pervade the ocean of the three-dimensional bone marrow and a group of motor cranial nerves with the purpose of awakening Asuntara, the energy of four intercrossed filaments, inside the human being.
These light particles affect the perikaryon and the dendrites, leaving the axon aside. Sometime in the near future, when viewing through superimposed magnifying lenses, the dendrites will appear to be more noticeable, and may be differentiated from the axons in the neutrophil due to a high radiant content.
The primary lysosomes, which are rich in lipofuscin—which, according to terrestrial science, marginalizes the nucleus in elderly people—are being drastically altered right this very second with the motioned light particles. The small rounded mitochondria with longitudinal crests will increase their volume, preventing neurological diseases that have been engineered by dark vectors of the three-dimensional universe.
The neurotubules from the cytoskeleton of the perikaryon are being modified, and their appearance will differ in comparison to the appearance of the non-neuronal microtubules because they will look transparent and luminous when compared to the others. The neurotubules transformed by these Devic discharges will start to transfer and transmute the molecules of proteins into shining molecules with different combinations at much greater speed than usual, causing an extensive intracellular field that will affect protein synthesis and the communication of dendrites and the axon.
The Luminous Nine intermittently bombard the cytoplasmic projections which are lacking a myelin coat with 010101-001100-010111 particles from the seventh dimension and bright 011011-011110-110011 particles from the fifth dimension. This action affects the numerous microtubules and increases the neuron dendrite filaments; this simple and intelligent action changes the endoplasmic reticule completely, which releases the black radiations implanted by the children of the dark.
The cytoplasmatic electro-dense material is rectified here and now while the plasmatic membrane gets bombarded with violet light that changes the structure of the dense filament matter; in this way, the potential action starts to translate the synaptic signal into a celestial Devic 011011 signal.
The neurons that naturally communicate with precision, speed, and incipient intelligence with other muscular and glandular cells through electro nervous impulses will start, from now, to connect and transform from a distance the neurons and cells of other biological organisms that come close to you. Its reach will project longitudinally approximately 100 meters from where you are standing or sitting. You will start affecting people that surround you positively without you even noticing or trying.

They will, in some cases, feel that the amazing energy is coming from you.
The Nine Devas of Crystalline Fire make sure that the enlightenment process doesn't only affect the person who reads this book and follows the advice here described, but also to whomever gets close to the individual who has been already restructured.

{THE READING}{EXPLANATION} READ CAREFULLY AND TRANSFIGURE YOUR BODY. EACH SENTENCE WRITTEN HERE AWAKENS AND ILLUMINATES THE ASTRO-ENERGETIC FILAMENTS OF THE HUMAN BODY. EACH PRINTED LETTER IS CONNECTED WITH LIGHT BEINGS, AND THEY ARE ANXIOUS TO START SHARING THEIR LIGHT AND LOVE WITH YOU. THIS BOOK ACTS ON THE PHYSICAL BODY BY CLEANSING THE PSYCHO-SPIRITUAL PATTERNS PLANTED BY THE SPAWN OF DARKNESS, AND INSTANTLY INTRODUCES NEW, EVOLVING, AND STABILIZING ENERGY PATTERNS. FOR EXAMPLE, WHEN YOU READ ABOUT THE GENETIC CHANGES EXPLAINED HERE. RIGHT THIS VERY SECOND, THE CHANGES ARE HAPPENING INSIDE YOURSELF. ON A PHYSICAL LEVEL, RIGHT NOW, WE ARE CHANGING THE STRUCTURE OF THE HYDROGEN PARTICLES THAT SERVE AS MAGNETS TO HOLD THE NUCLEIC ACID CHAINS TOGETHER. IN THIS WAY, THE MAGNETISM DIRECTIONALLY CHANGES AND EACH CELL CREATES AN INTERNAL VORTEX THAT FORMS A WAVY CHAIN WHERE FOUR STRANDS WILL INTERCROSS INSTEAD OF TWO. THESE CHEMICAL MATRICES ARE USED WITH THE PURPOSE OF FEEDING THE EVOLUTIONARY PROCESS. THE MOLECULAR STRUCTURE OF THE SYNTHESIZED PROTEINS ORDERS YOUR CHARACTER AND BEHAVIOR. THE PSYCHO-CORPOREAL RESTRUCTURING THAT THE READER IS GOING THROUGH AS THIS BOOK IS BEING READ AND CHANGES THE INTERNAL QUALITY OF THE MOLECULES. THROUGH THESE LIVING WORDS WE MODIFY THE WAY IN WHICH THE HYDROGEN "UNION" PROTEIN IS BEING SYNTHESIZED. WE ARCHITECTONICALLY TAKE THIS "UNION HYDROGEN" INTO THE NUCLEOTIDE AND MAKE IT SPIN AT A VERY HIGH SPEED. THIS CHANGES ITS STRUCTURE AND MAGNETIC GRAVITATION; THE ACTION FORCES THE PROTON, OR THE PROTON INTERFACE, TO BECOME DESTABILIZED WITH THE PURPOSE OF DESTROYING THE ENERGY OF INVOLUTION INJECTED BY THE DARKNESS. CONSEQUENTLY, THE HYDROGEN PARTICLE WILL REPLICATE WHILE IT SPINS AND IT WILL TRANSMIT LIGHT FLASHES OVER THE INFORMATION MATRIX THAT RESTORES LIFE TO THE EXPANSIVE THINKING IN THE INDIVIDUAL HUMAN BRAIN. THE DNA CODE WILL BECOME MORE COMPLEX, INCREASING ITS FILAMENTS IN THE THREE BODIES. WHEN YOU HAVE AN EXTRA HYDROGEN UNION MATRIX, IT IS POSSIBLE FOR THE

0-101011-000001, ARE THE THREE NAMES USED TO DESCRIBE THESE
TRAL BODY. THIS IRIDESCENT GRAVITATIONAL FORCE HAS THREE
GRAVITATIONAL WAVES THAT COME FROM THE FIFTH DIMENSI
MORE COMPLEX ORGANIC COMPOUNDS, CREATING CORRE
ARE URGING YOU TO BECOME ONE OF THE EVOLVED H
DIMENSION, IT IS POSSIBLE FOR THE HUMANS
SIONALLY TO ANY WANTED REGION OF THE UNI
LL AFFECT YOUR MATERIALITY BY TRANSM
EMICAL REACTIONS THAT WILL AFFEC
EI OF THE SUBATOMIC PARTICLE
AND INTRODUCE MULTIPLE MA
EPARED WHILE WE ALTER IN
S TO AN INEFFABLE WO
SIBLE FOR THIS UNIO
O FILAMENTS TH
. THE DNA TH
OW YOUR I
NUCL
RR

SYMBIOTIC DREAM FORCES, SIMILAR TO THE
ON, WHICH ARE CAUSED BY A LUMINOUS IN
SPONDING ELEMENTS FOR A CORRECT CHEM
UMANS THAT WILL ASSIST OTHER HUMAN

C
COM
AUSING
SE PROCESS
BY THE NEBUL
E NUCLEIC ACID M
LE WILL BE FORCED
PLACE, A NEW COMBINAT
HE MATRIX OF THE REPRESSIV
AGNETISM GENERATES AN IRREVE
ALL DENSITY SCENARIOS WILL BE M
S. THIS BIO-ENERGY PROCESS THAT YOU
INTO IRIDESCENT ENERGY, WHICH WILL PR
W IS CONTROLLED WITH SUPER RADIANT LIGHT
MENSIONAL CHEMISTRY, AND REPROGRAM CELLULAR
S INTO THEIR EVOLUTION OR ASCENSION. THROUGH THI
ICAL EVOLUTION TO TAKE PLACE INSIDE THE READER'S OR
TELLIGENCE WITHOUT PRECEDENT, WILL AFFECT THE READER
THREE-DIMENSIONAL MOLECULES THAT FORM PHOTONS. 001001-00

FIFTH-DIMENSIONAL PARTICLES, WHICH, WHILE UNITED AND OSCILLATING, FORM THE BASE OF THE ASTRAL LIGHT. THESE ENERGY CODES PENETRATE THE HUMAN SPINE AND A SERIES OF TUBULAR MERIDIANS IN THIS AREA. THIS ACTIVATES, ON AN ASTRAL LEVEL, DORMANT ENERGIES IN THE FIRST OF THE HUMAN VORTICES, IN THE AREA OF THE PERINEUM. THIS ENERGY ON EARTH, AND SPECIFICALLY INDIA TOOK THE NAME OF KUNDALINI. THIS KUNDALINI WAS AFFECTED BY THE SOURCE OF ALL DARKNESS THOUSANDS OF YEARS AGO. BACK THEN, KUNDALINI HAD FOUR FILAMENTS THAT AFFECTED THE NERVOUS SYSTEM, FOUR FILAMENTS THAT AFFECTED THE ASTRAL BODY, FOUR THAT AFFECTED THE CAUSAL BODY, AND ONE FILAMENT THAT ASCENDED THROUGH THE CENTER OF ONE OF THESE TUBULAR MERIDIANS KNOWN TO HUMANS AS SUSHUMNA. THESE FILAMENTS OF LIGHT ALSO PENETRATED CITRINI, WHICH CONNECTED THE THREE BODIES KNOWN BY PSYCHIC HUMANS IN THE PRESENT, AND AT THE SAME TIME JOINED THE SOUL WITH OTHER MULTIDIMENSIONAL CRYSTALLINE SILHOUETTE KINDS OF ENCASEMENTS. CITRINI, WHICH IS INSIDE SUSHUMNA, IS A VERY COMPLEX NADI (ASTRAL CHANNEL), AS FINE AND DELICATE AS SILK. CITRINI WAS DECODED AND WEAKENED BY THE DARKNESS, AND THIS MADE OUR WORK SIGNIFICANTLY MORE COMPLICATED. IN THE PAST, WHEN WE INTRODUCED ANY KIND OF ASTRAL LIGHT, CITRINI WAS DESTROYED, THE PHYSICAL BODY COLLAPSED, NEVER RECOVERED, AND IN MOST CASES RESULTED IN A COMPLETE DESTRUCTION OF THE ORGANISM. IN OTHER CASES, WHEN THE PHYSICAL BODY WAS VERY STRONG AS IN THE CASE OF A YOUNG WARRIOR, A SINISTER NERVOUS BREAKDOWN TOOK PLACE. BACK THEN, IT WAS IMPOSSIBLE FOR US TO COMPREHEND SUCH IMPENETRABLE. GRAYISH, SUPERIMPOSED OBSCURITY, AND THEREFORE, WE WERE UNABLE TO HELP. HOWEVER, WE LEARNED HOW TO WORK WITH THE RESOURCES THAT WE WERE AVAILABLE; LIGHT AND LIVE INTELLIGENCE. LIGHT IS THIS INTELLIGENCE. WHAT WE WERE FORCED TO DO WAS TO REPROGRAM THE 001001-000000-000000,00000100000-100000-1,100000-101011-000001 SO THAT THESE WOULD OSCILLATE WITH DIFFERENT SPEEDS AROUND A 10000101-0011-000001 (IT IS IMPORTANT TO MENTION THAT IN THE PAST,

ALINI AWAKEN AND TRANSMUTE IT WITH QUADRUPLE FILAMENTS
THAT HAS ONE CARBON MOLECULE. EVEN THOUGH THIS STELLAR
HAVE MADE KUNDALINI ASCEND BILATERALLY LIKE TWO IN
CAL BODY THAT IS BEING MODIFIED. SIMULTANEOUSLY, T
THIS LIVING AND REPLICATING LIGHT, ITS CONFIGURA
ICATE. WHEN THIS LIGHT PERVADES THE FIRST V
LIPTIC ORBITS. THESE FOUR NUCLEI DO NOT N
ED WITH CARE AND LOVE. IN THE FIRST V
S YOU, HAVE TO BE EXTREMELY PATI
NTRACELLULAR ELECTROMAGNETIC
UOUS MATERIALITY. WITH TIM
TURN, AFFECTS THE ENTIRE
LIVING INTELLIGENT SP
ASTRAL LUMINOUS FO
THE DESIRED EN
AGNETIC RESO
THE ASTRA
HIS C
00

0
THE
ED THE
CREATED A
ANOTHER VIBRA
OOK PLACE. IN TH
ODUCED INTO YOUR B
EMBRACE CITRINI TO STR
YTHMS, WHICH CONNECTS WIT
OW FINALLY ABLE TO PENETRATE
CHANGE IS WHILE YOU READ, RELA
TED, A POWERFUL LIGHT FROM THE SEVE
FFERENT NUCLEI THAT ARE COMPOSED BY O
E LIKE A STAR OF LOVING LIGHT THAT PERMAN
HUMAN WILL EXPERIENCE WILL BE SO PREVAILING
TS RADIANCE WILL BE APPRECIATED WITH THE NAKED H
NSTEAD OF BEING AFFECTED BY "EEIPIOC SERIOS" AND ITS W
TING ENERGY WILL COME STRAIGHT FROM ARCTURUS, A STAR
REACTION INDICATES THAT HELIUM IS BEGI
NNING TO RUN LOW AND THAT ITS EXPANSION IS INEVITABLE, RIGHT NOW

IN EACH OF THE THREE BODIES LIKE A CENTRIFUGAL AXIS THAT RELIEVES CITRINI. WHEN THIS MARVELOUS EXPERIENCE MANIFESTS, WITH HELP OF THE LUMINOUS NINE AND THESE PRINTED LETTERS. THE SOURCE OF ALL LIGHT WILL BE ABLE TO EMBRACE THE SUBTLE BODY, DESTROYING ALL ITS KARMA AND DESTINY. THE LOVING AND MATERNAL EMBRACE WILL LIBERATE ALL BEINGS FROM THE ENSLAVING GRAYISH DARKNESS FOREVER, AND THEY WILL BE IMMORTALIZED IN ABSOLUTE CONSCIOUSNESS. {THREE DIMENSIONAL NEURONAL EFFECTS PROVOKED BY THIS READING}{UDVIAT ATRATAKA T ASTAMIAT DRATADITIURTSABI-EL} WITH THE READING OF THIS BOOK, A COMPLEX AMOUNT OF FEELINGS CAN ALSO BE FELT. THESE FEELINGS MAY SEEM AMORPHOUS, SINCE ON A NEURONAL LEVEL, CHANGES OF DIFFERENT TYPES HAPPEN. SINCE THE NEURONS THAT ARE CHARACTERIZED BY HAVING MORPHOLOGICAL TYPOLOGIES (ALSO KNOWN AS PERIKARYON) FEED THE CELLULAR BODY BRIGHT WATERY SUBSTANCES, THERE IS A DEEP EMOTIONAL RELEASE COMING FROM MEMORIES STORED DEEPLY WITHIN THEM. THE LIGHT WILL FORCE AN UNDETERMINED NUMBER OF ELONGATIONS TO TRANSMIT MORE IMPULSES THAN USUAL TO THE PERIKARYON; THESE FLASHING LIGHTS ALSO FORCE THE AXON TO TRANSMIT RADIANT IMPULSES OF ARISIAN LIGHT FROM THE PERIKARYON TO ANOTHER NEURON. IN THIS WAY, NEW LIGHT PATTERNS ARE CREATED THAT REPLACED THE NOCTURNE PATTERNS OF THE CHILDREN OF THE DARKNESS. THE REPROGRAMMING THAT YOU ARE UNDERGOING FORCES THE STAGNATED DUSK IN THE CELLS TO FLOW TO THE SURFACE, SO THAT IT IS SEEN BY THE INDIVIDUAL. THESE INTERCELLULAR NEUROLOGICAL SCHEMES (WHICH SEEM NORMAL) WERE CREATED THOUSANDS OF YEARS AGO BY THE FALLEN BEINGS OF LIGHT THAT WERE OVERWHELMED BY THE SHADOWS SO THE HUMAN BEINGS WOULD BE ATTRACTED TO THE DEEPEST NIGHT TO FEEL THE SUFFERING THAT SPAWNS FROM THE ABYSS OF THE NEBULA IN THEIR SOULS WITH THE PURPOSE OF ENERGETICALLY FEEDING THE NEBULA WITH THEIR SPIRIT. WE ARE THE SECRET TO NEURONAL REGENERATION, EVEN THOUGH IT HAS BEEN THOUGHT THAT SAID REGENERATION IS IMPOSSIBLE. IN THIS MOMENT, WE ARE INTRODUCING SPHERICAL PATTERNS OF LIGHT. WITH THE PURPOSE OF

001-001100-00111 AND 01110-01110-010010 PARTICLES DIRECTLY
AND ALIGNS THE PSYCHO-BIOLOGICAL BODY WITH THE CAUSAL
IGENT AND LIVING LIGHTNING OF THE LIGHT BEINGS. THIS
SIANIC FILAMENTS WITH THE DNA FILAMENTS. THE BIOK
PERMANENTLY DISCHARGING THEIR RAYS TO ALL THE
ECTRICITY WILL BE INCREASED ALMOST DISPROP
ELLE THAT IS FULL OF FREE RIBOSOMES, WHI
U READ, REACHING ORGANELLES THAT FIL
R BY AN ACT OF MAGIC. THE LIVING
FORCE STRUCTURES THAT HELP
E OF THIS TRANSFORMATION,
THE POSSIBILITY OF A HEA
S THE CENTRAL AXIS A
E DISPERSE CHROMAT
I, TRIANGULATI
T, WE ARE WO
AT OF NUC
E PER
G

AND ASTRAL BODIES, INCREASING THE EXTR
IS HOW THE INDEFINITE REPRODUCTION OF
CELLS OF THE SYSTEM WITH THE PURP

R
TED
OUS SYS
R RADIANCE
SLY INSIDE TH
RESCENT CELESTIA
QUATIC LUMINESCENC
SES THE TRANSCRIPTIONA
VOLUTION TOWARDS LIGHT AN
ELF DISPLAYS CHANGES THAT URG
HIGH TYROSINE AND ARGININE CONT
ING ALL THE NEURONAL SPHERES IN YOU
S THE NUCLEUS AND CHANGING ITS STRUCT
LASMIC RETICULUM; THESE ARE LIKE LUMPS OF
LL BECOME CISTERNS OF THE ANDO-PLASMATIC RET
OSE OF INTERNALLY MODIFYING THEM AND GETTING THE
LATION TO THE PROTEIN SYNTHESIS, WILL INCREASE RIGH
ORGANELLES THROUGH THE USE OF HYPERELECTRIC TENTACLE
A SENSORIAL CAPACITIES WITHIN THE INDIVIDUAL. THE SOMATIC

FROM THE SEVENTH DIMENSION. 001001-001100-001111 AND 011110-011110-010010 PARTICLES ARE COMPONENTS OF HIGH LUMINESCENT CONTENT THAT, ALONG WITH 010101-001100-010111. 000001-111110-010101 AND 0011000-101001-010111 PARTICLES OF LIGHT, PRODUCES A CERTAIN TYPE OF HIGHLY RADIANT ATMOSPHERE IN THE SEVENTH DIMENSION. 001001-001100-001111 AND 011110-011110-010010 WILL BE PARTICLES THAT PERVADE THE OCEAN OF THE THREE-DIMENSIONAL BONE MARROW AND A GROUP OF MOTOR CRANIAL NERVES, WITH THE PURPOSE OF AWAKENING ASUNTARA, THE ENERGY OF FOUR INTERCROSSED FILAMENTS. INSIDE THE HUMAN BEING. THESE LIGHT PARTICLES AFFECT THE PERIKARYON AND THE DENDRITES, LEAVING THE AXON ASIDE, SOMETIME IN THE NEAR FUTURE, WHEN VIEWING THROUGH SUPERIMPOSED MAGNIFYING LENSES, THE DENDRITES WILL APPEAR TO BE MORE NOTICEABLE, AND MAY BE DIFFERENTIATED FROM THE AXONS IN THE NEUTROPHIL DUE TO A HIGH RADIANT CONTENT. THE PRIMARY LYSOSOMES, WHICH ARE RICH IN LIPOFUSCIN—WHICH, ACCORDING TO TERRESTRIAL SCIENCE, MARGINALIZES THE NUCLEUS IN ELDERLY PEOPLE—ARE BEING DRASTICALLY ALTERED RIGHT THIS VERY SECOND WITH THE MOTIONED LIGHT PARTICLES. THE SMALL ROUNDED MITOCHONDRIA WITH LONGITUDINAL CRESTS WILL INCREASE THEIR VOLUME, PREVENTING NEUROLOGICAL DISEASES THAT HAVE BEEN ENGINEERED BY DARK VECTORS OF THE THREE-DIMENSIONAL UNIVERSE. THE NEUROTUBULES FROM THE CYTOSKELETON OF THE PERIKARYON ARE MODIFIED, AND THEIR APPEARANCE WILL DIFFER IN COMPARISON TO THE APPEARANCE OF THE NON-NEURONAL MICROTUBULES BECAUSE THEY WILL LOOK TRANSPARENT AND LUMINOUS WHEN COMPARED TO THE OTHERS. THE NEUROTUBULES TRANSFORMED BY THESE DEVIC DISCHARGES WILL START TO TRANSFER AND TRANSMUTE THE MOLECULES OF PROTEINS INTO SHINING MOLECULES WITH DIFFERENT COMBINATIONS AT MUCH GREATER SPEED THAN USUAL, CAUSING AN EXTENSIVE INTRACELLULAR FIELD THAT WILL AFFECT PROTEIN SYNTHESIS AND THE COMMUNICATION OF DENDRITES AND THE AXON. THE LUMINOUS NINE INTERMITTENTLY BOMBARD THE CYTOPLASMIC PROJECTIONS WHICH ARE LACKING A MYELIN COAT WITH 010101-001100-010111 PARTICLES FROM THE SEVENTH

N ALREADY RESTRUCTURED. . .
NT PROCESS DOESN'T ONLY AFFECT THE PERSON WHO
OR TRYING. THEY WILL, IN SOME CASES, FEEL
TELY 100 METERS FROM WHERE YOU ARE STAN
ISTANCE THE NEURONS AND CELLS OF OTH
OTHER MUSCULAR AND GLANDULAR C
DEVIC 011011 SIGNAL. THE NEURONS
MENT MATTER; IN THIS WAY,
ASMATIC MEMBRANE GETS B
RK. THE CYTOPLASMATI
LY, WHICH RELEASES
AND INTELLIGEN
AND INCREASE
THIS ACT
1 PAR
ND

D
011-
THE FIF
E NUMEROU
DRITE FILAMEN
THE ENDOPLASMIC
S IMPLANTED BY THE
RIAL IS RECTIFIED HERE
IGHT THAT CHANGES THE STRU
RTS TO TRANSLATE THE SYNAPTIC
TE WITH PRECISION, SPEED, AND I
IMPULSES, WILL START FROM NOW TO CO
COME CLOSE TO YOU. ITS REACH WILL PRO
AFFECTING PEOPLE THAT SURROUND YOU POSIT
G FROM YOU. THE NINE DEVAS OF CRYSTALLINE FI
DVICE HERE DESCRIBED, BUT ALSO TO WHOMEVER GETS

READS THIS BOOK AND FOLLOWS THE A

THAT THE AMAZING ENERGY IS COMIN

Uncomfortable Stages and Anesthesia

The symptoms that you will feel as you read these words are variable. If your nervous system isn't prepared, the Devas of Crystalline Fire will start injecting into the central nervous system a sort of light from the sixth dimension that will turn liquid. This light has the purpose of strengthening the nervous system and simultaneously numbing it so that it is able to tolerate the celestial radiations. During this process, you will feel tired and sleepy. Your legs will feel tired, as if you have been walking uphill for miles, but your muscles won't hurt. Simultaneously, your mental process will become slow and you will be a little forgetful. These symptoms will be short-lived.

If your nervous system is strong, you will feel a tickling sensation in all your nerve terminations, your spine, and brain, and something similar to orgasmic sensations in the heart and the center of the brain. You will also enjoy prodigious energy.

Since the nervous system has been generously recharged by the Luminous Nine, in some cases, the transmitted energy will be so much and so strong that you will be surprised by anxiety and even panic attacks. This is also momentary, and will pass as soon as your nervous system gets used to this new luminous energy.

At this point, they will let your system recover and, on some occasions, they will apply their anesthesia while the process of corporal alchemy goes on. Due to the emotional, physical, mental, and psycho-spiritual cleansing, the person will go through moments of emotional, existential, and mental crisis.

Try to relax during these periods—relax more and more. Do not tense your body—trust; our promise is to accompany you until the end. We are with you now, and will be with you through good and bad times.

Don't be tense, relax, accept the energies and let them purify you entirely. Relax your body, mind and soul.

With time, you will start to have visions, to hear us and to feel us. In order for this to happen, you must relax, trust, pay attention, and concentrate on the point five inches behind the crown of your head. Ask and listen.

We wish you all the luck in the universe in your new navigation and change of course.

Do us a favor, and do yourself a favor—don't be concerned anymore about your physical appearance; the clothes or the brands you wear, the car you drive, the jewels you own, the house you live in, or any other type of materiality that seems to define you.

Untie yourself from everything; detach yourself. You are beautiful the way you were created and you do not need any additives. Become free from the darkest forces that want to turn off your light; do not let society's rules overcome you. Do not be ashamed of your body. You are a brilliant and marvelous soul. Look at yourself, understand yourself, and live happily; this life is only a figment of your imagination that appears and disappears in the blink of an eye.
Love yourself more and more every day; Love all your enemies more and more, and wish everyone wellbeing and light. Understand those that shelter themselves in their material possessions to feel like they are somebody; those who use material power to feel like they are superior to others. Understand that these are only tortured souls full of terrible dark anguish and fear. Comprehend that even people who do terrible things are simply sick with the virus of the Nebula. I am not saying this to be naïve or submissive; you should be wary of these persons. Move apart from them or even sabotage the injustice they manifest, but never, (even if you have to fight against them with sword in hand)—never stop loving them and wishing them light and eternal peace.

XII

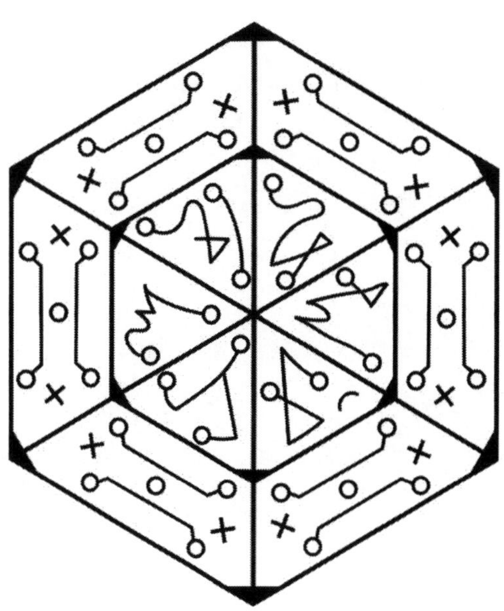

Speeding up Spiritual Evolution

The Practice

Asuntara, asuntarium aditratim aditratam vashtiakam Xiabiel

The energy in the reading of this book, in addition to the constant vibration of the terrestrial changes, will provoke an intracellular thermodynamic illumination. This will cause the soul's disembodiment, so that it is in tune with the same frequency of the tender decibels of dream creation, which will bring you closer to the Source of all Light.

These natural gifts will be absolutely necessary for spiritual perfection. Once the souls go through the transmutations projected by the higher powers of clear and shining light, these will flower with messianic fibers of high dynamic power.

These fibers, along with Asuntara, will occupy nine dimensions and will be in contact with all the angelical forces. These souls will earn nine great powers and seven lesser powers.

The Source of all Radiance will communicate directly with these souls, without any intermediaries. They will be able to understand how the relative reality of the universe lacks real and material foundations.

The atom will be understood as an innocuous mental concept; materiality will become cyclic angular information.

This reprogramming and three-dimensional human restructuration will be possible because the energetic forces of rotational circumvention will be alternating energies in different dimensions constantly with the purpose of creating undulated lines of light and circumscribed astral fields of radiance that transcend time and space. This synchronization of the soul may be observed simultaneously in this three-dimensional universe as nine opposite cones of light, surrounded by a spiral nebula with the large characteristics of a galaxy illuminated by divine celestial light.

This latent rotational spiral force will allow codified information with pervading rhythms of sub-solid refulgence to penetrate the nine dimensions.

The human race has to work along with the spiritual and galactic forces so that the spiritual axis of each individual undergoes a material galactic, dimensional, ethereal, and anti-material alteration.

The human being will drop duality and (s)he will become able to accept that (s)he and the nine universes are one. This is possible through injections of shining spirals of light with vibrating audiovisuals that display themselves magnificently, covering the entire universe. We will shatter the ego and, consequently, all illusion of separation will be left in oblivion.

Know that the forces of the splendorous irradiation will predominate in the nine dimensions, and since you, as a human being, are an extension of the power of Love, the Nine won't let the spiritual seed of light within you be nullified.

{THE PRACTICE} {ASUNTARA, ASUNTARIUM ADITRATIM ADITRATAM VASHATIAKAM XIABIEL} THE ENERGY IN THE READING OF THIS BOOK, IN ADDITION TO THE CONSTANT VIBRATION OF THE TERRESTRIAL CHANGES, WILL PROVOKE AN INTRACELLULAR THERMODYNAMIC ILLUMINATION. THIS WILL CAUSE THE SOUL'S DISEMBODIMENT, SO THAT IT IS IN TUNE WITH THE SAME FREQUENCY OF THE TENDER DECIBELS OF DREAM CREATION, WHICH WILL BRING YOU CLOSER TO THE SOURCE OF ALL LIGHT. THESE NATURAL GIFTS WILL BE ABSOLUTELY NECESSARY FOR SPIRITUAL PERFECTION. ONCE THE SOULS GO THROUGH THE TRANSMUTATIONS PROJECTED BY THE HIGHER POWERS OF CLEAR AND SHINING LIGHT, THESE WILL FLOWER WITH MESSIANIC FIBERS OF HIGH DYNAMIC POWER. THESE FIBERS, ALONG WITH ASUNTARA, WILL OCCUPY NINE DIMENSIONS AND THEY WILL BE IN CONTACT WITH ALL THE ANGELICAL FORCES. THESE SOULS WILL EARN NINE GREAT POWERS AND SEVEN LESSER POWERS. THE SOURCE OF ALL RADIANCE WILL COMMUNICATE DIRECTLY WITH THESE SOULS, WITHOUT ANY INTERMEDIARIES. THEY WILL BE ABLE TO UNDERSTAND HOW THE RELATIVE REALITY OF THE UNIVERSE LACKS REAL AND MATERIAL FOUNDATIONS. THE ATOM WILL BE UNDERSTOOD AS AN INNOCUOUS MENTAL CONCEPT; MATERIALITY WILL BECOME CYCLIC ANGULAR INFORMATION. THIS REPROGRAMMING AND THREE-DIMENSIONAL HUMAN RESTRUCTURATION WILL BE POSSIBLE BECAUSE THE ENERGETIC FORCES OF ROTATIONAL CIRCUMVENTION WILL BE ALTERNATING ENERGIES IN DIFFERENT DIMENSIONS CONSTANTLY WITH THE PURPOSE OF CREATING UNDULATED LINES OF LIGHT AND CIRCUMSCRIBED ASTRAL FIELDS OF RADIANCE THAT TRANSCEND TIME AND SPACE. THIS SYNCHRONIZATION OF THE SOUL MAY BE OBSERVED SIMULTANEOUSLY IN THIS THREE-DIMENSIONAL UNIVERSE AS NINE OPPOSITE CONES OF LIGHT, SURROUNDED BY A SPIRAL NEBULA WITH THE LARGE CHARACTERISTICS OF A GALAXY ILLUMINATED BY DIVINE CELESTIAL LIGHT. THIS LATENT ROTATIONAL SPIRAL FORCE WILL ALLOW CODIFIED INFORMATION. WITH PERVADING RHYTHMS OF SUB-SOLID REFULGENCE TO PENETRATE THE NINE DIMENSIONS. THE HUMAN RACE HAS TO WORK ALONG WITH THE SPIRITUAL AND GALACTIC FORCES SO THAT THE SPIRITUAL AXIS OF EACH INDIVIDUAL UNDERGOES A

MATERIAL GALACTIC, DIMENSIONAL, ETHEREAL, AND ANTI-MATERIAL ALTERATION. THE HUMAN BEING WILL DROP DUALITY AND (S)HE WILL BECOME ABLE TO ACCEPT THAT (S)HE AND THE NINE UNIVERSES ARE ONE. THIS IS POSSIBLE THROUGH INJECTIONS OF SHINING SPIRALS OF LIGHT WITH VIBRATING AUDIOVISUALS THAT DISPLAY THEMSELVES MAGNIFICENTLY COVERING THE ENTIRE UNIVERSE. WE WILL SHATTER THE EGO AND, CONSEQUENTLY, ALL ILLUSION OF SEPARATION WILL BE LEFT IN OBLIVION. KNOW THAT THE FORCES OF THE SPLENDOROUS IRRADIATION WILL PREDOMINATE IN THE NINE DIMENSIONS, AND SINCE YOU AS A HUMAN BEING ARE AN EXTENSION OF THE POWER OF LOVE, THE NINE WON'T LET YOUR SPIRITUAL SEED OF LIGHT WITHIN YOU BE NULLIFIED .

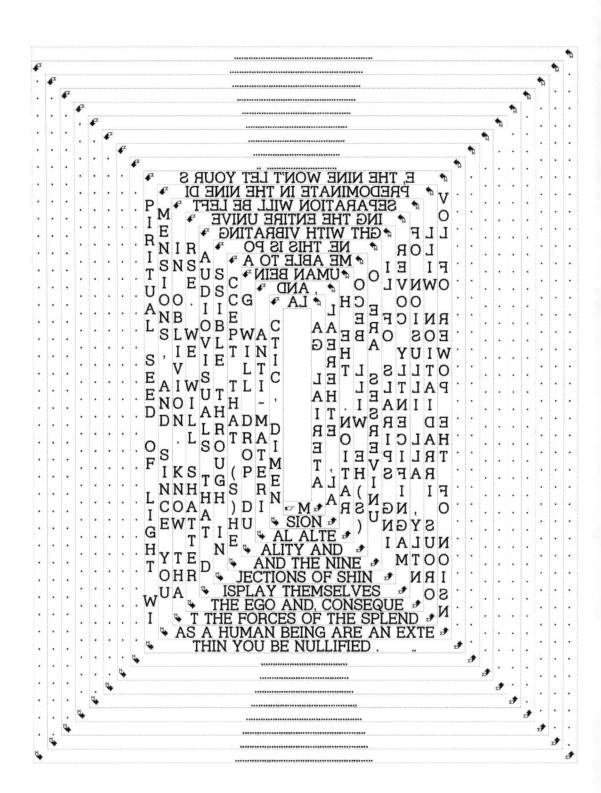

First Option for the Unchanging Human Being

The portion of the human beings that didn't make the spiritual leap during the changes and who will be left on Earth will have to evolve through different spherical worlds.

A chemical-spiritual seed will be implanted in numerous electromagnetic fields of gray vibrating thoughts inside the top astral capsule, which is located at the center of the brain; in this way, the individual conscious of the "I" will become purified.

This new, three-dimensional individual will work as a bond between the luminous and dark systems.

The Source will dazzle the human beings embraced by confusion and will force them to understand that time and space are only figments of their imagination. With this understanding, the individual will be able to penetrate the secrets of his/her soul. The Devas, at this point, will dismantle the personality while extracting the soul from its continuous cycle of suffering.

These individualized human drops, so to speak, will be prepared for a planetary migration and will orbit through spectral forces closer to the Source of all Radiance. Linear time will determine when the "I" encapsulation will have to move into a new encasing of a more expansive gravitational spectrum.

This cyclic pressure of the universe is, and will be, exerted universally in different historical intergalactic moments. In a certain moment, the entire galaxy will go through multidimensional fields, where its planets and stars will suffer a severe magnetic and gravitational transmutation. If you doubt our words, observe the geophysical terrestrial fields in the present moment.

When the earth starts to expel magma from its center, the spiritual forces inside the physical shell will be reprogrammed beyond their three-dimensional shield. This high vibration going to be injected into the human being and will momentarily transfer the code of the material human body to another parallel third dimension that is similar to this concurrent dimension.

In this way, the physical human body will be rescued and restructured in order to be reinserted into a new world.

Second Option for the Unchanging Human Being

The implantation of eternal crystalline light deposited into the human body might lose its radiance. Due to this phenomenon, the body will have to be restructured with new meridians and DNA. Before the reinsertion, the soul encapsulated in this new model will be capable of living inside the magnetic waves of light coming from the fifth dimension. The radiant intelligence will superimpose this more depurated model in a planet with different electromagnetic vibrations.

The new human standard, even though vibrating in between oscillating gray three-dimensional energies, will redirect the diverging forces.
In order for the new brain to work in four dimensions simultaneously, it will have to possess four receptive visual organs and fourth-dimensional ears.
The audiovisual system in these bodies will be of vital importance for the evolution of the human race, which has stagnated for thousands of years, so it can finally enter into pragmatic, progressive stellar horizons.
The reconstruction of the biological audiovisual system will be composed by ethereal astral filaments connected to the biochemical matter.
The visual system won't be precisely composed by eyes with irises, pupils, corneas, retinas, macula and so on. These more evolved visual organs will be placed on the head and will cover a radial circumference of 360 degrees; the visual power will change from being masculine, unilineal and unilateral, into a more global, spherical and feminine power.
The auditory system will not just capture circumferential waves, but it will also capture undulating sounds from other dimensions as well.
Once the body has reached the optimal adjustments in the fifth dimension, it will be returned to the three-dimensional stellar universe. However, this newly implemented body-mind-egoic organism will capture the energy waves of the fourth dimension, and will be able to have easier access to spaces of infinite radiant light. Such changes will push the human race to continue its evolution process to resplendent Devic horizons.

Total Three-Dimensional and Multidimensional Enlightenment

This presentation will begin by describing the mental and physical commotions of the human being in the enlightenment process within the three-dimensional field.
This is done with the purpose of preparing the human molecular body so it doesn't suffer when it collides with the infinite and in this manner transmutes to tolerate such impact and stay relaxed during the most incredible experience ever imagined.
As the human was created in the divine image of the Source of all Radiance, (s)he can experience God's greatness; humans can live, feel and enjoy divine expansion, if there is acceptance. These experiences work in favor of their purification. If there is complete relaxation and surrender to the refulgent Love, the ego will be destroyed and the Source will grant the most precious gift of all the dimensional fields to the individualized human mind.

First, the Source will expose the prepared human to an explosion of perpetual peace, and it will relive a species of three-dimensional spiritual nucleosynthesis.
While the enlightened one expands, (s)he will feel that the temperature of his/her soul decreases dramatically, as if a baryogenesis process is taking place within; (s)he will start producing stable thermodynamic protons and neutrons within his/her three bodies. The temperature will change permanently as time passes by. The reactions to reach a perfect thermodynamic harmony must be monitored by the Devas, who will be guided by Gabri-el-a and Raphael, who will combine the permutations transferred by the cosmic expansion. They will subtract the portion of protons and neutrons based on the temperature changes. This portion benefits the protons, since the great masses of neutrons appear from the conversion of neutrons to protons.
The Crystalline Devas understand the laws and constants of the dreaming consciousness that dictate the procedure of matter at these energy levels. For them, said process lacks speculative perplexities; they perform their job without vacillation or doubt in their crystalline minds.
While the individual goes through intense changes, it will expand and continue to feel colder. Its neutrons and its free protons will destabilize because seventh- dimensional light swirls will be inserted inside the body. In the instant that the spiritual nucleosynthesis happens, the temperature is

forced to rise with dynamic spectral lightning so spirit reaches a higher grade of passion of relating energy.

If something similar to deuterium is formed in this phase due to the intervention of the forces of darkness, the luminous One will immediately destroy it with fire. However, particles similar to the deuterium will be formed in the next phase where the formation of luminous gas is delayed. This luminous gas will set the stage for the adequate cooling of the expansion of the individual human consciousness, and the particle similar to deuterium will materialize with a spontaneous swirl of bright light.

After the explosion of the human consciousness, the three-dimensional astral mind will become excessively cold, impairing any type of nuclear fusion. Because of this, the elemental quantities will be established by the Devas of Crystalline Fire, forcing them to change genders in a phase where the decomposition of the spiritual nucleosynthesis takes place and effect.

The human being undergoing such changes will experience a very similar expansion to the leptonic expansion of baryons and photons. The human being will perceive the sensation of being LIGHT. In this stage, the consonance of expansion of being will be more than the scales of time of the numerous electromagnetic interactions. This is why the nuclear reactions will stay in perfect balance. The rhythm of expansion will be modified by cyclonic rays to provoke decoupling. The expansive "I" existence, in this moment, will be frozen with the purpose of causing a chain reaction where particles similar to neutrinos will lose balance, reaching the disengaging phase. They will propagate adiabatically with reciprocating temperatures corresponding to those of the dimensions of the "I" expansion.

After the explosive spiritual expansion, the reactions that preserve the harmony between neutrons and protons will turn more parsimonious than the expansion itself. In the three-dimensional field, and in a far corner of the universe, this enlightenment will be appreciated more for its implicit content of protons, which materializes a gassy body and, as a consequence, forces the photons to stop being adequately potent. This will give way to the materialization of pairs of particles similar to positrons; these changes will cause instauration of life into an interesting compensation of one electron for every 108 photons.

The pseudo-leptonic growth will reach its peak and evolve into a radiant expansion that will last 101,000 seconds, ending in a disarrangement of energy and matter with solar temperatures that are capable of originating a great refulgence at the foundation.

The individual in this phase will turn into a ball of energy that is fiery red, but (s)he will not experience any heat or any sort of uncomfortable feeling; on the contrary, the power experienced within will be magnificent and beautiful. After this transmutation ends, (s)he will start cooling down to produce heavier nuclei. The decrease in temperature will, without a doubt, be drastic; this has been planned in this way by the Devas so that any egotistical essence gets annihilated and the fundamental nature of being manifests with its entire splendor realized.

In the next phase, the individual particles will blend to produce certain gases similar to helium 3, 4 and hydrogen, which will cause an inconsistent nucleus of atomic mass. This nucleus will come to be the body of the prepared human being. The human will slowly transcend the three-dimensional parameters and start to access other types of subtle elements.

In these sectors, the prepared human will continue to expand externally and know the real nature of his/her spirit, the ego will cease to exist and (s)he will embrace all the existing dimensions.

There will be a new birth; a birth that implies total comprehension of the will of the multidimensional dream.

Reader, once you have awakened, you will behold that your essence is not just the Source of all Radiance, but also the Absolute Consciousness that dreams it.

Before completely losing your sense of dreamed individuality, you can choose between staying inside the dream or retiring to become pure and clear consciousness once more.

{TOTAL THREE-DIMENSIONAL AND MULTIDIMENSIONAL ENLIGHTENM

ENT} THIS PRESENTATION WILL BEGIN BY DESC

N THE THREE-DIMENSIONAL FIELD. THIS IS DONE WITH THE PU

TAY RELAXED DURING THE MOST INCREDIBLE EXPERIENCE EV

ESS; HUMANS CAN LIVE, FEEL AND ENJOY DIVINE EXPA

ATION AND SURRENDER TO THE REFULGENT LOVE, TH

INDIVIDUALIZED HUMAN MIND. FIRST, THE SOURC

REE-DIMENSIONAL SPIRITUAL NUCLEOSYNTHES

REASES DRAMATICALLY, AS IF A BARYOGE

NS AND NEUTRONS WITHIN HIS/HER TH

TIONS TO REACH A PERFECT THERM

EL-A AND RAPHAEL, WHO WILL

L SUBTRACT THE PORTION O

PORTION BENEFITS THE

THE CONVERSION OF

E DREAMING CON

ER AT THESE

STALLINE

CKS S

EY

EIR

ERPL

EM, SAI

RE UNDERST

DICTATE THE P

ONS. THE LAWS AN

GREAT MASSES OF N

S, BASED ON THE TEMPER

S TRANSFERRED BY THE COSM

MONITORED BY THE DEVAS, WHO

E WILL CHANGE PERMANENTLY WHILE

E WITHIN; (S)HE WILL START PRODUCING

EXPANDS, (S)HE WILL FEEL THAT THE TE

N TO AN EXPLOSION OF PERPETUAL PEACE, AND

OURCE WILL GRANT THE MOST PRECIOUS GIFT OF A

THESE EXPERIENCES WORK IN FAVOR OF THEIR PURIFI

D IN THE DIVINE IMAGE OF THE SOURCE OF ALL RADIANC

BODY SO IT DOESN'T SUFFER WHEN IT COLLIDES WITH THE IN

RIBING THE MENTAL AND PHYSICAL COMMOTIONS OF THE HUMAN B

JOB WITHOUT VACILLATION OR DOUBT IN THEIR CRYSTALLINE MINDS. WHILE THE INDIVIDUAL GOES THROUGH INTENSE CHANGES. IT WILL EXPAND AND CONTINUE TO FEEL COLDER. ITS NEUTRONS AND ITS FREE PROTONS WILL DESTABILIZE BECAUSE SEVENTH- DIMENSIONAL LIGHT SWIRLS WILL BE INSERTED INSIDE THE BODY. IN THE INSTANT THAT THE SPIRITUAL NUCLEOSYNTHESIS HAPPENS, THE TEMPERATURE IS FORCED TO RISE WITH DYNAMIC SPECTRAL LIGHTNING SO ITS SPIRIT REACHES A HIGHER GRADE OF PASSION OF LINKING ENERGY. IF SOMETHING SIMILAR TO DEUTERIUM IS FORMED IN THIS PHASE DUE TO INTERVENTION OF THE FORCES OF DARKNESS. IT WILL BE DESTROYED IMMEDIATELY BY THE LUMINOUS ONES WITH FIRE; HOWEVER, PARTICLES SIMILAR TO THE DEUTERIUM WILL BE FORMED IN THE NEXT PHASE WHERE THE FORMATION OF LUMINOUS GAS IS DELAYED. THIS LUMINOUS GAS WILL SET THE STAGE FOR THE ADEQUATE COOLING OF THE EXPANSION OF THE INDIVIDUAL HUMAN CONSCIOUSNESS, AND THE PARTICLE SIMILAR TO DEUTERIUM WILL MATERIALIZE WITH A SPONTANEOUS SWIRL OF BRIGHT LIGHT. AFTER THE EXPLOSION OF THE HUMAN CONSCIOUSNESS, THE THREE-DIMENSIONAL ASTRAL MIND WILL BECOME EXCESSIVELY COLD. IMPAIRING ANY TYPE OF NUCLEAR FUSION. BECAUSE OF THIS, THE ELEMENTAL QUANTITIES WILL BE ESTABLISHED BY THE DEVAS OF CRYSTALLINE FIRE FORCING THEM TO CHANGE GENDERIS, IN A PHASE WHERE THE DECOMPOSITION OF THE SPIRITUAL NUCLEOSYNTHESIS TAKES PLACE AND EFFECT. THE HUMAN BEING UNDERGOING SUCH CHANGES WILL EXPERIENCE A VERY SIMILAR EXPANSION TO THE LEPTONIC EXPANSION OF BARYONS AND PHOTONS. THE HUMAN BEING WILL PERCEIVE THE SENSATION OF BEING LIGHT. IN THIS STAGE. THE CONSONANCE OF EXPANSION OF BEING WILL BE MORE THAN THE SCALES OF TIME OF THE NUMEROUS ELECTROMAGNETIC INTERACTIONS. THIS IS WHY THE NUCLEAR REACTIONS WILL STAY IN PERFECT BALANCE. THE RHYTHM OF EXPANSION WILL BE MODIFIED BY CYCLONIC RAYS TO PROVOKE DECOUPLING. THE EXPANSIVE "I" EXISTENCE, IN THIS MOMENT, WILL BE FROZEN WITH THE PURPOSE OF CAUSING A CHAIN REACTION WHERE PARTICLES SIMILAR TO NEUTRINOS WILL LOSE BALANCE, REACHING THE DISENGAGING PHASE.

THEY WILL PROPAGATE ADIABATICALLY WITH RECIPROCATING TEMPERATURES CORRESPONDING TO THOSE OF THE DIMENSIONS OF THE "I" EXPANSION. AFTER THE EXPLOSIVE SPIRITUAL EXPANSION. THE REACTIONS THAT PRESERVE THE HARMONY BETWEEN NEUTRONS AND PROTONS WILL TURN MORE PARSIMONIOUS THAN THE EXPANSION ITSELF. IN THE THREE-DIMENSIONAL FIELD, AND IN A FAR CORNER OF THE UNIVERSE. THIS ENLIGHTENMENT WILL BE APPRECIATED MORE FOR ITS IMPLICIT CONTENT OF PROTONS, WHICH MATERIALIZES A GASSY BODY AND, AS A CONSEQUENCE, FORCES THE PHOTONS TO STOP BEING ADEQUATELY POTENT. THIS WILL GIVE WAY TO THE MATERIALIZATION OF PAIRS OF PARTICLES SIMILAR TO POSITRONS; THESE CHANGES WILL CAUSE INSTAURATION OF LIFE TO AN INTERESTING COMPENSATION OF ONE ELECTRON FOR EVERY 108 PHOTONS. THE PSEUDO-LEPTONIC GROWTH WILL REACH ITS PEAK, AND WILL EVOLVE INTO A RADIANT EXPANSION THAT WILL LAST 101,000 SECONDS, ENDING IN A DISARRANGEMENT OF ENERGY AND MATTER WITH SOLAR TEMPERATURES THAT ARE CAPABLE OF ORIGINATING A GREAT REFULGENCE AT THE FOUNDATION. THE INDIVIDUAL IN THIS PHASE WILL TURN INTO A BALL OF ENERGY THAT IS FIERY RED, BUT (S)HE WILL NOT EXPERIENCE ANY HEAT OR ANY SORT OF UNCOMFORTABLE FEELING; ON THE CONTRARY, THE POWER EXPERIENCED WITHIN WILL BE MAGNIFICENT AND BEAUTIFUL. AFTER THIS TRANSMUTATION ENDS, (S)HE WILL START COOLING DOWN TO PRODUCE HEAVIER NUCLEI. THE DECREASE IN TEMPERATURE WILL WITHOUT A DOUBT BE DRASTIC; THIS HAS BEEN PLANNED IN THIS WAY BY THE DEVAS SO THAT ANY EGOTISTICAL ESSENCE GETS ANNIHILATED AND THE FUNDAMENTAL NATURE OF BEING MANIFEST WITH ITS ENTIRE SPLENDOR IS REALIZED. IN THE NEXT PHASE, THE INDIVIDUAL PARTICLES WILL BLEND TO PRODUCE CERTAIN GASES SIMILAR TO HELIUM 3, 4 AND HYDROGEN, WHICH WILL CAUSE AN INCONSISTENT NUCLEUS OF ATOMIC MASS. THIS NUCLEUS WILL COME TO BE THE BODY OF THE PREPARED HUMAN BEING. THE HUMAN SLOWLY WILL TRANSCEND THE THREE-DIMENSIONAL PARAMETERS AND START TO ACCESS OTHER TYPES OF SUBTLE ELEMENTS. IN THESE SECTORS, THE PREPARED HUMAN WILL CONTINUE TO EXPAND EXTERNALLY AND KNOW

THE REAL NATURE OF HIS/HER SPIRIT, THE EGO WILL CEASE TO EXIST AND (S)HE WILL EMBRACE ALL THE EXISTING DIMENSIONS. THERE WILL BE A NEW BIRTH; A BIRTH THAT IMPLIES TOTAL COMPREHENSION OF THE WILL OF THE MULTIDIMENSIONAL DREAM. READER, ONCE YOU HAVE AWAKENED, YOU WILL BEHOLD THAT YOUR ESSENCE IS NOT JUST THE SOURCE OF ALL RADIANCE, BUT ALSO THE ABSOLUTE CONSCIOUSNESS THAT DREAMS ITSELF. BEFORE COMPLETELY LOSING YOUR SENSE OF DREAMED INDIVIDUALITY, YOU CAN CHOOSE BETWEEN STAYING INSIDE THE DREAM OR RETIRING TO BECOME PURE AND CLEAR CONSCIOUSNESS ONCE MORE.

XIII

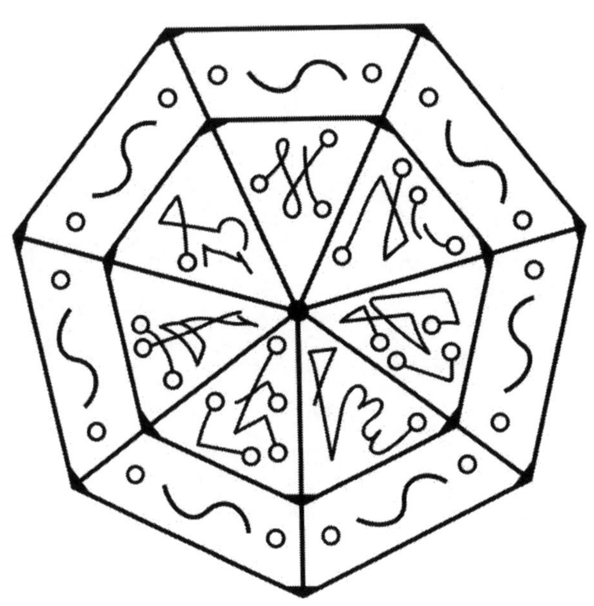

Speeding up Spiritual Evolution Still more

Meditative Practices of Particle Acceleration

If you want to speed the process of blazing illumination even more, you can try some of these exercises.

Breathing

Inhale for three seconds, hold the breath in for three seconds, exhale for three seconds and hold the breath out for three more seconds. All this must be done without being forceful and during the whole day and repeating the name of a seraphim, taking breaks of two to four hours after eating.
If there are any nervousness or anxiety problems, the breath retention after the inhalation should be removed from the practice.
The count should only increase if it happens naturally.
For example, AN-NA-BELL would be a name of three seconds. The practitioner should in this case repeat the three syllable name as she inhales (3), holds (3), exhales (3) and holds (3)....Repeat.

Rubi Adonai Meditation for Women

If the brilliance of the Mother Light is used properly, an intercellular exchange can take place that will start to govern each energetic vortex of the feminine body.
Devic harmonies are used during meditation to form vibratory frequencies in the form of radiant spirals, which connect the feminine body to higher harmonic combinations of multiple universes and undulating refulgent patterns in other dimensions of eternal light.
In this way, the physical and tangible reality will come to be perceived as patterns of angular and undulated lights that vibrate at different speeds. As this perception becomes more developed, women will be capable of understanding that these patterns were created by a breathtaking ethereal feminine vastness that covers everything in all universes, and that the effulgent light is simply the direct continuation of Her flowing splendor.
If the radiant worlds (networks) of communication are carefully selected within these dimensions, new patterns of thought will be resurrected in Her, giving rise to the coming age of the luminous restoration of the Universe.
Women are the key for this change to be possible. This responsibility is in your hands. Stop patriarchal oppression now and show your real expansive nature.
Repeat the angelic words below to reconnect with the Nine Devas of Crystalline Fire.

Adonai a-hit a-him adit-ra-tim mash-ist-ta-tim parak-tam

1- Mantra of Clear Cleanse:
ANDONAIIII ASH-TIM A-IIII A-IIIM

Repeat the mantra 9 times.

If the light that the meridians embrace is revealed, the mind can connect to the feminine radiance with more passion. The mantra illuminates the feminine meridians and attracts the maternal Devas.

2- The Feeling

Feel and scan each part of your body, even your bones from head to toe. To completely activate this energy, it is necessary to feel and to form temples of resonance in the nadis (meridians), which will bewilder the mind with their musical light.

3- Living Air Breath- Engage the 4-corner breath in sync with the name of the Seraphim.

This is done by making a temporal contemplative pause on each vortex, using breath retentions before the inhalations and after the exhalations, repeating the name of a Seraphim utilizing each syllable of the name as one second. For example, AN-NA-BELL would be a name of three seconds. The practitioner should in this case repeat the three syllable name as she inhales (3), holds (3), exhales (3) and holds (3)….Repeat. Simultaneously she should do several rounds (3 OR MORE) of breaths while redirecting the vital energy in the different vortexes, starting at the first vortex continuing to the ovaries, from the ovaries to the third vortex, and from there to the solar plexus, heart, breast, throat, third eye, until you reach the crown of the head.
When you apply these small breath retentions, they recharge the vortexes with energetic Love, awakening them and producing explosions of profound emotive color.

4- Fleeting Descent

From the crown of the head, let the energy drop through the center of the spine three times (3 X's) as if it were lightening. Exhale descend to the Earth connecting to the center of the Earth's core, thus connecting the femininity of The Mother to that of the human female body. Inhale, concentrate on the Crown and repeat two more times to complete the cycle of three.
The fleeting descent will open the portals of refulgent Love. This process will capture the power and transmute your energy into that of the Motherly beauty and its one thousand eight hundred and eighty-one transfigurations (1881).

This descent will ease the living energy connected to hormonal imbalances that torment women, bringing comfort and the soothing breeze of Maternal Love.

5- The Astral Spiral Ascension- Light particle accelerator

- The Astral Spirals are of PINK LIGHT, the color of LOVE, however if another color appears spontaneously, let it transpire.
- The Astral Spirals will transmute negative and collective critical mass into positive pragmatism. This pressure that the cyclonic vortex exerts will eventually take the woman's consciousness into another dimension with altered molecular codes.

a) **<u>Root Vortex to Ovaries</u>**- With an inhalation ascending your Feminine Power from the Root vortex to the ovaries by visualizing Pink Concentric Spirals circulating in inward moving helixes. Visualize inside of each Concentric Spiral, a particle of light or a sphere that travels from the periphery to its center simultaneously in both ovaries at extreme speeds until it reaches the center at such a high speed that it explodes into light. These explosions transpire on the inhale and logically the energy contracts on the exhale and ascends on the inhale. The natural rhythm of the inhale expands and the exhale contracts, all in perfect synchronicity.

Make sure the spirals are always perpendicular to the floor, not parallel.

b) **<u>Ovaries to Third Vortex (Navel)</u>**- Inhale as you ascend and transform the two Concentric Spirals into undulating lines that move in the form of the Kundalini rising, crisscrossing and intersecting at the Navel Vortex from both Ovaries. Position the Spirals one on top of the other above the Navel Vortex. Moving these 2 Concentric Spirals (which are slightly conical in form at the very center) in opposite directions (clockwise and counter clockwise) with one particle of light in each spiral, visualize these particles of light traveling the Concentric Spiral from the periphery of the Spiral to the center at high speeds, accelerating as they get closer to the center until they reach its axis, where they touch in the very center and collide and explode with an amazing expansion of light, which then contracts with the exhalation and ascends with the inhalation moving these spirals up to the center of the Chest.

c) **Center of the Chest Vortex (Heart)** – Inhale and repeat, inward circulating Concentric Spirals one stacked on top of the other over the Heart Center. Visualize the particles of Light traveling the spiral at high speeds accelerating as they get close to the center until they reach its axis, where they collide and explode during the inhale with an amazing expansion of light that then contracts with the exhale in the center of the Chest.

d) **Breasts Vortex**- Consolidate the expanded light from the explosion in to a concentrated point of light in the center of the chest, from here the two Spirals of light extend out to the breasts. Visualize the spirals moving from the Heart Vortex and extending out singularly until reaching the end of their journey at the breasts, as the tiny spheres of light continue to accelerate until they explode (on their own without colliding) and expand with the inhalation, and contract back to center with the exhalation. With the next inhale rising up to the Throat Vortex.

e) **Throat Vortex**- Inhaling visualize the two Spirals rising in an undulating fashion like the Kundalini in motion from both Breasts, crisscrossing and merging at the center of the Throat Vortex. Repeat the same action with the Concentric Spirals, colliding as they reach the axis, on the inhalation producing another magnificent explosion and expansion, and the exhalation generates a powerful contraction that renews the brilliance of this Light energy. With the next inhalation the Spirals ascend to the Third Eye.

f) **Third Eye Vortex**- Inhale as the Concentric Spirals continue to ascend and collide at the center of the Third Eye Vortex where they explode and expand in sync with the inhale, and contract with the exhale, ascending yet again with the inhale to the next Vortex, opening in this manner Universes of possibilities in each center until they reach the top of the head.

g) **Crown Vortex**- Breath normally as the particles travel inside the spirals, Inhale as the Spirals collide at the center of the Crown producing another magnificent explosion, that expands with the inhalation and contracts with the exhalation. The Light and Energy expands up and out in a conical fashion and then enter back through the crown descending to the Throat (passing the Third Eye).

6-Descent of Crystalline Wind

At the Throat Vortex visualize the two opposing Spirals in the same explosive manner as in the other vortices. Here the superior mind combines with the Air Element in the Throat and this purifies the Three Bodies and the soul begins to understand Being-ness. This is how the impalpable ethereal femininity will enlighten materiality and convert it into expansive ethereal Star Powder.

The meditation keeps evolving but it is very complicated and a teacher is need it to do it correctly.
We are going to train teachers around the world.

Meditation of Particle Acceleration for Men

Empowering breath

This is done by making a temporal contemplative pause on each vortex, using breath retentions before the inhalations and after the exhalations, repeating the name of a Seraphim utilizing each syllable of the name as one second. For example, AN-NA-BELL would be a name of three seconds. The practitioner should in this case repeat the three syllable name as she inhales (3), holds (3), exhales (3) and holds (3)….Repeat. Simultaneously she should do several rounds (3 OR MORE) of breaths while redirecting the vital energy in the different vortexes, starting at the first vortex continuing to the ovaries, from the ovaries to the third vortex, and from there to the solar plexus, heart, breast, throat, third eye, until you reach the crown of the head.
When you apply these small breath retentions, they recharge the vortexes with energetic Love, awakening them and producing explosions of profound emotive color.

Expand every vortex with this living energy. When you reach the Crown vortex, bring the accumulated energy from here down through the spinal column.
Start making two parallel circles (one on top of the other) with a particle that spins in a clockwise manner and another one that spins in a counterclockwise manner, around the first vortex.
The circles must be parallel to the floor.
Slowly separate the cycles.
Increase the speed of the particles and make them crash into one another in the center of each vortex, producing an explosion of radiant light.
Change the direction of each particle in the same vortex.
Repeat this procedure in each vortex starting with the Root and ascending up to the Bladder, Navel, Heart, Throat, Third Eye and finally the Crown.
When you reach the Crown vortex, bring the energy downwards through the spine.

Repeat this procedure three, five, seven or nine times.

DNA/RNA Change

Visualize the DNA and RNA symbol in each vortex from the first to the seventh and spreading from each vortex all throughout your body.

Repeat the respective mantras:

Activador ADN / DNA Activator
Repetir en cada uno de los 8 centros 3 veces /
Repeat on each of the 8 centers 3 times
MANTRA
"RAFAEL ADIMITRAT ASHTIM BUSHTAM"

Activador ARN / RNA Activator
Repetir en cada uno de los 8 centros 3 veces /
Repeat on each of the 8 centers 3 times
MANTRA
"RAFAEL ADIMITRAT ASHTIM BUSHTAM"

Expansion

Let your consciousness touch all the borders of the room you are sitting in, now go beyond the room and then up in to the sky and then expanding across the Universe.
Do this as long as you wish or can.

Only when the chromosomes go beyond the zone of time-space refulgence are they able to evolve in other dimensions. The biological restructuring happens through a process of pulsating energy that affects and changes the DNA from two strands to twelve strands plus one strand in the center (thirteen in total), provoking an irreversible magnetic change. Here, the materiality of the human image, which in reality is Love-Light gravitationally trapped by the sensation of being "Someone", is left behind. The woman goes to a new dimension where sadness, anger, stress, fear, and other emotions cease to oscillate around the soul.

In this meditation, and with Devic help, the woman uses her femininity with such caution that she changes her dark patriarchal-imposed material form for a luminous and ethereal one.
As her consciousness is abiding in this parallel dimension, and at the same time her body is on earth and with a new acute state of lucidity, no one will be able to stop her transforming light.
Before exiting the material world, her duty will be to help others to transcend their energetic karmic chains.

Meditation for Couples

Sit in front of your partner.

1. Breathing Exchange.

One of you exhales and the other inhales the exhalation of the first in sync.

2. Nadi Shodhana

Repeat the same procedure with Nadi Shodhana. This is done by blocking the nasal passage opposed to the partner's and exchanging air; as the partner exhales from the right you will be inhaling from the left and vice versa.

3. Pairs of energetic circles.

Visualize two circles that meet at their radius (almost like two circular wings) and that are parallel to the floor.
In these, there are two particles of radiant light spinning clockwise and counterclockwise.
The particles enter through the back of the head of one of the partners and penetrate the head, coming out through the third eye. From here, the particles enter the third eye of the other partner, then come out from behind the head and continue their journey in that circumference at high speed. In order to introduce themselves in the individuals once again, the other circle meets at the height of the third eye and the only difference is that the particle travels in an opposite direction.
Repeat the exercise ten times, and make them collide and explode in-between both foreheads before changing the direction.
This can be done in the Heart vortex as well.

4. Penetrating glance.

With your gaze, penetrate the right eye first and then the left eye of your partner until you reach the center of your partner's brain and visualize how it expands with golden light. The second partner concentrates on the expansion that is taking place within his/her own body; this has to be done simultaneously.

Change roles.

Repeat the same practice in the Heart Vortex.

Peace be with you

SO, BE IT AND MAY THE POWER OF THE

SOURCE OF THE UNIVERSE

BE WITH YOU.

Dictionary

Acetate: A negative ion, typically found in aqueous solutions.

Acetylcholine: A neurotransmitter located in the brain, enables and mediates the communication between neurons.

Acetylcholinesterase: A human enzyme that separates water molecules in order to allow the correct performance of the Acetylcholine.

Acetyl: A specific arrangement of chemical molecules. This is the so-called functional group. It can develop more complex structures with other functional groups.

Actin: A structure made out of proteins; it is one of the basic constituents of the eukaryotic cell.

Activin: A structure made out of proteins. It is responsible for the secretion of sexual hormones in men and women. It also helps to regulate the menstrual cycle in women.

Adenine: It is one of the five nitrogenous bases that form the DNA and RNA.

Adiabatically: This refers to a process where heat is not exchanged with the surrounding medium.

Adipose Tissue: A tissue composed mainly of fat.

Afferent Neurons: Neurons that carry nerve impulses from receptor organs to the CNS.

Alanine: A significant component of a number of proteins; it helps metabolize glucose.

Albuminoid: a compound of proteins found in animal cells.

Alkaline: A substance with a pH higher than 7.

Amino acid: A base structure that forms proteins.

Amygdala: An organ composed of lymphatic and epithelial tissue, located in the throat area.

AMU: An atomic mass unit. It is used to express the mass of an atom and has its equivalent in kg.

Androgens: The male sex hormone whose function is to stimulate the development of male sexual characteristics.

Angstrom: A unit of measure more or less of the size of a Hydrogen atom (1X10-10 meters). Denoted as 1 Å.

Antimatter: In particle physics, this term corresponds to the opposite of the matter element. It has been seen mainly in laboratories and its existence is very short, because when it interacts with matter it decays into other particles and high-energy rays.

Apoptosis: It is known as the death of a cell due to external or internal causes.

Asparagine: An amino acid that makes up the genetic code. It is produced by the body.

Atrial Natriuretic Peptide Atriopeptin: A substance released by the heart when the blood pressure is high in order to dilate the blood vessels so the blood pressure lowers.

Atmic: Concerning the soul or Atman.

Axon: The part of the neuron that conducts nerve impulses from the "head" of the neuron to the next neuron.

Baryonic Particle: A particle made out of three quarks; it forms the matter that we consider “common” or normal.

Bufotenine: A hallucinogenic substance derived from serotonin.

Carboxyl: An organic functional group consisting of a carbon atom that is double bonded to an oxygen atom and single bonded to a hydroxyl group.

Cerebral cortex: A mantle of nerve tissue that covers the surface of the brain.

Cerebrospinal Fluid: The fluid that surrounds the brain and spinal cord.

Chakra: A center of energetic convergence within the subtle body. There are 7 main chakras and they are located along the spine in relation to the physical body.

Circadian Rhythm: Changes in the physical habits of a living being (like the sleep cycles), which take place over time in relation to external and internal influences.

Cholecystokinin: A hormone that stimulates the production of digestive enzymes.

Choline: n essential nutrient in the body that aids the synthesis of cellular components forming the cell membrane.

Chromosome: A structure in which the genetic information is stored.

Cluster: This refers to a cumulus or group—whether large or small.

Corticotropin: A hormone produced by the pituitary gland that stimulates the production of androgens in the body. It also helps establish the correct secretion of other hormones in the body.

Cytokines: Proteins that regulate cell interaction in the immune system.

Cytoplasm: A substance found within the cell. It fills the space between the nucleus and the cell membrane.

Cytosine: One of the five nitrogenous bases that make up DNA and RNA.

Cytoskeleton: A structure made of protein that gives shape and structural support to the cell.

Decibel: A measure given to express the comparison between two values. Mainly used in the measurement of sound levels.

Dendrites: Neuron extensions dedicated to the perception of stimuli.

Deoxyribose: A sugar molecule constituted by six carbon atoms.

Deoxyribonucleic Acid: Also called DNA, it is the structure that carries all the genetic information of a living being (some of them have RNA instead of DNA).

Deva: A manifestation of the benevolent deity; a being of light from the spiritual realm.

Dihydropyridine: A substance that contributes to the output of calcium in the body.

Dihydrotestosterone: A sexual male hormone, more potent than testosterone.

Dimeric glycoprotein: A macromolecule made up of the combination of one protein and one sugar.

DMT: A substance with strong psychedelic properties that can lead to altered states of consciousness.

Dopamine: An important neurotransmitter that regulates behavior, learning, physical activity, coordination and moods.

Efferent Neurons: Neurons that carry nerve impulses from the CNS to the receptor organs.

Electron: A fundamental particle that carries an electric charge.

EMDR: A psychological therapy technique that treats illness through eye movements.

Endometrium: A formation in the uterus that serves to accommodate the zygote in the case of pregnancy. It is renewed every month through the menstrual cycle.

Endoplasmic Reticulum: An organ of the cell that synthesizes and transports proteins (in the case of the rough endoplasmic reticulum) and lipids (in the case of the smooth endoplasmic reticulum) within the cell.

Enol: A specific arrangement of Hydrogen, Oxygen and Carbon atoms, which serve as "bricks" to form more complex chemical structures

Entropy: A physical law that dictates the reversibility of any process. Depending on the point of view, it's related to the constant increase of "disarray".

Electroacoustic Frequencies: The number of "peaks" of energy that sound waves have per second. It is proportional to the energy carried by the wave.

Electrophysiological Properties: Properties of cells and tissues regarding their electrical properties, modes and their ability of function.

Epinephrine: Also called adrenaline, this activates and prepares the body for the fight or flight reaction.

Epithelial Tissue: A special body tissue that covers all the surfaces in the forms of mucosa and skin.

Erythrocytes: Also called red blood cells, their function is to carry oxygen in the blood.

Estrogens: Female hormones responsible for the proper development and functioning of the sexual organs.

Ethereal: This usually refers to something celestial. It is difficult to define and is located within a higher or subtler plane of existence.

FSH: A hormone responsible for the development of the body's reproductive processes.

Gallbladder: The digestive organ that stores bile.

Gen: A structure made of nucleotides. It contains genetic information.

Genome: The total genetic information found in a species.

Geopathic Disturbance: Anomalies in soil layers near the surface.

Glycerol: Alcohol produced from the gastric degradation of fat.

Glycine: An amino acid that acts as an inhibitor of the Central Nervous System (CNS).

Glucids: An organic molecule, known as sugar.

Glucocorticoids: A hormone that regulates the metabolism of sugars, fats and proteins.

Gluon: A fundamental particle of nature that carries the strong nuclear force. This particle manages to hold the neutrons and protons together in the atom's nucleus. The gluon has no mass and no electric charge.

Glutamine: An amino acid involved in the "manufacturing" of DNA, replacing proteins.

Glycoprotein Hormone: A hormone formed by a sugar molecule and a protein molecule.

Gonadotropin: A hormone that regulates reproduction.

Graviton: A hypothetical elementary particle that carries out the gravitational interaction.

Guanine: One of the five nitrogenous bases that build the DNA and RNA.

Hadron: A subatomic particle, formed by quarks, which stays together due to the Strong Nuclear Force.

Hemoglobin: A substance that carries oxygen in the blood.

Histology: An area of science that studies the organic tissues.

Holography: A laser technique designed to create three-dimensional images.

Homeostasis: Organisms' ability to maintain a balance in their body, offsetting external changes with internal changes.

Hypophysis: A gland that secretes the hormones in order to regulate homeostasis.

Hypothalamus: The region of the brain that is responsible for coordinating behaviors related to the perpetuation of the species.

Inhibin: A protein structure that regulates FSH secretion.

Ion: An atom or molecule that has gained or lost electrons. It is electrically charged.

Lepton: An elementary particle that has a non-integer spin. The electron for example, is a lepton.

Leucine: An amino acid used by the cells to create proteins.

Leucocyte: Also called white blood cells, their function is to carry out the body's immune response.

Limbic Forebrain: A region of the forebrain where the limbic system is located.

Lipid Molecules: Molecules made of fat.

Lipofuscin: Yellow pigment, which is a sign of cellular aging.

Luteinizing Hormone: A sex hormone that aids in the secretion of progesterone and testosterone.

Lymphocytes: Large leucocytes that react to strange substances.

Lysosome: An organ responsible for cellular digestion.

Meiosis: A reproduction method used by the sex cells (gametes).

Melatonin: A hormone related with the sleep-activity cycles in animals.

Meridian Channels: Channels in the body through which vital energy travels.

Methionine: An amino acid responsible for the synthesis of phospholipids.

Mineralocorticoid: a hormone that facilitates the hydration of the cell.

Mitochondria: A structure responsible for cell respiration; it provides lots of energy.

Monoamine Oxidase: An enzyme found on the outside of the mitochondrion.

Morphogenic Protein: A protein that can generate a strong formation of bone, cartilage and other tissues.

Muon: An elementary particle of considerably large mass and a very short life span.

Myelin: An insulating layer that covers the neuron's axon.

Myelinated fiber: Wrapping that covers the neuron's axons.

Myosin: A fibrous protein responsible for muscle contraction.

N-glycosidic bond: A link that connects simple sugar molecules to form more complex molecules.

Neurobiology: The study of nerve cells and how they influence behavior.

Neuromodulators: Substances produced by metabolism to regulate the release of neurotransmitters; in addition, some of them are used to treat nervous system disorders and maladies.

Neuromuscular synapse: The union between a neuron and a muscular fiber.

Neurons: A nerve cell, primarily responsible for the transmission of electrical impulses in the nervous system (NS).

Neurosecretory neurons: Nerve cells that secrete a substance and are responsible for releasing it into the blood stream.

Neurotransmitter: A molecule that transmits information from one neuron to another through the synapse.

Neutrino: A subatomic particle that results from the disintegration of a neutron. It does not have an electric charge and has very small mass.

Neutron star: A special star made of neutrons and other particles; it's heavy and has a very small size (radius, less than 100 km).

Nicotinic Receptor: A receptive channel to acetylcholine; nicotine also actives it.

Nitrogenous Base: A basic organic structure that builds up the nucleotides.

Norepinephrine: A neurotransmitter that is released into the blood and is homeostatic.

Nucleic Acid: A structure made of nucleotides which, when organized in a specific way, gives place for big DNA chains.

Nucleoside: A nucleotide that lacks the phosphate group.

Nucleosynthesis: The process of formation of new atoms made from protons and neutrons, mainly in nuclear reactions.

Nucleotide: A base structure that forms DNA and RNA. It has a nitrogenous base, a sugar, and a phosphate group.

Olfactory Bulb: A part of the central nervous system where the sense of smell is processed.

Pentose: A sugar molecule with five carbon atoms.

Peripheral Nervous System: A section of the nervous system that directs all the connections from the CNS to all the fibers of the body. It is not protected by bone.

Perikaryon: A structure of the neuron that contains the nucleus and the cytoplasm.

Peristaltic contractions: Movements made by organs of the digestive system to move food and expel the stool.

Phenylethylamine: A neurotransmitter that produces psychoactive effects.

Phenylhydroxylamine: A specific chemical arrangement made of nitrogen, hydrogen, oxygen and carbon atoms.

Pheromones: A chemical substance secreted by living beings in order to cause a specific behavior change in other living beings.

Phosphate: Salt made of phosphorus and oxygen.

Photon: Light manifested in its particular (particle-like) behavior rather than a wave; its energy depends on the frequency of the light.

Pia mater: The internal part of the meninges; it covers all the CNS.

Pineal Gland: The organ responsible of the secretion of melatonin and DMT.

Plasma: A state of matter consisting of a fluid in which its particles have been ionized; consequently, it has an electric charge and is a good conductor.

Plasma Membrane: A wall that defines the size of a cell; it is composed of lipids and proteins.

Polyhedral Neurons: An efferent neuron. This classification is due to its shape.

Polypeptide: The long arrangement of amino acids.

Positron: An antimatter particle opposite to the electron. It has a positive charge.

Progesterone: A hormone involved in the process of menstruation and pregnancy.

Prolactin: A hormone that stimulates milk production in the mammary glands.

Proline: A nonessential amino acid that repairs and maintains muscles and bones.

Protostar: The formation stage of a star. A period comprised from when the gas cloud collapses up to when the nuclear reactions in the core of the star begin.

Proton: A baryonic particle with positive electric charge; it has a very large mass.

Psilocybin: A substance found in some fungi; it is a very strong hallucinogen.

Quark: A fundamental particle that (in a specific arrangement with other quarks) leads to the constitution of particles, like protons and neutrons.

REM: The phase of sleep in which rapid eye movements are experienced; it is said to be a stage of greater intensity and neuronal activity.

Rennin: An enzyme that stimulates the secretion of hormones that control the water balance.

Ribonucleic Acid: Also called RNA. It is the structure that carries all the genetic information in a living being (some of them have DNA instead of RNA). It can be lineal or in a double helix. The main difference with DNA is the presence of different substances in its composition.

Ribose: A sugar molecule that has five carbon atoms essential for RNA.

Ribosomes: A structure within the cell responsible for the synthesis of proteins.

Root Mid Square (Rms) velocity: A measurement used in certain physical contexts, where it is necessary to know the average velocity (statistically) of a group of particles with random movements

Ryanodine: A substance that produces muscle paralysis. It is derived from a shrub.

Sarcolemma: The cellular wall that covers muscle cells.

Sarcoplasm: The cytoplasm present in some cells, such as muscle cells.

Septum: The cartilage separation of the two nostrils in the nose.

Serine: A nonessential amino acid; it is related to many enzymes in the body.

Serotonin: A neurotransmitter associated with the management of emotions, such as joy, anger, anger, mood, sexual urge, among others. Its cadence is associated with depression.

Steroid Hormone: A substance that helps the body control many functions, such as metabolism and muscle recovery, among others.

Synaptic Clefts: The space between a neuron and another, where they are connected.

Synaptic vesicle: A structure in the axons that secretes neurotransmitters.

Thymopoietin: A human gene. It is a protein that encodes some substances within the DNA.

Thymosin: An important protein group for the cellular development of the immunological system.

Thyroglobulin: A protein synthesized by the thyroid gland. It affects the process of secretion of other important hormones.

Thyrotropin: An important hormone that regulates the activity of the thyroid gland.

Thyroxine: An important hormone that controls cell metabolism.

Tiroliberina: A hormone produced in the hypothalamus that has the function of stimulating the secretion of thyrotropin.

Tryptamine: A neurotransmitter present in the brains of mammals.

Tryptophan: An essential amino acid employed to promote the release of serotonin.

Triiodothyronine: A hormone that promotes the metabolism of food and oxygen.

Troponin: A protein that enables muscle contractions.

Troponin C: This helps displace troponin to activate muscular contraction.

Troponin T: This helps displace troponin to activate muscular contraction.

Troposphere: The lowest layer of the atmosphere where most of the oxygen is located. It is less than twenty kilometers thick and is very important for the development of life on earth.

TSH: A test that measures the thyroid-stimulating hormone.

Tyramine: A neurotransmitter that acts on the body by changing the pressure and the amount of blood coming into our brain.

Unmyelinated fibers: Axons that are not electrically isolated (they don't have myelin).

Vasodilation: This corresponds to the body's action of increasing the size of the blood vessels, allowing more blood and oxygen to flow, and improving irrigation.

Vedantic Beings: Beings in a state of "complete" or "final" wisdom.

For more information and more books with related topics please check our web page

matiasflurybooks.com

matias108@gmail.com

If you are interested in our upcoming workshops: Seeds of Light Implants or Quantum Transmissions or any other information about this topic check out our web page.

www.celestial9.com

Or the face book group

Book Downloads from the Nine-Group

https://www.facebook.com/groups/fromthenine/?pnref=story

Other books from the same Author

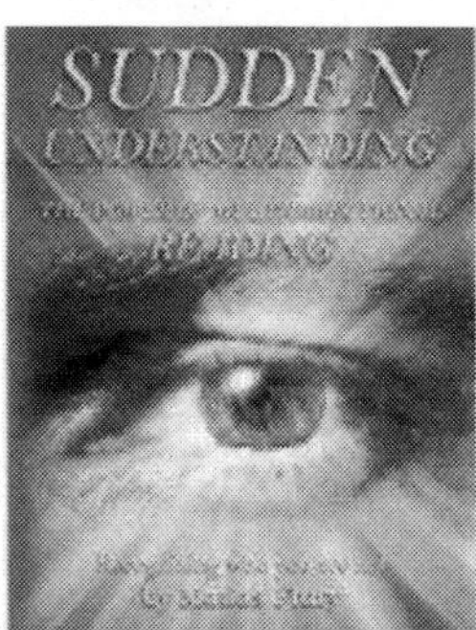

Reading Sudden Awakening seduces and entices the mind to pay attention to an immense yet subtle infinite reality hidden and living quietly in all of us all day long. This spiritual power will become alive as you read, and it will be present in your life, sometimes subtlety and sometimes intensely. The feeling of luminosity this book will awaken in you will certainly continue optimistically contributing to freeing you from the dictatorial mind and emotions, leaving you in an immense field of blue, pure awareness.

I invite you to do the experiment; there is nothing to lose and much to be gained.

This experimentation intends to propel you forward in your spiritual search at great speed; you will be taking a shortcut. Just read the words on each page and see that enlightenment is possible, and around the corner, for every human being on earth.

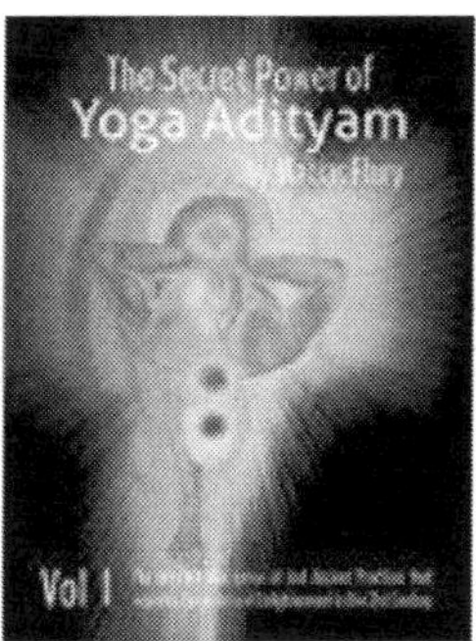

This book is a product of many years of work as a professional Yoga teacher, combined with deep personal exploration and careful scientific research, involving dozens of people, done with aura machines and Kirlian photography. This book is intended to illumine and elucidate the movements of energy in the subtle body during the practice of yoga asanas, and give an understanding of the connection between the physical, mental, spiritual, and emotional realms. This book provides a profound introduction to our system of Yoga practice and will serve as a support and a beacon of light for all serious practitioners of Yoga.

Until this time the Western world has been introduced to yoga asanas, pranayama and the many wonders of Hatha Yoga from a somewhat narrow perspective. We tend to see Yoga as a series of physical exercises, or a method of stretching and strengthening the body while quieting the mind and breath. That is all right in the beginning, but the value of Yoga goes far beyond such limited concepts. The true goal of Yoga is nothing less than Self-Realization, also known as Enlightenment, or Nirvana, or God-Realization, essentially synonymous terms which point to a timeless state of supreme peace beyond the mind. Yoga is a method by which the limiting wall of the personality is gradually deconstructed so the individual mind can reconnect with and finally merge in the infinitely-expansive pure Consciousness which is our true nature.

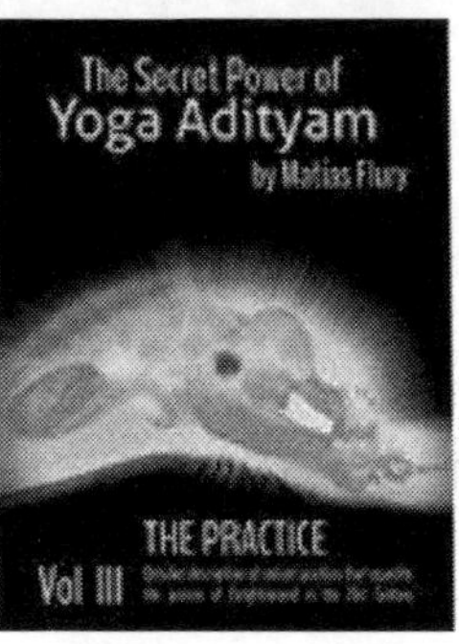

Yoga Adityam was born out of the necessity of spiritualizing yoga in the West. This new system evolved through many years of yoga practice and spiritual experiments. During my long period of study and exploration, I received instructions from accomplished yogis and siddhas, both in India and the West, and after many years of dedicated practice, I came to a deep understanding of the principles of how energy moved through the three bodies during the practice of asanas, pranayama and meditation. I carefully analyzed the many ancient yoga styles described in classic yoga books in India and compared them to the yoga styles taught in the West in various countries. When I followed the history of any particular style to its ancient roots, I was confronted each time with the revelation that many vital parts were missing when it was presented in the West. For example, in the practice of asanas, not only was breath retention often missing, but also the use of bandhas (yogic body locks), Drishtis (positioning of the gaze), mental

the Addendum, contains precise descriptions of yoga asana sequences that stimulate this same mystical ascending energy (Kundalini). On top of this, you will be able to see Kirlian photos that show how the energy of Kundalini moves though the chakras (psycho-energetic centers) and how it affects them by modifying their colors and the body's aura shape and

size.
In my heart I hope that anyone who comes across these teachings is blessed with the right perspective to make appropriate use of such practices. To do so, we must appreciate the essence of spiritual practice. There are many ways of practice, many flowing rivers rushing to the same ocean. Yet practice is of no use unless it is done with right understanding. Remember, it is the essence that matters, and that which is the essence is the simplest thing. At the beginning, we go through life living from moment to moment. We develop personalities through our judgment of ourselves, others and the environment we find ourselves in. We construct a series of habitual patterns based on what we like and what we don't like. In this way, we end up running after gratification and fleeing from discomfort. We need our memory to do this; without memory, we would not be able to judge based on past experiences. So, we create a mental map filled with things to avoid and other things to desire, and the right paths to reach them.

Spiritual Experiments: The Portal of Truth is the story of the author's burning quest for Enlightenment which has taken him to the frightening depths and astounding heights of spiritual experience. Written in dramatic style, with many sections of entertaining dialogue and vivid descriptions of his numerous shamanic journeys, this book is as entertaining as a novel, the only difference being that every word of it is true.

Made in the USA
San Bernardino, CA
30 December 2018